White House

Story

A

Memoir

By

Melinda Bates

ISBN: 13:978-1723100543
ISBN: 10:1723100544

Ense-DeVere Publishing P. O. Box 189010 PMB 111 Coronado, CA 92178

White House Story,

A Memoir

Table of Contents

Prologue ~ Goodbye To All That

I'm staring at the door to the Oval Office, about to go in for the final time, to say my farewell to the President. There's a peep hole in the staff door, so the President's assistants can see if he's deep in conversation with the Nobel Prize winner or movie star du jour, or if he's looking restless and waiting for someone to come in and break up the meeting. (He doesn't like to be the bad guy. That's what staff is for.) But I know there are no celebrity visitors today. Today it all comes to an end.

I glance at Betty Currie's desk and it's clear for the first time I can remember - no papers waiting for his attention, no schedules, no agendas. Tan packing boxes are everywhere, stacked along the walls, neatly sealed and labeled, reaching almost to the ceiling.

She looks plenty tired herself, and I notice Socks is not in his usual place lying by the French doors in the sun. Betty knows I'm looking for the President and we both turn to that door. It's closed.

"Is he with someone, Betty?"

"No, he's free, and I'm sure he'd like to see you - go on in."

I square my shoulders, tug at my suit jacket, and take a deep breath. I push open the white, paneled door and notice absently my hands are shaking. *Damn! This is going to be hard.*

The President looks up, gives a weary smile. "Hi, Melinda. I'm glad you came by."

He looks exhausted, his normal ruddy color faded to ashen. Of course, I've seen the President worn out before. We have all seen him beaten down more than once, and seen him recover - every time - even from the "troubles" of 1998. But never like this. This time his eyes carry the sad realization that now we are truly at the end. This time his weariness is shocking. For weeks he's exceeded even his normal hectic pace, getting little sleep and wearing out the staff. He's working like a madman to do, do, do, all the last remaining things that have simmered on his agenda, some for years, against time that is now run out. Eight years may be enough for some presidents, but not for Bill Clinton. He's been working to solve

America's problems forever, it seems. The idea that his time at bat is now over must be intolerable.

I laugh a little as I realize, I don't look that great myself. We've all been pushing ourselves to get one final thing done for him - the brilliant transition he asked for - and I'm about dead from the effort. Exhaustion is simply a garment we all wear, hanging loosely over our aching bones. We keep going with the promise that soon (soon!) there will be plenty of time to rest all we want.

It's Friday, January 19, 2001. At 11:59 a.m. on Saturday he will stop being President and become simply "Mr. Clinton." There will be a new sheriff in town, a new family up in the Residence, testing the mattresses and admiring the art, and a new man in the Oval Office, sitting at the *Resolute* desk, being addressed as "Mr. President." It's breaking my heart to turn over the Visitors Office, my baby that I have nurtured for all eight years with my time, energy, sweat, sacrifice, imagination and determination. But giving up the Presidency? I can hardly imagine.

He stands, stretches, steps to the front of the desk and reaches out to hug me. I go right into his arms and stay there for a moment. Finally, we pull apart, wipe our eyes, give a small sigh. I manage a sad grin. "This is finally it, Mr. President. I can't believe it. Where has the time gone? Eight years? It feels like only eight months!"

"Well, it's been a hell of a ride, hasn't it? A hell of a ride ... and I'm so glad you came along for the whole deal. What a time we've had. Who would have imagined all those years ago at Georgetown that we'd get to do ... this ... "

He looks down at the desk, gently brushing his fingers over the gleaming surface. His eyes are distant, looking either back at our amazing adventures, good times and bad, or forward at some imagined future; I can't tell which. Then he gives a little shake, smiles and says, "I'm glad to see you - I have something for you. Only the folks who came along for the whole ride are getting these."

He holds out a narrow, rectangular white box. I open it with careful hands. Inside, nestled on cotton, is a small gavel, about 7" long, made out of honey-colored wood, with a brass band around the crown. I take it out and hold it up to the light.

"It's beautiful, but, what is it?"

"Read the band," he says with a sly grin.

"President William J. Clinton, January 20, 1993. So, it celebrates your first inauguration?"

"It's made out of the wood they used to build the platform I stood on to take the oath of office. There are only a few, and I wanted you to have one."

I shiver, and the hairs on my arms stand up. Tears threaten my eyes again. This is our final gift exchange in the Oval Office, and it's pretty swell.

"Thank you, Mr. President, I love it! And I have a gift for you too."

I reach for the folder I'd laid on the desk. There hasn't been time to wrap my present, but he won't care. For years I've shopped on eBay for White House memorabilia, building my own impressive collection and buying things for the President's birthday or Christmas gifts. I can't compete in the gift area with his rich friends who keep him well supplied with expensive designer ties, or present him with paintings. But I seem to be the only one who knows how much he loves old books or publications about the White House and Presidents, and where to find them. I've gotten amazing things online, for very little money. His favorites are articles clipped from nineteenth century magazines, often with elaborate illustrations, about his predecessors or the White House. Sometimes I find these at flea markets, but eBay is my best source. I look there almost every day. I enjoy the hunt (and the shopping). This "going away" present is another of these historic documents, and his eyes light up when he sees it.

"Where in the world did you find this? 1885 - just look at these pictures of the House back then. This is great!"

"eBay, Mr. President. I've become an expert at online auctions for you."

Finally we have something to laugh about, and we pore over the article together for a minute, gently turning brittle old pages.

"These gifts are so thoughtful. Thanks very much. It will go either in the Library or maybe my new office up in Harlem. I'm glad to have it, and I'm glad to have had you here all these years."

He shakes his head, thoughtful again. "A hell of a ride, a hell of a ride... "

We look at each other one last time, each of us trying not to cry, reach out for a final, quick hug, and I walk out of the Oval for the very last time. Betty glances up as I leave, but I've already said goodbye to her. I guess she's seen plenty of these sad farewells, and knows if she says anything we'll both fall apart. Such a nice lady, and who knows if I'll ever see her again.

My heart is so heavy I have to clench my teeth and tell myself, W*alk. Just walk.*

Out into the crisp, cold air of the West Colonnade, glancing at the bare sticks of the Rose Garden, where the President loved to throw the ball for Buddy. Through the House, pausing for a last look at the China Room, Library and Vermeil Room, to set their details into my heart. I know it will be a loooong time before I'll see them again, if ever. Down the East Colonnade with a look out at the Jacqueline Kennedy Garden and the lawn stretching down to the South, the ghostly trees covered in frost. The little pool under the pear tree is frozen, and I know I won't see it when flowers bloom there again.

Down the hallway to our offices, now empty. My staff all gone. No reason for them to stay. All those people I have come to know and love over the years, gone to who-knows-where, and who knows when I'll ever see them again. I look at the empty chairs and blank computers and remember our normal, frantic pace, our laughter and dedication, our pride.

My heart's getting ready to be broken, and I can't let on - the Bush people are coming for a briefing and to get the keys. Time for all us Clintonistas (a word of scorn for them that we wear with pride) to move on out the door. Emotion has to wait 'til I'm out of here and safely in my car - if I can manage it.

So now I am the last one, waiting alone in my office. I'd like to send a few more emails from my impressive White House address, but the Archives people have shut that all down, so I sit in silence and stare at the blank walls, vaguely wondering how the new Director will decorate. It used to be so beautiful. In a couple of hours I'll turn out the lights and walk away from the most amazing and wonderful time of my life. A hell of a ride. A hell of a ride...

Want to know how you can tell if the signature on a Presidential letter is authentic or an auto-pen? The President's personal stationery is a very pale green, so anything on that paper is his actual signature. Now you know!

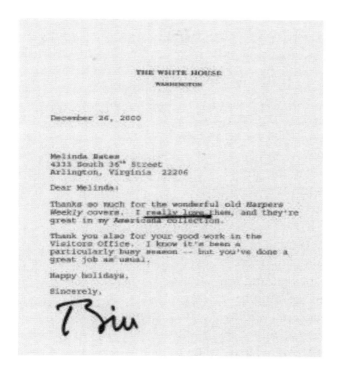

CHAPTER ONE ~ 1964 ~ IN THE BEGINNING

"Hi!" said the tall, skinny kid with the big head of curly hair. "I'm Bill Clinton and I'm running for freshman class President!"

You are probably hearing those words in your head in whatever American accent seems normal to you. But I heard those words in a rich Ozarks twang that was brand new - and grating - to me. I winced and tore my eyes away from my class schedule. My parents had neutral east-coast accents; most of their friends were diplomats and journalists. This drawly, twangy Arkansas-speak is harder on the ear than the soft Southern accents of Georgia and the Carolinas I'd heard in movies. To my mind it boldly announced *Southern hick alert!* Which is pretty funny when you consider the speaker was one of the smartest, most interesting people on the planet, and was eventually going to change my life.

But we were just kids of eighteen, and I didn't know that yet, so I had to firmly repress the giggle that threatened to cut our conversation short. Thank God my head firmly told my mouth, *No - no! Don't laugh. If you talk to this boy you will at least know **somebody** here.*

A reassuring thought. I had been at Georgetown University a whole day now, wandering around, muttering to myself, *Where is my next class? Do I have the right books? Am I smart enough to be here? Where's the cafeteria? Will I ever have friends here? Damn! How stupid was it to decide to be a day student? At least if I had a roommate I'd know somebody ...*

And then, more importantly, *Is my long straight hair long enough and straight enough? Is my skirt short enough? I wanna look great, but I don't want to look like every other girl in the freshman class!*

Now I had somebody to talk to, even if it was just for a minute. I squinted up at my new friend in the brilliant September light and smiled. I looked down and noticed he still held my hand in his. I've always noticed men's hands, even back then, and his were beautiful, the fingers long and slender.

"OK, tell me about it."

He dropped my hand and off he went about how this freshman class could be the first to do this or that or whatever. I wasn't really interested in college politics. In 1964 the world was virtually humming with possibilities, or so it seemed to me. I was finally an adult - no more nuns to boss me around - and could hardly wait to discover who I really was. I was pretty sure that would not involve campus campaigns, but this boy was just so nice, how could I not listen? I'd probably still have time to find my next class, and maybe he could help me.

So I nodded, and smiled, and pretended to be interested. I don't remember his words, or his platform, but I do remember thinking, *Good Lord. This boy has more smarts, charm and charisma than any person I've ever met - heck, any person I've ever heard of. And he's just a kid like me!*

In someone else this might have been intimidating, but there was nothing intimidating about Bill. He was friendly, open, and genuine. My smile became sincere - I liked him a lot.

When he turned to go, something happened that had never happened to me before, and has never happened again. Even after all these years the power of it is as clear as if we spoke just yesterday. He turned to go and my heart and my head spoke out to me, loud and clear: *This is an extraordinary person. He's going to do amazing and important things with his life, and I hope I get to watch it happen. He's going to make history some day!*

I can't tell you why I thought this, and you may think I'm making it up, but I promise you I'm not. It happened exactly like that. And I can also tell you that over the years when I've given speeches and tell this part of the story, there is often a person in the audience who comes up after to say, "I met him in Chicago in 1970 and had the same experience." Or, "I met him at Oxford and that's exactly what it was like…"

This is the effect Bill Clinton has on people. His brilliance and personality are a force field you can't resist. If you've ever been in the same room with him, you understand it. If you haven't, you may be thinking, "Oh, come on! I don't believe THAT! So here's a more contemporary example:

My friend, Howard was the only Democrat in a group of venture capitalists in Washington, in the late 1990s. Every time they met he had to take a lot of grief from the other members, who all despised President Clinton. One in particular, let's call him "Mr. Critic," really hated him. (Isn't that stupid? How can you "hate" someone you never met?) Then Mr. Critic was invited to attend a luncheon with the President.

The hotel ballroom was arranged for the President to speak from a lectern for twenty minutes, (oh, yeah, like THAT'S gonna happen with Bill Clinton!) and then move to the luncheon tables, where a seat at each had been left empty, so he could talk more intimately to the guests. Mr. Critic found himself next to the empty seat at his table. He listened intently to the President's remarks and chatted with the other guests. Then President Clinton came to his table, sat down, turned, and smiled at Mr. Critic, who later sheepishly told Howard that his head could not comprehend what his ears heard his mouth saying: "Mr. President, it's so great to meet you - I am one of your biggest fans!"

It's funny, but not unusual. Bill Clinton's intellect, curiosity, charisma, grace and empathy are legendary.

During our years at Georgetown I counted Bill a good friend. I took him to his first Judy Collins concert, and he so loved her music that years later he and Hillary named their daughter Chelsea after her song, *A Chelsea Morning*. We saw Bob Dylan perform in Gaston Hall, before an audience of no more than six hundred people. Most students hadn't even heard of Dylan yet. Bill repeatedly - and unsuccessfully - tried to set me up on dates with various friends at school.

I was in the Institute of Languages and Linguistics and Bill was in the School of Foreign Service but we had some classes together, including two with the famous Professor Carroll Quigley, the first man who ever demanded that I think so hard it made my brain hurt. (Write a 400-word essay about the history of man from the end of the Wurm glacier to the beginning of the Iron Age....) As a non-Catholic, Bill took a required class in comparative religion one semester, and the Jesuit who taught it invited him for a beer and burger in The Tombs, our college hang out..

"My son, I've been watching your work in class and wonder if you've ever considered that perhaps you have a vocation?" (As in, for the priesthood.)

"Well, Father, it's nice of you to think so, but, ah, wouldn't I have to be a Catholic first?"

Bill had been a Baptist since he was very little. There was a lot of good-natured kidding about THAT question. Talk about throwing yourself into your class work ...

In 1966 the school ran a contest to find the "sexiest voice on campus." I won. My prize was to get to record the daily phone updates for class changes or special events. I'd forgotten all about this long (long) ago, but to my great embarrassment, at a fancy event on the State Floor years later, the President's assistant, Betty Currie, whispered in my ear, "Melinda, what does 'FEDICAB' mean?"

I almost dropped my drink and stared at her in shock. "Well! I guess I know who's been telling tales to you!"

"Yes, he said you'd be shocked, but, what does it mean?"

"It's the acronym for the phone number students called to hear my "sexiest voice on campus" reciting the day's schedule. I cannot believe the stuff he remembers!"

He loved to tell these stories to take me by surprise at the oddest moments.

By 1967, a time of great unrest and upheaval in universities around the country, Georgetown was still a relentlessly stodgy place. I broke out into full-fledged rebellion against everything my wonderful parents tried to teach me and became the only hippie on our conservative campus. Years later, when Bill said he didn't smoke grass, I knew he was telling the truth, because if he had, he would have been smoking it with me. I'm not proud of it, I just think it's important to tell the truth.

While I was a hippie, Bill was already an activist, deeply involved in politics, volunteering and working in Arkansas Senator Fulbright's office, and carrying bags of food to terrified families hiding in their Washington tenements during the race riots. Still, we had a lot of fun together. I was never a girlfriend, but always a good friend.

During the 1992 campaign, NBC asked me to do an interview about what Bill had been like as a student and friend. The interviewer, pushing for a bit of background, asked repeatedly if we had dated. He was just sure there had been some grand romance, and if he pushed hard enough he could get me to tell him all about it for the Nightly News.

After a few rounds of this I got a little exasperated. With the camera rolling I leaned in, smiled and said, "Try to understand. It was the late 1960s. Bill Clinton was one of the truly nice guys on campus. As far as I was concerned, this immediately eliminated him from the realm of romantic possibility!"

Well, everyone in the room laughed, including the interviewer. I told myself, *Now he'll back off, they will cut that bit of tape, and we'll go on with more substantive things.*

Imagine my surprise - and embarrassment - that night, when Tom Brokaw introduced the tape, and those few moments were almost the ONLY thing they aired. I was mortified, but I guess there are worse things to be said about a candidate than "He was a really nice guy."

Over the years my friend went off to Oxford, then Yale, then back home to Arkansas and the beginning of his political career. We sometimes saw each other when he came to Washington, and we occasionally exchanged letters.

In the late '60s and early '70s I took my rebellion to serious lengths. For my twenty first birthday I took my Grandma's inheritance money and bought a motorcycle - not a dainty, girly bike, but a big *Triumph Daytona*, the one with twin carbs that went like the wind. I replaced the standard exhaust system with snazzy, hollowed-out chrome tail pipes, with no baffles - it sounded like a 747 taking off. I loved this. In fact, it was so loud the police in Georgetown started stopping me for disturbing the peace (and also, I think, for the novelty factor. The bike was big, I was small, and a GIRL, so what was up with that?) Eventually, they tired of it and warned me to just not drive through there anymore.

I'm only 5'3" tall, so my feet could just barely touch the ground on either side. At first I could only start it by standing next to it, kicking the starter, then swinging my leg up and over the seat. It looked stupid. Then one of the local motorcycle outlaws took an interest in me, the pretty "uptown" girl, and taught me how to start it while standing up on it, giving a swift, hard kick down, then gently rocking it off the stand and zooming away. I was so proud of that move! My favorite thing was to put on my semi-transparent shirt, with no bra, and go out on the bike to see how many accidents or near-misses I could cause.

Do you think I took myself too seriously ?

My poor parents. Such lovely people, who raised me, my sister and brother to be nice, civilized, intelligent people. I cringe now when I think of what I put them through. I don't know which was worse – that it was stupid, careless, self-destructive? All of the above?

In 1972 I got born again (halleluiah!) and married my long-time boyfriend, Darryl Bates. We must have been insane. He's a very nice man, but we were completely unsuited as mates for each other. I wish someone with a little wisdom had stepped in to stop us. We were trying to do the right thing and didn't know any better. But, from our troubled marriage came our best blessings, our sons, Shiloh and Noah.

In 1978, Bill became the youngest man ever elected governor of any state. I sent my congratulations with a note: "… and we know perfectly well this is only the beginning, as you move on to even more exciting achievements. Your friends are all proud of you!"

I spent my whole life in or close to Washington, DC. It's a great city, but people come and go; they don't usually stay. By the late 1980s, I was getting lonely. All my friends had moved away. I missed them. My kids were in school, and I had a great job at the

National Gallery of Art, but I needed friends too.

Then, in early 1988, I got a notice about our upcoming Georgetown twentieth reunion. I'd never attended a reunion, but this seemed like a good place to make or re-make connections. Since I lived close by, it was easy to volunteer to help the event committee. I was told to call Tim Chorba, a graduate of Georgetown College, about participating.

You have to understand - way back in the late '60s, the "East Campus," where Bill and I studied, was as separate from Georgetown College as East and West Berlin. Somewhere over on the other side of the campus I vaguely knew they were studying for a liberal arts degree, while we were specializing, as were students in the Business School, or Nursing. I never knew any of those boys, never dated any, never took any classes with them and didn't think much of them.

So, I didn't know Tim and he didn't know me. I had a hard time persuading him to allow me to help the committee, but he finally, reluctantly, agreed. How silly was this? Life rule #26: never, EVER turn down an offer of volunteer help for your project.

A group of us gathered one night in the Alumni House to call classmates around the country and encourage them to attend and donate to the school. I reached Governor Clinton in Little Rock, and we happily chatted. He said he couldn't wait to see us all. I was surprised at how easy it was to reach a governor - I would have expected layers of staff to get through, but it was just a trooper, and then Bill. Maybe it's an Arkansas thing? I was pretty persuasive with my other calls - I'm effective with a message I believe in - and eventually made a good impression on Tim. I never imagined this would turn out to be important later in my life.

As part of the 1988 festivities, the University invited Governor Clinton to address all the reunion attendees. Try to remember the days of Ronald Reagan, a president who never spoke publicly without notes (unless he was making up a story) and had to be prompted about most topics if taken by surprise. People called him the "great communicator" but many of us wondered if he knew (or cared) enough about anything to speak about it with real passion.

In this context of low expectations, Gov. Bill Clinton spoke to us about America heading into the next century. "What kind of country will we be? What kind of country are we leaving to our children? What can we do to make it a better world? What should our foreign policy be? How can we help people rise out of poverty and join the middle class? How can we strengthen the middle class? How can we make college affordable for more people? What do we do about health care? How do we make the American dream a reality for people struggling to move their families out of poverty and into a stable middle class?

He asked, and answered all these questions, and more. He talked about the issues and problems any governor faces and how similar they are to those a president must solve. He spoke from his heart, without a single note, for two hours. I know, I know - it sounds like a looong time, but it was fascinating for anyone who cared about the future of America. I don't think a single person left the room. This was clearly a man who'd spent his life thinking about and dealing with the many difficult challenges confronting a true leader. It was a thoughtful, impressive performance.

After the speech, Bill and a few of us old friends had a quick meal in the Tombs, the dark, basement campus beer and burger joint that had been the scene of many of our most productive college discussions. I told Bill, "I've been a Republican all my adult life. These roots go back to Abraham Lincoln. Literally. My great great grandfather ran on the Lincoln ticket for an office in New York City in 1860 and 1864, and I have his badge to prove it. But, if you run for president, I'll not only vote for you, I'll work for you. You should be president."

He laughed and gave me a serious look. "Well, you know, I might need to take you up on that offer sometime."

I was sure he would.

Finally, in the fall of 1991, Gov. Clinton announced he was running for president. George Bush's approval ratings were at ninety percent, and there weren't a lot of Democrats around willing to take him on at first. People forget how bold this decision was.

In Washington, I was delighted my friend was finally

running, and looked for a way to help without leaving my job (now running events at Macy's) and family to work in Little Rock. I found it with other Georgetown classmates, working under the direction of Tim Chorba, now a senior partner at the well-known lawyer/lobbyist shop of Patton Boggs, LLC. Once again I had to prove myself to him. At first he didn't remember me from the 1988 reunion efforts, and was reluctant to include me in the campaign. But as I reminded him of our telephone project he suddenly burst out, "I do remember you! You're the woman who gives great phone!"

Tim, who went on to much grander things as US Ambassador to Singapore, and is therefore quite dignified, insists he never said any such thing. But I remember what I remember.

At that point I was warmly welcomed as a campaign volunteer. We had a great base of operations in the Patton Boggs conference room. We'd meet and distribute lists of names and phone numbers, get reports about money raised, plan events - it was fun! Still, I missed being part of the work in Little Rock or on the campaign trail. It sounded like the most excitement ever. You could see the crowds on the evening news and sense the electricity surrounding the candidate. I tried to imagine what it would be like to actually be there, in the center of all the energy. It seemed amazing and far removed from what we were doing. Then I'd shake my head and get back to the drudgery of making more calls.

My parents raised us to be responsible citizens, and I voted in every election since I came of age. But this was my first experience working in politics - and the presidential race is the biggest game of them all. I was so green I actually thought once the next fund-raising event was over, we'd be "done" with all that. As in, *OK, I can make fifty more phone calls now 'cause once this next dinner/luncheon/brunch/whatever is over, we'll be done with fund raising!*

Go ahead, roll your eyes here. Talk about clueless ... It took me six months (six months!) to come to the forehead-smacking realization that fund-raising NEVER ends. It just goes on and on and on forever. So we kept calling to plead for money and kept running events and kept talking about what a great president Bill Clinton would be.

I was new to this kind of cold calling, but I passionately believed in Governor Clinton and his agenda for America, so it wasn't difficult to talk to people. And, after all, we had the shared Georgetown experience. I usually received at least a polite and often cordial reception. But I remember speaking to one classmate, a doctor, who snarled at me, "I wouldn't vote for Bill Clinton if he promised to appoint me Surgeon General!"

"OK, I'll put you down as not a fan..."

A year later, in the summer of 1993, when our Georgetown class had its twenty-fifth reunion at the White House, we briefed the President on this remark, so when the reluctant doctor went through the receiving line the President could greet him with "George! I wanted to make you Surgeon General but they told me you were not interested. What a shame!"

Fortunately, this was the minority view. There was a great response from classmates who were generous with money and promises of support. But to the general public, for a long time, Bill Clinton was simply, "Governor Who?" I mean, how many people had heard of the Governor of Arkansas? How many people could imagine the Governor of a small, poor, rural state could run and be qualified to be president? As an East coast snob myself, it was a stretch to visualize anything important coming from Arkansas - and I KNEW him.

In the summer of 1992 the campaign was so desperate for money you could "Be Bill's Running Mate" on a jog to the White House for free and have brunch with the candidate at the *Old Ebbitt Grill* for $250. In today's world this is chump change in politics at the Presidential level, but in 1992 he needed every penny.

When brunch ended, the candidate stood and shook every hand, including the waiters. A few of us classmates waited over at the side, watching. We saw how he connected with each person, turning on his intense attention and megawatt charm. Unlike every other politician I'd ever seen up close, when he's talking to you, he's talking to YOU, and no one else in the room matters. (The usual politician behavior is for them to be looking over your shoulder to see if there's anyone more important in the room who they should be paying attention to.) You are the focus of a virtual supernova of charm, and you're just going to get pulled in.

I turned to Tim and said, "You know, if we could only figure out a way to get him to interact with each voter for just a minute, he would win in a landslide."

Fortunately, Bill and his advisors were able to figure it all out without my help – they created town hall meetings, which were a whole new way to campaign back then. Once he got up in front of those folks and started talking and looking into the camera at the people at home, his victory was assured.

At a fund raising dinner with some Georgetown friends.

CHAPTER TWO ~ I HAVE A DREAM

For a year we labored on behalf of our friend. Every moment I wasn't working at my job I was doing something to help the Clinton campaign. In all that time I never once thought that if he won, I might get a job in the new administration. Not once. Like most people I assumed all the jobs in the White House went to foreign and domestic policy experts, numbers crunchers, lawyers and the like. Since I am none of those, I never imagined there could be a place for me. I worked because I believed in Bill Clinton's agenda, and his willingness to work heart and soul to accomplish it. I believed in his decency and his dedication to making ordinary people's lives better. I'd seen these things since we were both eighteen and was happy to have a small part in making the dream of all those years become a reality.

All our efforts finally ended on election day. No more calls, no more events, even (oh happy day!) no more fund-raising. Now only the voices of the voters would determine the future. I stood in the little curtained voting booth in the Fairlington Elementary School auditorium staring at the ballot before me. It was a strange feeling to see at the top of the ticket the name of a friend; someone I'd known for most of my life, someone I'd worked my hardest to help put into the most important job in the world. I shook my head in disbelief, muttered a little prayer and pushed down firmly on the button.

I don't remember a thing about the rest of the day, but I sure remember election night. It came in a delirious haze of excitement. It was finally decision time. Thank goodness my husband drove us to the party at the Women's National Democratic Club. At that point I hardly remembered my own name, so I can't imagine where we would have ended up if I'd been in the driver's seat. All of us who worked so long and hard together were glued to the multiple TV screens doling out the news in bits and pieces. I could feel the adrenaline tingling in my fingers. I was tempted to take a nice, stiff drink, (it seems to work for everyone else!) but my limit is one glass of wine - not nearly enough to knock down the anxiety rising in my gut.

Slowly Dan Rather and Tom Brokaw called the states for one candidate or the other. We agonized over the total of electoral votes. We cheered for some states and groaned for others. We held our breath, watching the tally, state by state. Finally, the magic number, 270, flashed on the screen. We let out our breath in screams of joy, pounding each other on the back with stunned faces. "He won! He won! He did it! He's the next President!" The numbers clearly said so, but believing it was another matter. It took a while, at least for me, for it to sink in.

I'm sure it's exciting to work on a campaign you support and win, but it was a lot more than that for me. This was not just a politician I admired, but a man I'd known since we were both barely able to vote. He was a dear and caring friend. He laid out a vision of our country I believed in. And now the American people said they believed in it too and trusted him to make it happen. It seemed incredible – the kind of news you only think you hear, until you shake your head to clear it. Presidents are older men – our fathers' and grandfathers' generations. How could one of **us** be President? And not only one of us, but a DEMOCRAT, for the first time in 12 years. We staggered home very late, not drunk on booze but on the sheer excitement and wonder of the moment.

It's a good thing I didn't have to go to work at Macy's the next day. I had the day off from special events and concierge duties. I hadn't slept a wink and I had an adrenaline hangover - a new and unpleasant experience. But, when I did get up, I had a sudden thought, for the very first time: *Boy, working for Candidate Clinton was the most exciting thing I've ever done. I loved it! Now that the campaign is over, I wonder if there's a way I can continue to make a contribution to **President** Clinton's agenda.*

I'm not an ambitious or competitive person, and this wasn't a typical thought for me, so it took me by surprise. Then I realized I had no idea how to do anything about it. *Maybe I should go to the Library, take a look at the "Plum Book."*

This is a bible to Washington political types and wannabes. It lists all the "plum" political jobs a President gets to fill with friends and supporters, hopefully well qualified for their positions. (At least they were in the Clinton administration.) Victorious campaign workers pore over its pages like pagan priests over the entrails of a slaughtered goat.

As a lifelong Washingtonian I vaguely knew about the Book but had never seen it and ended up at the Arlington County Central Library. "Do you have the Plum Book," I asked?

I bet I was the first of many to request it - it was only the morning after the election. The librarian produced the book and I leafed through it. I saw positions for lawyers, policy experts and … numbers crunchers. Damn! Just as I expected. Then I found a page listing the "Executive Office of the President." Here were the names, titles and phone numbers of about a dozen White House officials. One of these was "Janet Johnson, Director, Visitors Office." I photocopied the page and returned the book to the librarian, who asked, "Did you find what you wanted?"

"Oh, I sure hope so!" I replied.

Back at home I settled in my favorite chair and studied the page again. I'd never heard of the White House Visitors Office, but I was an expert on visitors' services from my four years at the National Gallery of Art in the 1980s. As an exhibition supervisor I designed ticketing systems, arranged crowd control, hired, trained and scheduled staff, and worked to accommodate the (literally) millions of people who came to the Gallery for shows like *Treasure Houses of Britain, Impressionist Treasures from the Soviet Union,* and *Japan, the Age of the Daimyo*. My first day (FIRST DAY) on the job I had met the handsome Prince and exquisite Princess of Wales, who walked up to me and began a conversation about tourism in Britain. (As if my opinion mattered.) This was more conversation than most people at the Reagans' state dinner at the White House had gotten! When they floated out the door I thought, *I am REALLY going to like this job*,

And I did.

Over the next four years I met royalty from all over the world, movie stars, theater and opera stars, and the famous people mentioned in the *Washington Post Style* section. One day, Jackie Kennedy sat down next to a colleague in the East Building and slipped off her flats to rub her aching feet. The next, the Crown Prince and Princess of Japan arrived for a performance of the most bizarre music you ever heard. In *Ga-Ga-Ku* the notes actually bypass any buffers to hit the pain centers in the middle of your brain. Every American in the room made that little sucking sound you do when fingernails screech down a blackboard. But the Japanese guests were in heaven. I loved all the amazing and creative things that happened at the Gallery on a daily basis. It was a privilege to be there.

I even learned to enjoy working with the sometimes-difficult public. Yes, I loved the Gallery, and when it was time to move on I assumed I was leaving the best job I'd ever have. After all, where else could I work in such beautiful surroundings? What other work could I do that would be this much fun, where I'd have such interesting colleagues, meet royalty and movie stars? I couldn't imagine what my future would be, but it was time to move on in 1990.

Now I looked at the name on the Plum Book page and wondered if the people in the *White House Visitors Office* did the same kind of work. Of course the easiest way to find out would be to call and ask, but I didn't want to do that. Whoever Ms. Janet Johnson was, she knew as well as I did she, and her beloved boss, George Bush, had just lost their jobs. Calling her to ask about it seemed too much like rubbing salt into an open wound. The idea made me squirm. I'm a softie. (Or, at least I was then.) *No, I can't do it. I just can't. She must be horribly depressed right now. Maybe next week ...yes, definitely next week!*

The next day I returned to work at Macy's and listened to phone messages from people wanting information about events we advertised. One call was from a Ms. Johnson, and gave her phone number. I certainly wasn't thinking about the *Plum Book* when I returned the call and was shocked almost speechless to hear the phone answered, "White House Visitors Office."

I gulped and asked for Ms. Johnson.

"We'll see if the Director is available, one minute."

Oh my God. Literally. *Oh my God.*

Now, you can believe anything you want, but I'm a Christian, and believe, without question, God knew I wasn't comfortable calling this lady, so He arranged, out of all the millions (billions?) of calls in Washington that day, for her to call me. And really, how could it have happened by chance? No, the universe shifed and the stars aligned for me in that moment. Next thing I knew, we were chatting. "Yes, Ms. Johnson, how can I help you?"

"I'd like information about the children's event you advertised for next Saturday, please."

When we finished, I said, "I've never heard of the White House Visitors Office before. I used to manage visitors' services at the National Gallery, and I wonder if it was similar to what you do. Would you mind telling me about it?"

"Of course," she said nicely, "I'll be happy to."

And that's just what she did, describing their work with some detail. I was madly taking notes on my side of the conversation and at the end said, "Thank you for telling me about your office. Under the circumstances I hope my questions haven't upset or offended you."

She knew exactly what I meant and laughed, "Not at all. The only thing that will bother me is if you come and take my job away from me, but there's not a darn thing I can do about it!"

We hung up. I stared at the phone without seeing it and whispered to myself, *Oh my God, there IS a job at the White House I'm perfect for. Now, how am I going to get it?*

CHAPTER THREE ~

HOW AM I GOING TO GET THAT JOB?

I was useless in the office for the rest of the day. I'm sure people spoke to me, and I answered; I'm sure I accomplished my tasks; but it all seemed very remote to me as I sat at my desk staring into space. Inside my new tunnel-vision I had a new goal, a new passion, a new obsession. I knew I was qualified for the White House job. I had all that experience at the National Gallery. I even learned to love working with the public, not just when they're being polite, but especially when they were rude and demanding. After all, any idiot can respond to rudeness with rudeness. The challenge is to make it all a game, responding to rudeness with kindness and graciousness (and a laugh you're careful to keep on the inside).

I finally drove home from Macy's in a daze, thinking, *That's my job. I know it. I have all the right experience ... but, I don't know how to even ask for it. I bet there are thousands of people who'd kill to get that job, probably as well qualified as I am ... now I know what I want, but what do I do next?*

Remember, Democrats had been out of power, wandering in the political desert for twelve interminable years of Republican control. There were legions of bright, talented people who devoted their entire lives over the last year to electing Bill Clinton. Now, those hordes were going to descend on Washington like locusts descending on Pharaoh, demanding their rewards for all the twenty-hour days, the nights crashed on someone's sofa, the year-long diet of stale pizza and cold coffee, the days on the road busting their butts setting up a candidate drop by or photo op, the family events missed, the career advancements foregone. All these sacrifices because they believed in the candidate, or the agenda, or because they saw a chance to change the world, and their own place in it, for the better.

And where would they all end up? There weren't enough jobs in all of politics to take care of these folks. Although it sure was satisfying to think about how much fun it was going to be to take some plum jobs away from the Republican incumbents who held them for so long -. not that I'm petty, or anything.

Some of these job seekers, because of their academic or career credentials, would end up in Cabinet agencies, pushing the bureaucrats to line up with President Clinton's economic or agriculture or housing agenda. A select few would land at the White House itself, the Promised Land of political life. That's where I wanted to go, and I knew I'd have to act fast, before they gave **my** job away to someone else.

Because my life had not followed a real career path, I had never needed a resume. But I knew I'd need one now. So my first step was to create an attention-grabbing document, something to show how absolutely, brilliantly perfect I was for this particular job. I began to write, and rewrite, laboring over the document for a month. Finally, early in December, I knew I couldn't tweak it anymore; it was ready to go. I made twenty copies and handed them to my friend, Tim Chorba, who was traveling regularly between Washington and the transition office in Little Rock.

"Melinda, I promise. I'll put one of these on each desk I pass. It will end up in the right hands - I promise."

Now it was time to sit back and pray, but I was surprisingly calm. I already thought of this job as "mine." I'd found it in such an amazing way, and I'd taken the action necessary to claim it. Now I just had to wait for the universe to line up with that reality. This may sound easy, but I assure you it wasn't.

I waited through all of December without hearing a word. I searched the mail every day for a sign that didn't come. I started to stake out the mailman. David Dunn, a friend of Tim's who heard about my job search, kindly put me in touch with two ladies who had worked in the White House for Ronald Reagan. Carol McCain was Senator John McCain's first wife. She was close to the Reagan family and had held the very position I wanted – Director of the Visitors Office. Gahl Burt had been Nancy Reagan's Social Secretary. These ladies knew a lot about how a White House works, what the jobs are, and what it's like to work for a President you love and believe in. They didn't know me from Adam, and, besides, I was a Democrat.

Nevertheless, they invited me to lunch at the Jockey Club, where Washington society meets and eats. I didn't move in those circles, but, as it happens, my then father-in-law had designed the interior of the club. So I felt right at home in the dark, wood paneled room with the hunt prints on the walls and the red and white checked tablecloths. The diners filling the adjacent tables spoke in the quiet, languid tones of the very rich and very important.

Carol and Gahl, in their chic and expensive suits, spent an hour sharing stories of their White House years. They laughed, they reminded each other of events and people they'd known. They showered me with kindness and information. Carol briefed me on the Visitors Office in detail. Gahl suggested if I were seeking some White House job, working for the First Lady could be exciting and rewarding. But I didn't know Hillary Clinton – yet. And I was focused like a laser on one specific job.

Finally, at the end of an hour of interesting conversation, Gahl gently asked me the obvious question we had avoided: "Melinda, do you have any reason to think you're going to be selected for this specific job? Have you heard from anyone about it?"

I looked at them across the table, so bright, so reasonable, so gracious. I smiled and said, "No, there's no concrete reason I can give you that would make any sense. I haven't even spoken with anyone about it. But I know in my heart I'm going to get this job. That's the only way I can explain it."

I expected a look of pity. Instead they looked at each other and gave a little nod of understanding. They got it. Somewhere in the universe doors were easing open, and I was surely going to step through. I felt more hopeful than ever.

Still, there was no actual news about my position. I waited and prayed. Christmas came and went. I'm sure I decorated and cooked and had a lovely time with my family, but I don't remember a moment of it. Washington was electric with excitement over the incoming administration – a new party, a new generation, a new direction! Remember, Washington is a one-industry town: Politics-R-Us. Everything important revolves around political power - who's got it, who's gonna get it, and who's now out of the game. In New

York it may be money and culture, in LA it's entertainment, I guess in Houston it's oil. But in Washington, it's all politics, all the time. And there's nothing like a new administration coming to town to set hearts racing and pundits pontificating.

Social Washington was falling all over itself to figure out who was going to be important enough in the new team to invite to their parties. The Washington Post *Style* section was full of stories about the new players. We hung on every morsel of news, every name dangled like pearls from the transition office, for clues about what the new White House would be like.

The press were desperate for stories to uncover the "real" Bill and Hillary Clinton. In the absence of any actual news, they were reduced to stalking the one family member they could get to – Socks the cat. Yes, paparazzi from all over the world, planted themselves outside the Governor's Mansion, crawling around on hands and knees. They stuck their long lenses through the iron fence to get a shot of the black and white kitty, who didn't know he was about to become the nation's most famous pet. Luckily, he has a sweet and placid temperament, and didn't mind the attention. As to whether he understood how ridiculous it all was, who can say?

By mid-January it was almost time for the inauguration, and I still hadn't heard anything. Tim swore he'd put my resume on every possible desk. I tried to imagine what the transition could be like, but I really didn't know. The press was full of stories about mountains of resumes coming in from across the country and piling up on desks in Little Rock. The figure I heard was 40,000. How would the right person ever find mine, in all that chaos? But I knew, I just knew, it was going to work out somehow. That job was mine!

Finally, it was January 20. The transition team had sent me tickets for various events, so at least I was on **someone's** list. I felt very emotional about my friend's inauguration as President of the United States. It was difficult to believe a man I'd known since we were eighteen was now assuming the most powerful position in the world. At forty-c
seven, I didn't feel old myself, but was Bill, the same age, old enough (seasoned enough) for the challenges ahead?

We Baby Boomers never even acknowledged middle age as we sped right through it on our bikes and roller blades, our tango shoes and yoga mats. So, how could one of us now be old enough to be President? You can know something with your brain and still have trouble accepting it as reality. This is how I felt on Inauguration Day, 1993.

I wept when I saw Bill and Hillary on the Jumbotron as he made his sacred vow, his hand resting on the Bible in Hillary and Chelsea's hands, their faces glowing with the excitement and promise of the day, and the days to come. I was overcome with joy, disbelief, and hope for the future. That, and the fact my nose and toes were frozen, but I didn't care.

When I got home I was surprised to find the mail had come. *I thought Inauguration Day was a holiday. Where did these letters come from? Bills, bills, a catalogue, more bills, and, wait, what's this one - from the office of the President Elect!?*

My throat closed, my breath came short, and my hands were shaking as I opened it. I unfolded the heavy cream paper, noted the classy gold seal at the top, took a deep breath and began to read: "Dear Ms. Bates, We are pleased to have received your resume, we're keeping it on file, and we promise to let you know if a suitable position comes up."

I read it twice, three times. I thought exactly what you are thinking - *a kiss-off letter! The transition team sent me a kiss-off letter! It wasn't even signed by Bill.*

My gut twisted. My heart hurt. A voice in my head yelled, *No, no, no, NO! That's not the right answer. I'm supposed to be a part of the new team! I have so much to offer on that one, specific job - **my** job! How could they send me a kiss-off letter?*

I dropped into a chair, too shocked and depressed to stand.

Months later, when I had a better understanding of the almost total chaos reigning at the overwhelmed transition office, I realized ninety five percent of the people who sent in their resumes never got any response at all. So, receiving any letter from them was actually a good sign. But I didn't know this on January 20, and I was devastated.

Still, we had a big evening ahead of us, and I was determined to celebrate. I'd helped our university class arrange a dinner in Georgetown, for classmates and friends from the campaign.

I offered to get a life-sized cardboard Bill Clinton so we could all take our first pictures with the new president. I was out voted – but they were wrong. It would have been a fun part of the evening.

My husband, Darryl, and I dressed in our best, I in my custom-made gold gauze evening gown, he in his tuxedo.

We looked pretty swell that night, and I thought I did a good job of hiding my sadness and disappointment about the job. But later, when I saw all the photos we took, I had to laugh. Around me, everyone is delirious with joy, while I, well, I'm smiling, but I still look as if my best friend **and** my dog just died. I've never been any good at hiding my thoughts and feelings, and I'm a terrible liar. You just have to look at my face to see the truth.

We had a great meal in Georgetown, then piled into mini-buses to head downtown for the Arkansas Inaugural Ball. Maybe you harbor some secret ambition to attend an inaugural ball? Maybe it sounds exciting as all get out to you? After all, how many of us get to go to a "ball"?

Well, lean in and let me disabuse you of that thought. Inaugural Balls are not really "balls." They are more like huge cocktail parties, held in immense, drafty, cavernous and unattractive spaces that have been tarted up on the cheap with lots of crepe paper bunting and flags. You can't wear real evening shoes, because you're walking on concrete for hours and your feet will never recover. You can't check your coat because the line to get it back is several hundred people long. So, you stand around, you get a drink, you greet friends (who are hard to find in the dark room) and you enjoy the musical acts. That's about it. Unless you like getting drunk - there's a lot of that too. Doesn't appeal to me. Everybody ought to get the chance to go once (because it's still an experience, and so you can say you went) but nobody would want to go twice. And that's the honest truth.

There are many different Inaugural Balls all around Washington, and the new President and First Lady are expected to make an appearance at each one. We knew they'd come to the Arkansas Ball, but we didn't know when. When we arrived, we found it a happy, rowdy, chaotic mix of revelers, many already well into the getting-drunk stage of the evening. We learned we had just missed the Clintons, who had visited, danced a dance, schmoozed a little while, and left. This is so unlike Bill Clinton I could hardly believe it.

What? How did that happen? Hillary must've gotten the Secret Service to arm wrestle him out of the ballroom, otherwise he would never have left all these friends! Well, we missed seeing them, but, hey, look over there - it's Chuck Berry, and he's a blast from the past. And anyway, we're here to celebrate a moment in history for our friend, who's now the most powerful man in the world. Let's try to wrap our minds around that thought, and forget about the damn job. I'll get over it. Like Scarlet O'Hara, 'I'll think about it tomorrow' ...

The next day, Thursday, was the Clintons' first public event, a widely publicized and nationally broadcast open house. This was a tradition in nineteenth century White Houses, but it hadn't been followed for a long time. The Clintons wanted to re-introduce it, as a way of demonstrating their commitment to being stewards of the most open and accessible White House ever, a House that truly belonged to the people. It was the first expression of a theme we'd come to hear from them often: honoring the past and imagining the future.

There was so much excitement in Washington and around the country about the new President and First Lady that everyone wanted to go. The National Park Service invited people to send in postcards, which they did by the thousands. Then cards were pulled out of a barrel in a drawing, and those people got to go.

I was at home, depressed and sulky, sullenly watching the event on television. *How could they not have picked me for the Visitors Office? I know I'm the perfect person. How could they give **my** job to someone else? It's just not right. Whine, whine, whine ...*

It was very upsetting, but I still wanted to watch every moment of the event. I'd been thinking about the White House for months now and seeing it on the television was pure torture. It looked beautiful and mysterious, hugged by large evergreen trees, the white stone gleaming in the cold air, as a long line of excited visitors shuffled in.

Then the cameras took us inside. The Clintons and Gores stood in a beautiful oval room, with scenic colonial-era murals on the walls and a fireplace behind them. They looked so young, so energetic (after twelve years of old men), so attractive and glamorous. Their smiles were blinding. I couldn't help smiling back, but I still couldn't understand why I wasn't there to help run the event.

But I wasn't, and the crowds appeared to be happily flowing through the receiving line. Then the cameras cut to what was happening outside. Outside was ... not so great. Outside thousands of people were lined up in a very disorderly way, looking like a crowd about to turn itself into a mob. Someone came in and spoke briefly into Hillary's ear. She shook her head, then took the President by his arm and turned away from the cameras to the back of the room. She whispered into his ear, but she forgot she was wearing a microphone, so everyone out in television land heard her tell him, "It's a real mess outside. People who should have gotten in, did not. And people who shouldn't have gotten in, did. It looks like we screwed all these people!"

They conferred for a moment, then stepped outside to the South stairs to greet the crowds waiting in the cold. This was not an auspicious beginning for the new administration. You don't want to look incompetent at hosting an open house, for goodness sake, when the whole world is looking to you for new leadership and fresh ideas about national and international affairs.

When we saw this happening, my husband turned to me and said, "Why haven't they called you? If you were there, this mess wouldn't have happened. This is what you're so good at!"

I stared glumly at the chaotic scene on the television. "I dunno, Darryl. You know they know all the smartest, most talented people in America. I guess they picked someone else for the job (**my** job). But, you're right – I would never have let that mess happen!"

Well, it turned out a whole bunch of people at the White House were also pretty upset about this screw-up on the very first public Clinton White House event. Twenty minutes later our phone rang: "Hello, this is Janet Green calling from the White House."

I grabbed Darryl's arm and calmly said, "Yes?"

"I'm calling about the job of Director of the White House Visitors Office."

"Yes?" I replied, gripping Darryl's arm even harder.

"Have you interviewed for this job?"

"No, I haven't" I answered, still calmly. But inside I was on the verge of hysterics.

"Oh, then have you spoken to anyone about this job"

"No, I haven't."

"Well, it's really strange, because I haven't been told to talk to you, or to interview you. I've been told you are the person for this job, and we need to get you in here right away."

I now had Darryl's arm in a death grip, but I managed to reply, in a level voice, "I'll be happy to come in; when is convenient for you?"

This was my first experience with an ability I didn't know I had - to be excited or even frantic on the inside but show only serene competence on the outside. It surprised me - and it turned out to be one of the most important qualities I'd bring to my new job.

As the call ended, we agreed I'd come to the White House on Saturday morning, and hung up. I turned to Darryl, let go of his arm, which was now turning blue, and began to leap up and down, there in the bedroom, screaming at the top of my lungs, "I got the job! I got the job!" Other than my kids being born, it was the most exciting moment of my life.

CHAPTER FOUR ~ MY EXCELLENT ADVENTURE BEGINS

On Saturday, the twenty third of January, I carefully dressed in my best black wool suit and white silk blouse. I was so nervous I put my fingernails through my pantyhose twice before I managed to get an intact pair on. I had to re-apply my lipstick three times, because I kept smearing it outside my lip line. *Damn!* I looked at the eyeliner and thought, *no way, I'll have to go without. I think I can manage some mascara, though. Not too much. I want to look professional and polished. Professional and polished.*

It took ten minutes just to fasten my pearl necklace, as I fumbled around with the stupid clasp. Then, because the universe thought I wasn't already nervous enough, my husband, who had taken our only car for some client business, didn't get it back until the very (very!) last minute. Darryl is a great guy but can be clueless about that pesky "time" concept. I was standing in our living room hyperventilating into a brown paper bag and staring frantically out the window when he finally showed up. I had to choose between taking the time to tell him what he'd just done to me and getting the hell out the door. I chose getting the hell out the door.

The streets were slushy with old, dirty snow. I hated having to wear a coat over my nice suit, but it was too cold to go without. One advantage from working at Macy's - I had a closet full of great clothes. I drove to the White House, anxiously looking for the South West Entrance. Although I was born in Washington, and lived there all my life, I'd never been to the White House before, and was ridiculously relieved to find it. (Hint: it's an enormous white house right in the middle of town.)

I gave my name to the Secret Service officer at the gate, with a big smile. I figured I'd be working closely with these men and women and wanted to make a nice impression. He looked at me quizzically, and handed me a visitor's pass, with a large, red "A" on it, and a chain. Then he waved me in to West Executive Avenue, the closed-off street between the West Wing and the Old Executive Office Building (now the Eisenhower Building). At the time I thought he was just curious but realized later they needed to memorize our faces as quickly as possible, so they could tell who was who in the hordes of new staffers.

I parked our aging Volvo station wagon, with the license plate "UPPITY"(our little joke. Darryl wanted "YUPPIE" and I had to gently explain we were too old and too poor to qualify), put on my game face, straightened my jacket, walked into the ground floor of the West Wing and presented myself to another officer sitting at a desk there. He called Janet Green in the Office of Administration, and she quickly came to get me.

We shook hands and I noted her unremarkable suit (hey! I worked at Macy's!), short brown hair and determined, focused look. She smiled and indicated I should follow her to a narrow stairway leading up from the lower level to the first floor. The hallways were humming with activity as people came and went from offices behind heavy wood doors. It looks nothing like the West Wing of *The West Wing*. All those offices with glass partitions - we called it the "Hill Street Blues West Wing." But that was a long way in the future. On this first trip I was too excited to notice much, although I did see some interesting paintings I hoped I'd get to examine some time - just not now. Now I had to make a great impression on my new bosses.

We walked down a hall to the office of David Watkins, Janet's boss and the Assistant to the President for Management and Administration. You may vaguely recognize his name, but not remember why. David was the (boneheaded) Presidential aide who took *Marine One*, the unbelievably cool Presidential helicopter, to play a round of golf in Maryland. As it happens, the helicopter crew HAS to fly on a regular basis to keep their skills sharp and check out the machine, so David's trip wasn't really as stupid as it seemed. But in Washington, as we were all about to learn the hard way, perception is more important than reality. MUCH more important than reality. So, shortly after he played that course, he had to resign. I don't remember anyone expressing any particular distress at his loss, but that was all later.

David waved me to a seat and the three of us sat together and began to talk about the Visitors Office. I was well prepared for this meeting, thanks again to the kindness of Carol McCain, and her niece, Melinda Andrews (now Fitzwater). On Thursday evening, after the call from the White House, I first phoned two hundred of my closest friends to tell them I got the job. (I GOT THE JOB!) Then I called Carol and asked if she had time to brief me in detail about the office. She seemed almost as excited as I was and told me to show up at her house the next afternoon. There was no reason for her to be so kind to me, other than her own inherent decency. It would have been just as easy, and would have been pretty tempting to anyone else, to let me start out on my own and maybe fail. These are two very classy ladies.

My friend Marc Hoberman, who worked with me at Macy's, went with me. We spent the entire afternoon reviewing everything from a rough diagram of the office to a rundown of how the tour ticketing system worked. They gamely tried to explain the Easter Egg Roll, but I confess, at that point my eyes started to cross. It's hard to concentrate on anything when adrenaline is pumping through your body every few minutes. But I memorized everything I learned, so on Saturday morning when David and Janet began to talk about the work of the Visitors Office, I quickly demonstrated I was already an expert.

"The current system requires the Members of Congress to ... but I think we can improve the process pretty quickly by... " *Ha! I came here prepared, and I'm going to be great at this!*

After a few minutes they sat back, exchanged glances, and breathed a sigh of relief.

After we reviewed tours David's face turned even more serious. I wondered what was coming next. "Let me tell you, Melinda, Janet and I have been working here on the transition for the last three months. Twenty-hour days of briefings with President Bush's people. I think we covered it all and I'm now an expert on how the White House works - domestic policy, foreign policy, economics, you name it. When I thought we couldn't take in one more piece of information I asked my final question: 'What is the single most difficult thing to manage at the White House?' I expected to hear something about Congress, or the Cabinet Agencies, or even the press, but no. The answer was, 'If you can pull off a successful Easter Egg Roll, you can do anything here.'"

David gave me a searching look. "And, now, Melinda, the Egg Roll will be **your** responsibility."

Inside I thought, *Gosh, I wonder how the heck I'm going to pull that off?* But I nodded, smiled, and confidently said, "I'm looking forward to it!"

Finally, David leaned in, lowered his voice a little and said, "We have been told we have a problem," (read: not staffing the Visitors Office, screwing up the first public event) "and that YOU are the solution."

Thank you, Mr. President! Again I gulped, and nodded that I was, indeed, exactly the right person for this job. I may have mentioned I'm not particularly ambitious, or competitive, or boastful. I prefer to let my work speak for itself. This is not any smarter in Washington than it would be in New York or LA, but it is how it is. This was now my second experience with that level of self-confidence and it was a revelation.

Oh, gosh, the stakes are incredibly high, but I bet I can do it. I KNOW I can do it. And I bet it's going to be fun – the most fun ever! I'm going to work my ass off to do a good job for the Clintons. Now, when can I get started?

On Monday morning I returned to the White House for the first time as an official staff member of the new administration. This time I braved the cold in my very best dark blue suit, the one with the gold pinstripes on the skirt. I picked a sparkly pin from my extensive collection of vintage rhinestone pieces and added it to the lapel. I bet the original owner of the 1940s never imagined a woman in a job like mine.

Again I entered on the West side of the House, but this time Janet escorted me through the West Wing, down the West Colonnade that runs along the Rose Garden, and into the "Palm

Room" (a small, corner, garden room). She pushed open tall, double glass doors and I followed her into the Ground Floor of the White House itself, along a rich red carpet with a gold border.

About mid-way down there was a Secret Service officer, in black pants and white blouse, who nodded at us as we went by. Janet and I both said, "Hello" and kept walking. I later learned from a Lieutenant this immediately differentiated us from the departing Bush people. They treated the USSS like furniture, never even acknowledging their presence. He told me he once conducted an experiment by greeting the same Bush aide in the same place every morning for a year. And every morning for a year she ignored him. Not us. Right from the beginning we were friendly, respectful, and made it a point to learn their names and faces. This was noticed and appreciated.

We passed some dark wood doors and I wondered what was behind them. I saw a small elevator lobby on the left, then a large oval room on the right with colorful murals on the walls - the one from the open house event. Opposite was a white marble staircase, with a silver railing, leading up to the State Floor.

I can't wait to see the rooms up there. I think the tours start down here. Goodness, the rug is spotless, the marble floors are shiny, and it smells so good - furniture polish? This House is well cared for. And look at the flowers in every room! I love flowers. I wonder who arranges them.

Next, a room on the right with First Lady portraits, (*Look - there's Nancy Reagan in bright red!*), a small room on the left filled with bookcases and books, and in front of us a pair of striking bronze sculptures with wild West themes, one of which looked like a Remington as we breezed by.

 We left the White House itself through a pair of ivory-painted doors and entered the East Wing through its corresponding corner room, then walked down the glass-walled East Colonnade that

runs parallel to the Jacqueline Kennedy Garden. (Republicans call it the "First Lady's Garden." Petty.)

Janet may have spoken, but I didn't hear her through the humming in my head: *This is too confusing. I wish I could leave a trail of breadcrumbs to mark my path.*

The Colonnade ends at a desk staffed by a Secret Service officer, and a huge bust of President Lincoln. If you jog to the left, you can go either up the stairs to the Social Office and Military Office, or down a short flight to the East Reception Room and the hallway to the Visitors Office suite. The hallway is paneled with wood and was then bare. Later we filled it with blown-up photos of the President and First Lady giving speeches, visiting the troops, or honoring distinguished Americans. I still have some of those photos, mementos of the exciting things we did there every day.

Janet briskly marched up to the woman sitting at the reception desk and asked for Janet Johnson, the departing Director. Then she turned to me, nodded and said, "Good luck! Let us know what you need once you figure it out," and left.

OK , here I finally am, and now it's up to me to get the job done. I'm in the White House, the most important place in America. I ought to be shaking in my shoes, but really, I can't wait to get started. I'm sure going to give it my all.

I stood up straight, smiled at the receptionist and looked expectant. Janet Johnson came out from her office on the right and greeted me pleasantly, if not warmly. She showed me into her office (which was about to become mine), and we sat down for what must have been a painful conversation for her. I hadn't planned to talk about how I got the job, her job, and was truly shocked when

the first thing she said was, "Have you come here from working at Macy's?"

"Why, yes, I have," I stammered. "Are you remembering a phone conversation the day after the election last November?"

"Oh, yes, I am," she said with a laugh. "In fact, when we hung up I turned to the person with me and said, "I have just spoken with my replacement.""

That took me from stammering to speechless. I'd known in my heart God was going to open this door, but I had no idea Janet recognized it in our conversation.

Next she briefed me on Visitors Office operations in a general way. We talked about Congressional ticketed tours, group tours, guided tours, self-guided (unguided) tours and special tours.

"Once we got the election results," she said, "we stopped making any promises to Congress or anyone else about how things would be done after January 20. Everyone understands you'll probably make changes, but no one knows what exactly you'll do. There are a lot of pending requests people are anxious about, and you need to let them know pretty quickly what you plan to do about all these tours, and how."

I appreciated Janet's help. She didn't have to stay to help us get started. I'm by nature a person who believes the best about people - until they prove me wrong. Janet Johnson was kind to me and I was kind to her in return. Over the years I consistently refused to be quoted saying anything critical of the Bush I Visitors Office, even though I was sorely tempted. Then a former FBI agent wrote a horrible book about his so-called experiences in the Clinton White House, full of lies and distortions. I would never have purchased or read that book, but one of my volunteers did, and photocopied the pages about us in the Visitors Office. Janet was quoted saying some nasty and untrue things about us. I was so disappointed - especially since I had carefully refrained from saying anything the least bit critical about them. Oh well. Lesson learned. This also helped me realize if someone was willing to lie about the relatively unimportant operations of the Visitors Office, I could be damned sure the rest of what he wrote was a lie also.

Then Janet invited me to see the rest of the office and meet the other two ladies who stayed to help us get started. Just outside of the Director's office was a space large enough for two desks, facing each other, with a path in the middle to the reception desk. Beyond was a large room, filled with sunlight from tall windows and five workstations.

Tracy Presock and MaryAnn Smith greeted me warmly. "Welcome to the most important and exciting time in your life. We hope you're ready for it!"

Considering they had all just lost their own important and exciting jobs, I thought they were amazingly gracious. There was a third young woman in the office, Holly Holt. Janet explained that Holly was not a Bush person. She appeared at the White House ten days before, offering to volunteer in their office. Somehow she figured out the regular staff were all leaving, there was still work to do, and a competent volunteer would be welcome. Holly came from Denton, a small town in Texas, where she worked on Gov. Ann Richards' campaign. Janet was careful to say she hadn't promised Holly a position. Staffing the office was entirely up to me.

I was curious about this pretty young woman, just out of college, who found a way to get a head start on a highly desirable White House job. We talked a little about the Richards campaign, and I could see for myself how smart she was. She had already shown initiative and resourcefulness and was charming in a genuine, small-town kind of way.

The clincher came when I asked, "So, Holly, you already know how to work the ticketing systems? They seem pretty complicated."

"Oh, yes, I've been doing that since I arrived. I'm already an expert."

"OK then, you've just become my first hire, welcome to the Clinton Visitors Office!"

I thought she'd be an asset to the office. I didn't know then she'd be a vital part of everything we did for the next eight years and I'd come to love her like a daughter. I watched, encouraged and mentored her through a variety of White House jobs, but she always came back to us in the Visitors Office.

The more I learned about the office, the more I knew I wanted to bring Marc Hoberman on board. He was my colleague at Macy's, but before that he had a lifetime of work in the upper reaches of academia, while I had never worked in an office. He understood how technology could help us modernize our procedures. I knew he'd bring skills and experience we'd desperately need. But I literally couldn't figure out how to hire him. I asked Janet (Green) and David, and they told me I had to work with the National Park Service - ask them for resumes, find people to interview that way and select staff from their lists. I was puzzled by this and thought it couldn't be right. (There are some advantages to having spent a lifetime in Washington.)

The Visitors Office is an odd duck. Years before, for political reasons, President Carter promised to cut the size of the White House staff. Sadly, President Clinton made the same dumb ass promise. Read my lips here: there are never enough people on the White House staff to get all the work done. Cutting the staff just makes people's lives that much more stressful and difficult. And, what's the gain? Do you think people in Iowa really care how many people work in the West Wing? How silly. And incredibly counter-productive.

Anyway, Carter technically did cut the size of the staff, but one way he accomplished it was to remove everyone in the Visitors Office, except the Director, from the White House staff list. Then he forced the National Park Service to hire them and delegate them back to the White House. Typical Washington chair shuffling.

But the Park Service isn't supposed to be a political entity, and we were, of course, highly political. How could I depend on them to send me resumes I'd be interested in? Actually, I knew I'd never get the staff I wanted that way, so I just waited a couple of days and then asked, of all people, Janet Johnson.

She looked surprised and said, "Why, you just find the people you want, however you want to find them, and then you tell the Park Service they are the ones you want, and they hire them for you. It's pretty simple."

So that's what I did.

I hired Marc as Associate Director. He really wanted the title and it was the best I could do for him, since I couldn't offer much money to go with it. Sometimes people think anyone who works at the White House makes a huge salary, but that's wrong. I started, in 1993, at $40,000, which was what my predecessor had made, and more than my salary at Macy's. Of course, like most people who worked at the White House, I wanted my job so badly I would have paid them to let me work there, just for the honor and excitement of it. But, since there's not much of a monetary reward, everyone wants an impressive title that tells people at parties how important you are and looks swell on your resume later in life.

Oh, and the business cards, on creamy white stock with the gold embossed Presidential seal at the top. Those are a huge perk. It was always fun to hand one of those to someone who didn't know what you did and watch their reaction. I still have a box in a drawer somewhere in Baja, that I can't bear to toss. They're just too beautiful, and, I guess, too full of memories.

Even your internet address reveals your status: melinda.bates@A1.eop.gov. The "eop" part stands for *Executive Office of the President*, and it was fun to watch even experienced Washingtonians puzzle over it and finally ask what it meant.

Just as Bill - Mr. President - selected me to run the Visitors Office, Hillary chose the Deputy Director, Robyn Dickey. Robyn had worked at the Governor's Mansion in Little Rock. When David Watkins told me she was the person for that position I quickly said, "You mean, I get someone who knows who's who in Arkansas, and knows how the Clintons like things done?"

"Yes, that's it exactly."

"Great! How soon can she get here?" I asked, while thinking, *This is perfect! She sounds like just what the Visitors Office needs. I can handle the Members of Congress, social and philanthropic Washington and the diplomatic corps. But I can guess how difficult it's going to be to take care of the Arkansans. I've read they're already calling by the hundreds about "a visit with Bill and Hillary," and the truth is, I haven't the faintest idea who any of them are. They can tell me they're his closest friend ever from kindergarten, and for all I know, they are! I have no clue. But Robyn will.*

Also, I'd been friends with Bill most of my life, but never worked for him. And I'd never even met the new First Lady. I had no idea how they liked things done, so learning I'd have a colleague who did was a real relief. I couldn't wait to meet her.

Robyn was closing up her life in Little Rock and didn't arrive in Washington until February. In those first, few weeks, I filled the other office positions with capable young women I knew who worked on the campaign: Carla Duryea and Christine Maloy. Mark had a smart friend, Claudia Derricotte who came to be our receptionist. She had the extra advantage of being African-American. I'm Hispanic (my mother was from Puerto Rico, with a Puerto Rican father and Cuban mother.) It's good for government to be diverse! They all brought the same excitement and determination: *We're so grateful to have this opportunity we'll gladly do whatever it takes to do the best job possible. We're working in the WHITE HOUSE.*

I was happy and relieved to make such a good beginning with these hires.

In all the different positions I've had, at the National Gallery of Art, at Macy's, at the White House, and later in the event business, I always, always considered it a privilege to mentor the young people who worked for me. The more I could teach them, the more competent or even expert they could become, the better for our work and the better for them as they moved on with their own future careers. It has been very satisfying to have so many of these young people come back to me later to thank me and tell me they learned so much I was "the best boss they ever had."

When people left the Visitors Office I always produced a glowing reference and printed at least twenty copies on White House letterhead paper for them to use throughout their careers. Here are some of my staff and my favorite USSS officers –

CHAPTER FIVE ~ WE SETTLE IN

In the midst of all our frantic activity I took the time to think about how our suite looked, as well as how it worked. I've always cared about my surroundings. I'm incapable of moving in to any space and not decorating it to suit myself. This included the closet I wallpapered with a zebra print, the wall I painted glossy black, and the paper flowers I cut out and applied to the bathroom walls of my first apartment. What can I say? I was twenty one!

As I've grown up, my taste has changed, (you may be thinking, thank God) but the impulse is still the same: If I can make it beautiful, I'm so much happier in it. Chaos and ugliness make me miserable.

Our suite was neither chaotic nor ugly, but it was boring and inefficient. I poked and prodded the National Park Service to provide new cubicles for the three young women who worked in the large, bright room on the West side. They spent their hours answering phones and reserving tour tickets - pretty dull, I thought, so I wanted their area to be functional and attractive. At least we started out with great geography - ground floor of the East Wing, with high ceilings and tall windows overlooking lawns, trees, flowers, squirrels and birds. One of the most beautiful and exclusive spaces in the country.

As for the rest, I used my own resources - my husband and the Bates family treasure trove of antiques. Late one night, early in February, Darryl watched me stagger in the door. He took my briefcase and led me to a chair, where I collapsed in exhaustion.

"I think it's obvious," he said, "you're going to spend a lot more time in your new office than you do at home. Let's see if we can make it beautiful for you."

"Oh, Darryl, you're a prince! That will be so great."

"We have to start with a plan of the space - do you have one?"

"No, but I'll ask around to see if I can get it."

There actually is a White House decorator who works on senior-level offices, filling them with nice nineteenth century antiques, art, and not-valuable White House mementos. I think she was pleased to find a soul mate as far as creating beautiful interiors, but she didn't have much to offer me. And, she didn't even have a floor plan. So Darryl came in to the office one Saturday, and together we marked off the measurements on his ubiquitous graph paper.

Then we looked at the paint - cream, off white, and ... cream. Very safe. Very boring. I wanted to liven it up a bit, but obviously, nothing shocking. I asked the White House painters, but the only choices were cream, off white and ... cream. So, the next Saturday, Darryl and I arrived with a couple of gallons of pale green paint for the trim, some drop cloths and paint brushes.

"Do you think we'll get in trouble for doing this ourselves?" he asked, as he dipped a brush into the tray. (Not that he cared.)

"I can't say for sure," I giggled, "but just to be safe we're gonna close all the doors, curtains and blinds. What they don't know won't hurt us."

Darryl has always been a rule-breaker at heart, so painting part of the White House on our own made perfect sense to him, and he cheerfully opened the paint and started on some door trim. I hit the baseboards and chair rail. Next to the cream walls it looked very nice - and nothing any reasonable person could object to. I was pleased when we finished late that afternoon, carefully put away the evidence of our unauthorized decorating, and closed the doors.

The next weekend, armed with his new floor plan, Darryl brought in some pretty, paneled double doors for my office and the doorway between the reception area and Marc's space. They worked much better than the cheap, flat, single doors we replaced, not to mention how much better they looked. I asked the White House Curators if we could donate the doors, so it would be official. It was my first experience with a lesson we'd all come to learn well: ain't nothing simple at the White House.

Rex Scouten, the Chief Curator explained it to me. "Well, Melinda, that's actually harder than you'd think. 'Donating' things to the White House is a legal matter that can take months to approve. I don't think you'd want to go to all that trouble over a couple of doors."

"You're right, but is there any other way to do this?"

"We can't tell you this officially, but suppose you 'lent' the doors to the White House, and then, when you left, you just forgot to take them back? At that point who would know - or care - where they came from? What do you think?'

"Fine with me. That's what I'll do." And that is what I did!

The next phase of our plan was to load up Darryl's Rent-a-Wreck truck with antiques - and he had really nice ones. The Bates family has been in the design business since, oh, forever, and always had the most beautiful things lying around or in storage somewhere. He brought me an elegant, eighteenth-century loveseat with a red damask, down-filled cushion Socks came to love to sleep on. We put it under the window that looks out to the trees, flowers and birds on the north lawn.

A pair of large, dark wood cabinets went on the west wall on either side of the new doors. I used them over the years to stow the endless piles of mementos people gave me. Opposite the window we put a pair of delicate, English, tall cabinets with glass fronts that he set up with a faux green marble counter between them for my computer. A large, gilt framed mirror went on the east wall, opposite the door. Over the years I had a lot of fun observing people who came into the office, looked at the mirror and then couldn't stop looking at themselves - adjusting a tie, patting their hair - when they were supposed to be looking at me.

The White House supplied a coffee table and the desk, in golden wood, not very practical (more a table than a desk), but it worked with the other cabinets. A pair of red, Chinoiserie arm chairs and a skirted table in the corner completed the furniture. It looked so nice that when senior people came in I could almost hear them thinking, *How come Melinda got such a great office? And, where did these antiques come from? I'd like to have a mirror like that in MY office ...*

All the walls were initially bare, but I soon began to receive large color photos of me and the President or First Lady chatting at

Noah and Darryl help me move in

some event, or watching a crowd, or heading out to the helicopter. When the celebrities started coming, I always got a copy of the "money shot" - the celebrity du jour with POTUS (President of the US) in front of the *Resolute* desk. This historic desk was made from the timbers of a British ship, *HMS Resolute*, trapped in the ice up in the Arctic, in the early 1850s. American sailors found her, congress purchased her and had her refitted, and sent her back to Queen Victoria. When the ship was decommissioned, the Queen had the desk made and sent to President Hayes in 1880. George Bush (I) used the desk in the Treaty Room, in the Residence. President Clinton, remembering the iconic photo of President Kennedy with his young son playing in front of the desk, brought it back to the Oval Office.

The White House Photo Office sends out these photos, and pretty soon I had a "collection." So I framed a bunch and hung them in rows on the West wall. A couple of years later, when I got to fly on Air Force One, I received a flight certificate. I was so excited about the trip that I framed this, the menu, a photo of myself picking up the "secure phone," and even the paper napkin with the AF1 logo. When I was promoted to Special Assistant to the President, I received a large, calligraphed document, signed by the President - this was my "commission," which only staff at my new level and above received. I'm very proud of it. An Army officer in the Military Office told me it meant I was the equivalent of a three-star general. Imagine that!

Between the antiques, the light-filled space and - most important - the East Wing location of our little bit of White House real estate, people who came to visit or meet with me got the impression I must be a pretty important person. When visitors stood in my office, looked around and looked at me with a little more respect I felt it necessary to explain:

"You have to understand. The White House is just like real estate. The single most important thing is location, location and...LOCATION. So proximity to the President is everything. There are people far more important than I am, happily working out of offices the size of closets over there in the West Wing, as close to the Oval as they can get. We have to be here, in the East Wing, because our work requires us to be close to the East Entrance - for tours and events. Isn't it great how that worked out?"

With my office done, we created better desks and work spaces for Mark, Holly and Claudia. In the entry way by Claudia's desk we hung a pair of colorful pictures of the Inauguration by Peter Max. He signed them for us and now they hang in my house in Baja, Mexico.

Since I'm a cat lover, I quickly fell in love with Socks, the Clintons' black and white kitty with the sweet personality. He had to be on a leash almost all the time, but if he came to visit us we could close the outer door to the suite, remove the leash, and let him roam. A couple of years later Mark thought to ask the Gift Unit (the folks who receive and catalogue all gifts to the First Family) if by chance they had received a scratching post for Socks, and if so, could we please use it? We thought they'd send, you know, a POST, maybe a couple of feet high, with some carpet on it.

 I was astounded when the laborers wheeled in a huge box. We peeled back the cardboard to find a...construction ... about four and a half feet tall. It had a heavy base, a thick trunk, and was topped by what looked like a large mailbox with openings on each end, all of this covered in thick red, white and blue shag carpet. Its gaudiness was astounding - but what did I know? Socks loved it at first sight. He lept up the trunk into the little house, quickly

discovering that he could lie there, with his nose peeking out one end and his tail hanging out the other and snooze all afternoon. And, thanks to the carpet and his claws, if we wanted to take him out to greet someone and take a photo, he didn't have to come unless he wanted to. It was a, um, striking addition to the office.

I loved Socks and loved having him in the office. His personality was very un-catlike. He was willing to be held by strangers, and to have flash bulbs popped in his face. He never once hissed or scratched. And, he was wonderful with children. We once hosted a group of disabled children who came to see the President. Shockingly (sarcasm alert!), he was running late! To pass the time, we took the children out to the South Lawn, and slowly walked around the driveway, looking at the gardens and the House. As we headed up the West side, towards the Oval and the Rose Garden, we could see Socks, on his long tether, under a huge oak tree. That's where he spent the day in good weather. The children all pointed and laughed. Any other cat would have headed away, to peace and privacy under the trees by the pool. Not Socks.

I was pushing a little girl in a wheelchair, and as we got closer, Socks stood up, made the mandatory cat-stretch, and sauntered over. We stopped, and when he reached us, he looked up at the child and jumped into her lap, where he sat, purring, as she lavished him with love. You can imagine how excited the children and their parents were. I don't think their visit with POTUS was nearly as memorable as their experience with his cat.

When we left the White House, Socks went home with Betty Currie, the President's assistant, who loved him too. He had a very nice life, and I wonder if he ever dreamt about his glory days as the most important cat in America.

Robyn's space was a different matter from the rest of the office. It was a nice sized room located just outside the suite door, and she quickly arranged it to suit herself. I want to be clear here: I love Robyn Dickey and think she is one of the smartest, most talented people I've ever worked with. She pulled off extraordinary events for the President and First Lady. I am still in awe of her accomplishments. Her only flaw, as far as I can tell, is that she is incredibly messy.

Messy to a degree I had never seen before (and I'm the mother of two boys!) Maybe "chaotic" is a better word to describe her office, with its piles of papers, books, agendas, photos, and stuff all over the chairs, floor, even her desk. Fairly soon these piles were so high there was only a little trail of carpet left, leading from the door to her desk chair. I used to stand in the doorway and shake my head in dismay.

How can she work like this? It would drive me NUTS to have an office this messy. I'd never get a thing done. But, I'm not her mother, and she always gets the job done - brilliantly. So, take a deep breath and walk away, just walk away.

Once the President was practicing a speech in the Family Theater, which is just up the hall from the Visitors Office. He stopped by to say "hello," glanced in to Robyn's office, then recoiled in shock.

"Good Lord. Whose office is this?"

"It's Robyn's, Mr. President. I know it's a little, um, different, but it doesn't seem to slow her down any."

He stepped inside, on the little trail of carpet, and looked around some more, shaking his head. Then he moved to her desk, looking in vain for an inch of space to write her a note. Giving up, he just stood there, hands helplessly outspread. The photographer who always accompanied him took a step in and snapped a picture. A day later it came to Robyn with a note from the President, "To Robyn, with appreciation for all her work and her neat-as-a-pin office."

All the new staff came on board as quickly as possible, so we could get started with the President's work. The two outgoing Bush ladies were a real help, but they greatly amused Marc and me by trying to teach us their system for tracking group tours. You'll think I'm making this up, but I'm not. Their "system" consisted of a large, red leather-bound book. The book had lined pages ('cause that's easier to write on). They wrote on the lines with pencil ('cause you can erase it when there are changes). If they needed to add more group names to the page, they put them on *Post-It* notes. Really. I swear! Remember, this was in 1993, not 1893. There were some primitive computers in the office, but I don't think anyone really thought to use them. If you had a green eyeshade and a quill pen, you'd have been right at home in the Bush I Visitors Office.

Marc and I were speechless. We didn't know whether to laugh or cry - and we didn't want to do either because these ladies were being so kind to us. We appreciated the time they generously gave us, but we knew the minute they left the red book was going to its new home in our "archives," a place of honor in a cabinet drawer. We were determined to start a modern and professional process, and we knew we'd use technology to create it.

Over the next eight years, as we repeatedly pushed to update our systems, we occasionally took out the red book and slowly turned its pages to laugh and remind ourselves of just how far we'd come. I was sad to see it go into Clinton archives, in January, 2001. I'm pretty sure no one else would understand what it represents, while for me it was a symbol of our hard-won achievements.

So, updating this antiquated process was our first priority. Marc immediately began work to design and implement a new, computerized system. But he was starting from scratch and had the huge disadvantage of having to work with the National Park Service bureaucracy. The term "change averse" was invented for these folks. Aaagh! I get it that some people are afraid of change, hate change, avoid change. But even if you think this way, could you at least just get out of the freakin' way while the rest of us try to move the world forward? I mean, what is **wrong** with people like that?

We asked for better computers for the girls working on ticketed tours, and they said, "Sorry, no money." This surprised me. No money for a priority White House request? Really? Well, can you give us better software? How about some nice dividers so they each have a little bit of privacy? No? Oh, come on, I'm sure you can do this. After all, it's for the WHITE HOUSE ...

Eventually they did provide all these things, but not without a struggle. You may wonder why I didn't use my own budget to supply what we needed - a sensible question. But, I didn't HAVE a budget. Remember, I was the only person in the Visitors Office on the White House staff. Everyone else worked for the Park Service, so whatever they needed had to come from the Park Service. The things we needed to coordinate our special events did come from the White House, but I never saw a budget, or had to reconcile costs. I told my bosses what we needed, and they gave it to me. The assumption was that a person directing a vital White House office would be smart enough to know what she needed and could be trusted to use resources wisely. I never asked for anything for myself, ever. Only for the things we needed to do the job for the President. And I don't remember anyone ever turning me down, except when we ran into regulations about "the procurement process" that tied up our efforts late in the final term.

This work took many months of long and exhausting days for us all. Sometimes I felt as if we were physically wrestling the new system into being, or giving birth with a long and difficult labor to a baby who just wouldn't come. I don't think a single part of it came easy. Something as simple as my signature was a challenge. It took forever to get an electronic version up and running.

Until we did, I had to sign every one of the hundreds and hundreds of letters we sent out every week. In the beginning, we didn't have any of the volunteers or interns who later were such a help. This meant many nights Marc and I worked until midnight, with him generating the tour response letters, me signing them, and then both of us tediously folding them and inserting them into envelopes. I had thought (hoped) Claudia would be more of an assistant to me, but the volume of letters and calls was so great she had to become the office traffic cop – directing everything incoming to the right person to deal with it. Thank goodness she was always calm, gracious and on top of whatever was coming at us.

I had to learn to be an executive, without any training. (I'd never heard of that section in Barnes & Noble!) I had to figure out even the simplest things. At first, everyone was so eager to help me that when anyone took a phone message she'd immediately march in and lay it on my desk. I'd look up and thank her. This created constant interruptions to my work. After a week of this I ordered in-boxes for everyone and told the staff to only interrupt me for emergencies. (They'd know what those were. They'd usually involve screaming.) Everything else went in the in-box for me to pick up when the time suited me. Baby steps at time management, but I could see there were other offices where people never figured these things out and chaos ruled.

Then I had to keep telling the staff to stop trying to protect me from bad news. They didn't want to tell me when someone called to complain about something, or when someone screwed up. OK, that's not happy news, but it's likely important news for the head of the office. If I didn't know something went wrong, how would I know to fix it? And, I never shoot the messenger – so tell me!

***

When things get really tough at the White House, and people are exhausted and stressed out, what keeps you going is the inspiration you draw from the President himself. His plans and dreams for America, the agenda he sets to reach those goals, the strategy he'll follow, and the excitement of knowing you have your own part to play in the most important "game" in the country. It's heady stuff.

You could look at the Visitors Office and think, "Oh, those people just coordinate tours, how important could that be?" That's exactly what those aides thought in the transition - and remember how well that went? Over the next eight years I worked with plenty of White House people who didn't understand our relationship with Congress, and what it meant to the President. But the Clintons understood, from day one, and frequently told me how pleased they were with how I ran the office.

The reality was, we spent our days interacting with Members of Congress and their staffs, on access issues that were important to them. Our real job, which I liked to describe as "herding cats," was to keep the Members happy, because happy Members will support the President's agenda and not complain, or, at least, not complain so much. They are, by God, a very whiny lot, even under the best circumstances. And, welcome to Washington, where it's NEVER, EVER, about what you HAVE done for me. It's only EVER about what are you GOING to do for me now?

Early that first week the President called all the new staff together to the East Room for our first general meeting. At least, I assumed it was the first of many to come, but it turned out to be the ONLY time it happened. He just got too busy.

So far I'd spent all my time in the Visitors Office itself, and didn't yet know the layout of the House. But I managed to make my way up the marble stairs to the State Floor, where I found a large, excited gathering of people who were all totally jazzed to be working for the President, IN the White House. I looked around the room, paying special attention to the famous portrait of George Washington, and near it, the Whistler portrait of Teddy Roosevelt. Like any President, he looks powerful, but his eyes are sad and he seems irritated. I learned later the President and the artist didn't like each other and squabbled about what location to use for the picture. They were walking from room to room when the President started to go up a flight of stairs from the State Dining Room, saying, "The trouble with you, sir, is you don't know what you want!"

Whistler replied, "And the trouble with YOU, sir, is you don't know how to pose!"

At this, Roosevelt spun around in a rage. Whistler said, "Wait! That's just what I want!" And that's the picture we see. The sadness is there too, from the loss of his first wife, the pain he never really got over. These are the details and stories I was eager to learn more of, but this morning there was too much excitement in the room to focus on art.

I was happy to see how many in the crowd were women and minorities. The President kept his promise to have a diverse administration. The men were all in suits, dress shirts, and ties. Among the women, those of us who were "of a certain age," wore business suits, silk blouses, understated jewelry, pantyhose and heels. The younger ones wore comfortable-looking pants suits, with open-collar shirts, and flat shoes. I envied them. Their shiny, straight hair hung in their faces - a look I never learned to like. It seems unprofessional and distracting to me for a woman to keep pushing her hair back, in what my staff called "the co-ed flip." My hair grows forward and is so thick there's no way to keep it out of my face except headbands and clips. I don't love the look, but it's neat and professional, and works for me. At least I don't resort to Republican helmet-head!

People who had worked together on the campaign spotted their friends from across the room and fell on each other like long lost brothers and sisters, with little shrieks of joy. I didn't see anyone I knew, so I started introducing myself: "Hello, I'm Melinda Bates, and I run the Visitors Office in the East Wing. We work with the Members of Congress on tours and coordinate the larger events. I worked on the campaign from here in Washington. What do you do?"

There was a lot of happy chatter until suddenly everyone hushed. The President was walking down the cross hall towards the low podium, accompanied by Hillary, the Gores and Mack McLarty, Chief of Staff.

We turned to listen. I was so excited I had to hold onto my hands to keep from jumping up and down like a child. (*I can't believe I'm here! I can't believe I'm here!*) And I'm sure I wasn't the only one thinking it.

Mack spoke first, then Tipper, then Hillary, then the VP, and finally the President. Outside of church it was the best preaching I've ever heard. Each one spoke to us about the challenges ahead.

"The American people have taken a chance with us."

Well, really, them. But we now represented them.

"People voted to change not only political parties, but generations, and agendas. The work ahead of us is going to be the hardest thing we have ever done, or ever imagined doing. The people may have voted for change, but that doesn't mean the government is going to just roll over and welcome it. Each one of you is going to have to reach deep within yourself and find a way to be smarter, wiser, more compassionate, more patient, and more creative than you have ever imagined being. It's not going to be easy. But it is going to be a heck of an adventure we'll all get to take together."

I brushed tears from my eyes, hoping no one noticed. It's easy to be caught up in such a moment - it was so inspiring. But inside, inside ...

I understand this is the most wonderful opportunity I'll ever have. But, I wonder if I'm up to the challenge they're laying before us. I knew I'm smart, but I can already tell the Clinton White House is full of brilliant people. Can I measure up? I'm starting to understand how high the stakes are, on every single little thing we do. Can I be sure the Visitors Office will always be an asset to the President? What if we screw up and hurt the agenda? And, Oh, please, Lord, don't let me fail here! You opened this door, now please help me do the best job anyone has ever done for a President.

This was the first time I heard the exhortation I soon learned to expect to hear from the President and Hillary almost every time I saw them: **"What are we doing today to make people's lives better? What are you and your office doing to make the world a better place? We only have a little time here, and we've got to make it count."**

I got goose bumps. More tears came to my eyes. *That's it! That's the heart of everything. We're here to make people's lives better, pure and simple. I'm going remember this.*

Over our eight years, every time I heard this, no matter how tired or discouraged I was, no matter how tired or discouraged THEY were, it gave me a fresh wind, and a renewed sense of the mission we shared. It made me proud to be part of making a better world for all of us. And watching both Bill and Hillary wear out teams of people half their age, working tirelessly, never stopping even for a bit of rest, reminded me that surely I too could keep working well past the exhaustion stage – to make the world a better place.

CHAPTER SIX ~ GETTING MY BALANCE

I can't speak for any other White House entity, but in the Visitors Office we did a lot of scrambling around in those first weeks to figure out what we were supposed to do, how we were supposed to do it, and who we'd work with to accomplish it. Not only were there were no manuals explaining all these complicated relationships and structures, but even the computers were empty of records. The Archives people had taken them all and left us with new -and completely blank - hard drives. Great!

After the nice Bush ladies left, we were on our own. I knew right from the start we'd be making significant changes. It just would have been nice to know our starting points better. At least once we got all staffed up we could get a handle on the tours. (Man, those phones NEVER stopped ringing.)

We almost never worked directly with the public, as that would have stepped on Congressional toes. People who wanted to visit were told to contact their Representative or Senator. Then that office wrote or called us about individual tickets or group tour reservations.

Holly, Carla Duryea and Christine Maloy, working in the large, open office, dealt with hundreds of calls and notes each day, while I plowed through thousands of group tour request letters. We figured out once I read 24,000 letters a year. 24,000! We also worked with the National Park Service rangers who managed the tickets for same-day, self-guided tours. The lines for these could be horrendous.

And this was just the tour part of our job. Looming over us was the Clintons' first Easter Egg Roll, in only a couple of months. Remember? "The hardest thing to do at the White House?" Based on what I heard about Robyn, she seemed to be the right person for that job. This left everything else to me, not least of which was figuring out what the President and First Lady wanted from us. After all, it was their house!

Early in February I went to my first private meeting with Mrs. Clinton (First Lady Of The US = FLOTUS), in her new West Wing office. It was odd that as well as I knew Bill, I'd never even met Hillary. Over the years when he came to Georgetown or Governors' Association events she always stayed in Little Rock with Chelsea. It was always a treat if he had time for a cup of coffee and a visit. The classmates who knew Hillary found her a little distant – until the campaign.

Bill's dearest friends, the men who were his roommates in college, volunteered to take turns traveling with him. He needed someone around who had no agenda other than his well- being. They were absolutely trustworthy, men of good judgment. They could be relied on to watch out for him, try to curb (a little) his need to connect with every blessed person he met, and help the schedulers keep him more or less - well, OK, mostly less, but that's just how it is - on time. They did this throughout the campaign, and Hillary came to value their devotion to their friend, and their willingness to put their own lives on hold to help him. Relations got a lot warmer as the campaign went on.

You can't blame her for being cautious. Candidates are surrounded by people who say they're really, truly your very best friend, with only your well being in mind. But they're often lying. They have their own agenda, and they're tryin' to hook their wagon to your star. Sometimes it's tough to tell who's in the game for which reason.

I was only just beginning to feel comfortable in the East Wing, where First Ladies traditionally have their offices, and the White House itself, with the public rooms tourists see on tours, and guests see at events. Unlike a lot of other people, who spent all their time in their offices, I had the perfect excuse to be in the House all the time - we needed to see how people moved through the House and understand what they saw and how it was presented to them.

But, while this is true, the real reason was that I was so thrilled to be working in the White House that I loved getting up from my desk and just going for a little walk - to the State Floor, for example, for a close look at the art, or architecture. Or to watch the tourists - sorry, "visitors" - as they slogged through, faces lit up with excitement and wonder at their ability to set foot in "America's House." It was work, but, damn, it was fun!

The West Wing was still *terra incognita* to me, and I wished I had a little map. I assumed the edges would be labeled, "Here there be dragons..." My biggest fear was wandering off course into some secure area where I didn't belong and upsetting the Secret Service. I knew the Oval Office was somewhere close by, but I hadn't seen it yet. It's on the first floor and I was going up to Hillary's office on two.

Although I knew in my head I had every right to be there, walking through the House, or into the West Wing, and I had my little staff badge to prove it, and my purposeful walk I hoped made me look as if I belonged, my interior conversation went like this: *For God's sake, how did I get here? It's a fluke - a mistake. I'll never be smart as everyone else here. Sooner or later - maybe sooner - they're going to find that out and I'll be asked, ever so nicely, to leave. Maybe I should save myself the embarrassment, and just offer to go ...* I now know this is called "imposter syndrome" and it's sadly common in women.

But I was careful to keep my fears at bay and to always present a serene exterior. I noticed my colleagues all did, and I never knew if they were really sure of themselves, or if it was an act - like mine. Over time I discovered for myself which ones were justifiably confident, and which ones were blustering their way through. I was glad to discover there weren't many of the latter. And, of course, over time I grew into my responsibilities, and (I think) got good at the job myself.

I walked through the first floor of the West Wing and up the narrow stairs to Hillary's office. The First Lady's traditional domain, the Social Office, was just upstairs from us in the East Wing. But Hillary broke with precedent by staking her claim to an office in the West Wing itself, an action that caused a lot of talk in Washington. (Shamefully, some of it about a woman knowing "her place." Every time I heard or read that, I wanted to punch in a smug face.) I might not have met Hillary yet, but it was obvious to any thinking person her "place" was wherever the hell she wanted it to be.

I knocked on another of those dark, paneled wood doors and entered the small reception area. Hillary's assistant, Pam, a woman with masses of curly dark hair, merry eyes and a no-nonsense attitude smiled and waved me to a seat. I wondered, *What is her job like? Is Hillary a difficult boss? I guess I'll soon know for myself ...*

In a moment the inner door opened. I saw a light-filled, feminine office, in shades of blue and sunny yellow with touches of coral. A large desk sat under a window, and there were flowers - tulips I think - on a skirted table. Hillary greeted me warmly. I don't remember the hairstyle of the day, although I think she had given up headbands by then. I don't remember the color of her suit, or her jewelry. What I do remember was the force of her intellect and personality, her warmth and her piercing blue eyes.

How great - Bill found a woman who is his equal! I can already tell she's amazing. I hope I get to work closely with her - I can tell she's going to make history here.

Hillary comes to the Visitors Office

Over time I'd get to know and treasure her kindness, thoughtfulness and loyalty, but today she was my new boss who would expect smart and thoughtful answers to her questions. We sat together on the rose and white striped silk sofa, and she quickly got to business, asking me for a briefing on the Visitors Office. I told her about the antiquated systems and technology we found, and the goals we set to improve it. She listened intently.

When I finished, she asked a few more questions about our interactions with the Members of Congress, who were our real constituents. She didn't need me to explain how important the tours were to those folks. Unlike other inhabitants of the West Wing, she understood we were about more than just making tourists happy. People on the Hill were very nervous about the changeover to a Democratic administration. The Republicans were afraid they would get no tours for their constituents. Some Democrats thought now they would get every tour they requested. There was no way we could make that happen.

"Everybody wants to come see YOUR White House. We're getting calls and letters from all over, people saying they didn't want to see the White House under Reagan and Bush, but now they're very excited to visit a White House where a Democratic president lives. Then we've got the Members' offices calling by the hundreds demanding tours for constituents. There's a lot of pressure, but we're creating a new system to enable us to track tours requested and tours granted, so we'll know whose turn it is next. That way we can treat all the Members fairly, so veterans from Montana, and Girl Scouts from Georgia, and middle-schoolers from Massachusetts will all have a fair shot at having a tour scheduled. It's going to take a lot of work, but it will make the office much more efficient and professional."

In hindsight - which is the ONLY sight in politics - I look at the naive optimism behind our backbreaking efforts to be "fair" and want to laugh - or weep. Not because we didn't accomplish our goals, because God knows we did and I still have the scars to prove it. No, it's because it was really pointless. The way Washington works is simple: our friends didn't care if we were "fair." They knew we'd treat them well and would probably have preferred we treat our enemies badly. And our enemies (make no mistake - they were truly enemies) never believed we were "fair," no matter how much we did for them. So, if that was going to be how it played out, what was the point of all our efforts?

I think this was really more about my own, internal compass, than it was about what was politically necessary. It was the right thing to do. Or, maybe not. It did do us some good to be able to emphatically defend ourselves when we were attacked. It always just amazed me when we had to. But understanding this was a loooong way away, and at the moment I had an evangelical commitment to our goals.

Hillary nodded her approval, then sat for a moment, thinking.

"That's a good beginning, Melinda, but it's important you understand what we expect from the Visitors Office. This is the people's House. The President and I are determined to make this the most open and accessible White House ever. We're counting on you to make it happen."

"And that's exactly what we're going to do, I promise you."

She smiled, stood, and offered her hand, then turned back to her desk. "Sounds good. I'll want you to keep me posted on your progress. Just remember: the most open and accessible White House EVER."

There were times over the next years when the things we tried to do were difficult, even seemed impossible (the President wants WHAT?!), but I remembered my promise and kept plugging away on our little corner of reinventing government.

Back in my office, I thought about the changes we were already making, and considered if there were other things we should be working on. *Just converting to a computerized system will give us information we currently lack. I know the Bush Visitors Office didn't have it either. How had they tried to manage being "fair"? Had they even tried? How much can you do when your system is penciled notes in a red book?*

When a Senator from Alabama, or a Congresswoman from California called to complain they had gotten "no tours" from our office and we "had to help them right this minute with this very important request," we needed a way to quickly know if their claim was accurate. Because it turns out, most times it wasn't.

Thank God Marc knows what he's doing, because I know what I want, and what he and I think will work for us, but I don't know enough about computers to know what we can make them do for us. He does. I guess I'll turn him loose on this project and keep everyone else out of his way.

At the end of the first six months we finally had an adequate system allowing us to be timely in our responses and, most important, to actually keep track of the tours scheduled. This probably doesn't sound terribly exciting to you, but we were over the moon with joy about our success.

We also created the first ever "Manual for White House Tours" for Congressional staffers who scheduled tours. OK, it wasn't *Anna Karenina*, but it was a really useful little booklet, and, best of all, there were all our names, right in the front under the White House seal. Who wouldn't like that? We hoped at least some of these folks would read the manual and realize they didn't need to call us with every little question. They could find the answers for themselves. Of course, they'd have to actually read something - you know, learn something - to do their job better, and many tour coordinators couldn't be bothered, when it was so much easier (for them) to just call us and ask the same dumb question over and over.

We quickly learned which offices assigned tour responsibilities to an experienced and capable person, and which delegated them to the recent college graduate daughter of the Senator's college roommate. Or the child of his biggest campaign contributor. Or, the staffer he was sleeping with (there were plenty of those). There really was no other possible explanation for the complete cluelessness of so many of these Hill staffers. Dumb as dirt, some of those folks. We enjoyed working with the former; we detested the latter.

While we were happily working away in our exhausting days to re-invent White House tour systems, we made a major mistake that publicly embarrassed the President. In the grand scheme of things it was probably not the biggest problem the President had (you think?), but it was plenty big to me.

We were so convinced of the brilliance of our plan, and the obvious ways these changes would benefit the Members and their constituents, that we gave no thought to **selling** our ideas on the Hill. In fact, it never even occurred to us (read: *me*). We thought our new system was so obviously better than what they had, they'd all just smile, and say, "Oh, boy! This is great! Thanks so much! We love it!" when we brought it on line. Wow, were we ever wrong.

Washington on the whole is very change-averse. Capitol Hill is pathologically resistant to change, no matter how demonstrably better the change may be. They don't care what you have done for them - if it's different from what they know, they don't want to hear about it. They may try to excuse this resistance by calling it "tradition," but it's really about being afraid of any kind of change and being unwilling to invest any time or effort into adapting to new ideas and processes. It's pathetic, but it is the way things are, and we should have figured this out and planned for it. But we didn't. I didn't.

So, when word started to leak out about our plans to change a system they all knew well, (were "stakeholders" as the bureaucrats say) the poop hit the fan. When we talked about how our new process would allow folks from all over the country a better, fairer shot at getting a tour, the Republicans spun that into ludicrous, overly-zealous, politically correct, Democrat "diversity" – a word we never used.

When we explained how much fairer the new system was, the people who benefited the most from the old system cried "foul." Who were we to change something that worked so well – for them? The serious people in Congressional offices understood what we were doing, but satisfied people don't raise a stink. Unhappy people do. Oh, and people who see an opportunity to score political points.

In early June we were finally bringing the new system online and were blissfully unaware of the discontent we were about to face. I was a happy person. We had worked night and day for six straight months to create what we knew was a better way, and I thought we might finally get to rest, just a little. On June 6, my oldest son, Shiloh, was to graduate from high school. For the first time in six months, I was going to leave the office before 9:00 p.m. to attend his graduation. That morning I received a call from *Roll Call,* the Capitol Hill newspaper. I was in a rush to get out of the office, and thought they were calling for a comment on something else. Rather than call them back myself, I passed the message to the Press Office, told them what I thought it was about, asked them to return the call, and left the office. Big mistake.

Two days later I found myself the subject of a truly nasty frontpage article about the new White House tour system. In a long story, full of critical quotes from anonymous Republican staffers, our system, our baby we had labored over so long and hard, was described as a fiasco. A nod to ridiculous Democratic principles like "diversity," and "fairness," that was going to needlessly upset the perfectly fine process that had served "so well" for so long.

Oh, and, the story said, "Ms. Bates had been called for a comment, but had not returned our call."

Well, yes, technically true, but it sure sounded sinister.

"Had not returned our call." Doesn't that sound like a person with something to hide, dodging the righteous press? Well, now you know better. And, of course, the press uses this as a scare tactic all the time: *Call us back or you'll be sorry when you see the story we're writing about you.* Point taken!

This was my first personal experience with nameless, groundless accusations, and it hurt like hell. It's one thing to get criticized when you screw up. It's another to be targeted unfairly. That's pain AND outrage. I was angry, although I realized it was a valuable introduction to how public life really works. Then to rub it in, a few days later, as I walked up East Executive Avenue past a couple of thousand tourists on the way to my office, every blessed one of the Secret Service Tour Officers I passed stopped me to say, "Hey, Rush mentioned you on his program this morning!"

Oh, swell, I thought. *Now I know where their political preferences lie. But did it have to be ALL of them?*

My tiny consolation was he got the story directly from *Roll Call*, without crediting them, and then changed it to make us sound even more incompetent. So, I figured, if he had to lie to make bad news about something as relatively insignificant as White House tours, then you can be darn sure what he said about the important things was a damn lie too.

I sat at my desk stewing over this mess and muttering to myself about the willingness of the press to use un-named sources - sources with a bone to pick - to tell a story. And why, for heaven's sake, had the timing been so urgent they had to go to press without connecting with me? There was no excuse - except that they knew they had a nice, juicy little hit piece on the new administration, and couldn't wait to go with it. Oh, wait, it's largely false? And the reporter's too lazy to look for the facts? No problem.

For the first time I understood, on a gut level: in Washington, perception is MORE (much more) important than reality. Our new system was a major improvement on an antiquated, unresponsive and unfair process. But this reality was beside the point. What was important was that we LOOKED stupid, and we had made the President look stupid. I was mortified and furious.

Even worse, I had a new boss, Patsy Thomasson, who I hadn't even met yet. Now all she knew about us was we had screwed up our mission and were probably incompetent. Patsy called us to come for our first meeting, and Robyn, Marc and I headed over to the West Wing, determined to vindicate ourselves. I kept reciting in my head, *We're right, we're right, we're right to do this. We're right, damn it!*

Patsy is an attractive woman, with dark brown hair, sparkling dark eyes, and creamy skin. She was an old friend of the Clintons (as so many were) from Little Rock. Years before she worked in Washington for Congressman Wilbur Mills, who came to a bad end when he had a drunken frolic in the Tidal Basin with the red headed stripper, Fanne Fox (an unusually sexy scandal for Washington.) Later, when we had time to know each other and become friends, I asked her why the people from his Arkansas district kept re-electing a known drunk to Congress.

"Well, Melinda, everyone on the Hill and everyone back home knew the person in Congress who knew the most about the U.S. budget was Wilbur Mills. And the person who knew the next most about the budget was Wilbur Mills – drunk. So, that's why he had a very long career."

"Okaaay. I get it!"

Thanks to the Hill article and the fuss from Congress, our first meeting was strained. Well, I couldn't blame her. She knew - or thought she knew - all about our supposed screw-ups. She knew nothing about our successes. Marc and I briefed her on the status of the Visitors Office we found, our plans to wrench it into the current era, and the great new system we created.

She listened skeptically, asked a few questions, then sat back with a pained look. I knew we were right to have done what we did, but that wouldn't mean much If I hadn't persuaded her of it. She thought for a moment, started to speak, stopped herself, thought again, tapped her pen on the desk.

Finally, she looked me dead in the eyes and said, grimly, in her Arkansas twang, "Well, Melinda, you may have created a brilliant system, but you all did a piss-poor job of selling it to your own constituents – the Members and their staffs!"

I was mortified. I'd never even heard the expression "piss-poor" before, but it didn't take a genius to understand her point. I got the message, loud and clear, and I couldn't argue with it. She was right. It hadn't even occurred to us we **needed** to sell it to them. And that says a great deal about how naïve we were.

"Look," I pleaded. "I know we screwed up, but we're going to fix it - I promise. We're already arranging visits to Capitol Hill to meet with Congressional staff. We'll let them tell us directly what they're worried about, and we'll explain how wonderful the new system is, and how it's gonna make their lives easier. I know this will work. I can be very persuasive. And it's not as if they ALL hate us. I believe it's almost all Republicans who are complaining. They just hate us all, whatever we do. We have Democrats on our side, and the Republicans who really understand the system can see it's going to work for them as well. We can't roll over and live with the old system. We can't. You've got to let us have a shot at fixing this. The President said he wanted us to reinvent government wherever we found it failing, and that's what we did!"

She grudgingly said she'd let us try, and waved us out of the room. As we walked back to the East Wing, I told Marc and Robyn, "I guess it went as well as we could hope for. And the truth is, I can tell I'm really going to like Patsy – once this all blows over."

Soon after, we did go to the Hill for a couple of meetings. Even without the mess we'd made, it would've been a good idea. It's difficult to demonize someone you've met and talked with and know to be a well-intentioned person. Some of our questioners were pretty hostile, coming from Republican offices accustomed to getting whatever they wanted from the Visitors Office. They were afraid those days were over - and they were right.

I was surprised any congressional office would risk making enemies of people in the White House Visitors Office. After all, we controlled a very important resource they were desperate to get, access to White House tours. Did they think we weren't taking notes about how people had behaved with us? As I said, dumb as dirt ...

But we were honest and persuasive, for those who were open to listening. God knows after six months we knew our program backwards and forwards, so we had no trouble waxing eloquent about its features and benefits. I think I may have promised at some point that if they'd just try out the new system, they'd not only get tour tickets, they'd also lose ten pounds and meet the love of their life.

Or, maybe not.

We made some friends and began our reputation as straight-shooters who were professional, gracious, and helpful to deal with. Over time, even our "enemies" came to respect us, and I was proud of that. You can never make everyone love you but coming out well on the respect side is a pretty good result too.

I can't say I enjoyed this experience much, but it was a useful eye-opener for me. This was a flap about something relatively inconsequential: TOURS - not nuclear policy. How much more would the folks on the Hill dig in against the really important changes the President was making in domestic policy, economic policy, foreign policy and all the other urgent issues we faced. And this was true even though the Democrats had a majority in both Houses.

I'm sorry to tell you, the people you send to Washington are mostly gutless wonders - go along to get along. They may not start out that way, but it doesn't take long for Washington, and the appetite for power, to corrupt even decent people. We were amused observers of this every election cycle, when new Members of Congress took office behaving like more or less normal human beings. But they are then surrounded by staff, lobbyists, and favor-seekers who all tell them, "You're right. You're absolutely right. Your judgment is impeccable. You're brilliant. In fact, you're the best thing to ever happen to government. Oh and, by the way, please vote for my client's bill - it will surely make America a finer, better place for everyone, even though it absolutely violates every promise you made before getting here. Oh, and, here's a small token of my regard to help in your next campaign."

And so they cave. Some in a few weeks, some in a few

months, but almost all of them do cave. It's so sad. I used to wonder what the folks back home would think if they saw the nice neighbor man they sent to Washington behaving like an over-privileged, arrogant jerk with us to try to get some favor. I hoped they'd be shocked and appalled, but the truth is, for many people, if bad behavior was what it took to get what they wanted, then they was just fine with it. And I haven't even gotten started yet on the Arkansans!

I run the helicopter departures

During those first, truly chaotic weeks, a parade of visitors came to introduce themselves to me, people we'd be working with in various Visitors Office responsibilities. I not only needed to meet them, I wanted them to know me, my background at the National Gallery of Art, and my lifelong friendship with the President. The career credentials established that I wasn't just some clueless crony with no experience, stuck into a plum White House job I was unsuited for. My credentials were perfect for the Visitors Office. (See: "heck of a job Brownie" ...)

My friendship with the President established that, if it were necessary, I had political cards to play, either to help myself or the Visitors Office agenda. This would be good news to any outside entity we worked with. They'd understand I could pull some serious strings to make things happen outside the regular system if I needed to. Sometimes I could see visible relief on the faces of my new colleagues when they understood they weren't going to have to baby sit some unqualified hack. It made me laugh. I guess they'd had some bad experiences with people who preceded me.

Almost the first person in my door was United States Secret Service Lieutenant Jeffrey Purdie, from the Special Operations Section. He was assigned to lead the Tour Officers and assist the Visitors Office with our tours and events, and the Social Office with their events. Jeff is a nice looking man, then in his thirties, with sandy blond hair. He usually wore a suit instead of the Uniformed Division's normal black pants and white shirt. Jeff explained he was new to the job too. Every time an administration turned over, the USSS officers who had worked closely with the outgoing administration were reassigned elsewhere, and new men and women came to work with the new President's team.

Made sense to me. Obviously, people who worked together for a long time formed friendships that might make it uncomfortable to work with a new group. He asked me how I'd like to be addressed: "Mrs. Bates, Ms. Bates, Melinda?"

"Won't we be working very closely together, for long hours, under stressful circumstances?"

"Yes, we sure will."

"OK then, I think 'Melinda' will do fine. I look forward to working with you and the Special Operations officers. And I guess we all have a lot to learn."

Jeff Purdie was not only one of the best people I've ever worked with, he is one of the best people I've known. I loved working with him, because he quickly learned I value the truth far more than false good news, and he'd tell me the truth even when it was bad news. This is shockingly rare in government. No one wants to be the bearer of bad news, even though it might be what we most needed to hear.

So Jeff was someone I quickly learned to trust. He respected and supported the work we wanted to accomplish and his team's part in making it happen. He brought enthusiasm, humor, and a can-do attitude to the table every day. He was a joy to work with, and I came to love him like a brother. God knows, I spent more time with him than with my own husband.

A few years later at the annual USSS Director's Christmas party, I was talking to the Chief of the Uniformed Division when he casually mentioned, "You know, Lt. Purdie is about to be promoted and moved to another job."

I almost dropped my drink and cookie. I'm sure my face turned white and my eyes rolled up. I grabbed his arm and blurted out, "You can't do that to me! What will I do without Jeff?!"

He raised his eyebrows and gazed down at me in surprise. I realized how this must look to him, so I quickly removed my hand, composed myself and said, "Oh, I'm sorry - please forget what I just said. I'm very happy for Lt. Purdie to be promoted. It's just, he's done such a great job with us, and we'll all miss him."

The Chief gave me a long look and said, "I promise you'll be pleased with the Lieutenant who will replace him."

"I'm sure I will. The Secret Service always sends us your best men and women."

And they did. They sent me Bryant Withrow, who was also smart, capable, a pleasure to work with, honest, and always willing to go beyond what we could reasonably ask in order to get our crazy jobs done. Another great guy.

My next favorite new colleague was Mel Poole, the director of the National Park Service's White House Visitor **Center**. I know it's confusing, but this is a separate thing from our White House Visitors **Office**. In 1993, they had only a little southern-style building on the Ellipse they used to hand out the day's public (unreserved) tour tickets. But they were building a new Visitor Center, a nice museum and visitor area a block away from the White House, in the Commerce Building.

Mel is a slender man, then in his mid-thirties, with dark hair, a wiry build, and mischievous eyes. He's direct and irreverent. Since I'm the same, I liked him right away. He was not very respectful of his agency's chain of command and complete bureaucratic inertia. I could tell it drove him crazy to come up with great ideas to make their work more effective or to provide better customer service, only to have them all shot down by people who never set foot outside their offices to see what Park Rangers and the public really needed. I thought it might help him if he could go back to those offices and say, "The White House is asking us to do xyz, so we really need to make it happen."

Wouldn't you think that would light a fire under someone's lazy ass? Well, sometimes it worked, but surprisingly often it didn't. I mean, really! Of course they were too smart to simply say "no," at least in any way you could trace back to any specific desk. Bureaucrats don't get to stay in their cozy jobs if they stick their necks out. Oh, no. When you don't want to do something, you play the bureaucracy game! You set up a committee to examine and discuss the issue, and have meetings, with "stake holders" (a ridiculous word they made up), and write reports for everyone to review. Then you have more meetings to review the results of the first meetings, and on and on and on. That way no one has to do a damned thing to make any changes. And the best part? You can't point the finger at any one person as being responsible for obstruction. It may be wrong, wrong, wrong, but it's very effective. Every long-term bureaucrat knows how to play this game.

All of this was a big surprise to me. I was so naive I thought everyone would respect that Bill Clinton had won the Presidency, and so, um, wasn't he supposed to get to set the agenda in Washington? Weren't the agencies (State, Education, Interior, etc.) supposed to stand up and salute when he said to?

I'm sorry to tell you this is laughably not true. At the top are cabinet secretaries and their direct aides who are the President's men and women, but not far below this level are the (literally) tens of thousands of worker bees who don't give a damn what the new people want. It's not even about being politically opposed to the President's agenda. It's more a desire to do as little work as possible, while staying safe and anonymous in their secure government jobs, so they can eventually get their secure government pensions. So, why would they work to help change happen? Change (even the most wonderful change) is the **enemy**.

Mel was a master at working around the system at the Interior Department, and soon confided his secret to me: "Sometimes it's better to go ahead and do what needs doing, and ask forgiveness after, than to wait around hoping for permission that never comes."

I was pleased he trusted me enough to admit this to me, and came to find it useful advice. He was also totally on board with our efforts to improve the tours and the ticketing process. He quickly became my favorite partner in crime as we pushed and prodded the bureaucrats to reform our little part of government.

Then circumstances handed me the perfect opportunity to demonstrate our commitment to the tours. The USSS Tour Officers told me that every time the President left the complex, the Park Police insisted on shutting down the tour lines way in advance, so it cut tour access dramatically. When they complained, the Park Police told them the equivalent of "tough."

There's a big rivalry between the two law enforcement agencies. They really don't like each other. Actually, they despise each other. It's one of those macho things. Anyway, when the USSS told the Park Police the White House was concerned about interference with tours, the Park Police officers laughed and said, "We don't believe anyone in the White House gives a damn about these tours."

When the Sergeants from the Tour Division told me this I got annoyed. "OK, if it happens again, you come get me, and I'll go out and complain in person."

A few days later the Park Police cut the line and screwed up tours again, and the USSS officers came to tell me. I got up from my desk, beckoned to Marc to come along, and followed the Tour Officers out to East Executive Avenue, where I could see for myself the gates were closed, and nobody could get in. I spotted Mel, and a **really** large Park Police Lieutenant, a giant of a man, so I walked over, trailing Marc and the USSS Sergeants, who hung back a little to watch what happened.

"How do you do, Lieutenant? I'm Melinda Bates from the White House Visitors Office. What seems to be the problem here? We want to get these tourists into the House."

"We had to shut it all down because the President's due leave soon."

"Yes, but isn't he leaving over on the other side of the House?" - I started to say, when he loudly interrupted me, "What do you care about who gets in on these tours?!"

Marc, Mel, and the other Park Police officers gave a collective gasp.

I'm 5'3" tall, and had to look way up at this tall - and bulky - officer. I'm pretty sure he expected me to stop and take a step back, but instead I took a step closer to him, locked eyes and said, with a sweet smile, "Lieutenant, we'll get along much better when you get a lot politer."

He looked shocked. Mel and Marc looked shocked. The USSS Sergeants looked impassive, (it's their job, after all) but shifted on their feet. No one expected me to talk to him like that. Hell, I hadn't expected to talk to him like that. But I guess his momma had raised him to have a little respect for a woman, so he just backed right down (to my great surprise) and said, "I'm sorry. What did you want to say about the tours?"

"Great, now, let's talk about how important they are. The President and First Lady both personally told me they want this to be the most open and accessible White House ever. How can we work together to make this happen?"

We discussed this pleasantly for the next few minutes and reached a compromise I thought would solve the problem. As Marc and I walked back to the office, Mel tagged along, apologizing over and over, "Melinda, I'm so sorry, I had no idea he would be so disrespectful. I'm so sorry!"

"Mel, don't give it another thought. I don't hold the Park Service responsible for what one Park Police officer said. Don't be silly! I'm not mad at you! I'm not even mad at him. I'm sure we'll all work well together now that we know each other better."

Mel finally walked off and Marc and I continued up East Executive Avenue. He seemed unusually happy so I looked at him quizzically. He was practically buzzing.

"What?" I asked.

"This is so great!" he blurted out. "I was wondering if you could do the job, and now I know you'll be great at it. Standing up to that officer ... I'm so proud of you!"

From Marc this was great praise, and, to tell the truth, I had surprised myself too. I'm not normally confrontational, but this time it just came up out of me when I needed it. The Tour Officers didn't say anything other than "Thanks," but I could see them looking at me differently in the next days. Word got around, and it was good for me and the Visitors Office. I'd stand up for our mission. I could be counted on. And, on a more basic level, (excuse my French) "Don't uh, screw with me." In fact, a few days later, Lieutenant Purdie hung a sign in their break room: "Melinda Bates ain't happy - ain't NOBODY happy!"

I had to laugh. It wasn't about me personally, but about the work we had to accomplish together. If they respected me as much as liked me, or if they respected me INSTEAD of liking me, I'd be fine with that. And just to drive the message home, behind my desk I hung a beautiful old painting of a grim-faced Chinese empress. My husband, Darryl gave it to me, with it a little sign to hang below, reading, "Don't Mess with the Empress."

So Mel and I were completely on the same page - opening up tours as much as possible. Other people gave our goal a lot of lip service, but Mel was the one I could count on to deliver. A couple of years later he took a posting to the Catoctin Mountains, just outside Camp David. I was heartbroken. I knew I'd never get such a good partner again - and I was right. After Mel the NPS made sure

I got people who were lukewarm - at best - about our supposedly shared mission. It got to be like pulling teeth to get them to do anything.

None of the Park Directors who followed Mel came close to his ability, and some were difficult, indeed. One was a nice man who came to our weekly meetings and appeared to take careful notes. My plan was to foster a sense of teamwork and encourage the NPS and USSS to produce the very best result by working together. I prefer to work this way, and I believe it helps and encourages each person to perform better than they realized they could. At least, that was my goal. This one director, though, was beyond any encouragement I could offer. He was so unproductive I joked with Marc that he must be writing his grocery list when we thought he was taking notes and assignments, since nothing on our mutual lists **ever** got done. It was both infuriating and sad.

In 1995, the Park Service unveiled its long planned White House Visitor Center in the ground floor of the Commerce Department, just a block away from the White House. They had been working on it for years before we arrived, but our first chance to see it came just before the official unveiling. Marc and I walked around the beautiful space with notepads, making lists of all the mistakes we saw. For example, they misspelled the name of famous artist Gilbert Stuart. Oops! They also had produced some very strange captions, that we found insulting to the President.

For example, a photo of four Presidents was titled: "President Bush, President Ford, President Carter and Bill Clinton." Um, no, it's **President** Clinton! The caption of a photo of the State Dining Room with a past social secretary and a military social aid made it look as if the military officer was on the First Lady's staff. Of course, he wasn't. Things like that. All in all, we presented them with a list of about thirty mistakes to correct before they opened to the public. To us this was a no-brainer. They had to fix things or risk looking stupid. Who would question that?

Well, the National Park Service did. They futzed around for weeks and finally sent me a memo. I guess they didn't have the guts to face us with their unhelpful response.

"Thank you for pointing out the error in Gilbert Stuart's name. We will fix it this week. As for the other changes you request, we have reviewed them and don't agree with your suggestions. All the captions were vetted by National Park Service historians and by the White House Curators. The installation is complete, and will not be changed."

I couldn't believe it. Weren't they even embarrassed? I called Mel, knowing he wasn't in charge, but at least he'd tell me the truth.

"Mel, have you seen the list we sent up? Their answer makes no sense. What can they be thinking?"

"I know. I know. But, here's the deal. They're saying there's no money to correct anything else."

"OK, well, then, how about we come down there with a label maker and stick correct captions over the wrong ones for you?"

He laughed. "No, although I'd enjoy seeing you do that, they won't allow it. The truth is, they think most of your changes are partisan, political notes. We're just gonna have to live with it."

"Political? Are you joking? They're about factual errors!"

"Oh, I get it, but I can tell you, we won't win this fight. They're dug in and that's the end of it. I'm sorry."

And, yes, that's how it stayed. I would have been mortified to display these. I would have thought the Curators, who had vetted the captions, would be mortified. Even the Park Service itself should have been mortified. But, they weren't. This was a real eye-opener for me. Anonymous bureaucracy at its worst.

A year after we all left the White House, I had a little time with one of those NPS flunkies who made my life so difficult. To my astonishment he went on and on about how much he missed us (!), how great it had been to work with competent people, as opposed to the dumb bunnies the Bush White House had appointed, how difficult his job was with those incompetent lightweights ... It was satisfying and surprising, but, oh, too little, and way too late.

CHAPTER EIGHT ~ MEET THE USHERS,

AND

MY FIRST PRESIDENTIAL EVENT

After the First Lady, the most important person I met in those early days was Gary Walters, the Chief Usher. It's OK – I'd never heard of the Ushers either.

Tracy Presock, the bright young woman from Bush I, who stayed to help us, sat me down to explain it: "The Ushers are the most important people you never heard of. Five men and women, career NPS employees, run the House and take care of the family, the historic structure and its priceless contents. They make the trains run on time. They manage the teams of cleaners, electricians, plumbers, horticulturists, butlers, carpenters, chefs, florists, maids, cooks and laborers who keep the House in tip top order. I probably didn't even list them all. There's a lovely man, Mr. Muffler, who goes around the House every week setting and winding every clock, and fixing all the little things that can break or fail in an old house. His son Rick is one of the calligraphers in the Social Office."

"You're going to work closely with Gary, so it's important to start off on the right foot. Unfortunately, he had no respect for Janet (Johnson, the Director who just left) so he won't come to the Visitors Office to meet you. Would you mind going to his office to meet him?"

I thought, *Aren't we all here to serve the President the best we can? His attitude seems arrogant to me, but, sure, if it helps, I'll meet him on his terms.*

"OK Tracy, no problem. please set it up for me. And, thanks for the briefing."

I probably shouldn't have agreed to go there. I should have politely invited him to come to see me in MY office. Because, over the next eight years, he never ONCE came to me. He set up our relationship balance right from the start. Sneaky!

I walked along the East Colonnade to the Ground Floor hallway. About two thirds of the way through there's an elevator lobby on the right, and a small, spiral stairway next to it. The elevator goes up to the top two Residence floors. This is how the First Family comes and goes from their "house" up there. The Ushers' Office is up one flight, in a corner of the State Floor no one ever notices. Over time I got to be very familiar with that space.

But Gary also had a private office, one more flight up, so I kept climbing, until I reached a small room with a low, worn sofa, where I sat, with my knees tucked up almost to my chin, and a desk and chair. Gary is tall, slender, and had an anonymous gray face above a perfectly forgettable gray suit - do they all go to bureaucrat school to learn how to look like that? Since staying in the background was a major part of his job, this helped make him perfect for his position. In fact, although he always looked appropriately professional, I sometimes thought he must have a closet full of identical gray suits to wear over and over. Well, I do remember an occasional brown suit too. I know I'm not being kind, but he deserves it.

Gary, you see, turned out to be a constant, nagging, duplicitous, backstabbing thorn in my side. Of all the lying, untrustworthy, unhelpful people I encountered in Washington, Gary was about the worst. After all, he'd been at it a long time. He was a US Secret Service officer for years before moving to the Ushers' Office, where he worked for years before becoming Chief Usher. He'd been around for a looooong time and had perfected the technique of looking you in the eye with great sincerity, promising to help with whatever you needed, and then going off and doing the opposite. Not because there was any real reason not to help you. Oh no. He did it just because he could.

There was really no other explanation - I know because I tried to figure it out for years, often from a position of banging my head helplessly against a convenient wall, muttering, "That bastard! What is his PROBLEM?"

We held meetings, made plans (with his input), believed we had everyone on board, and then, at the last minute, he'd hit us with, "Oh, no, we couldn't possibly do THAT. The White House has NEVER been used that way before. I'm sure Mrs. Clinton wouldn't want that ... "

But only when it was too late to regroup and plan an acceptable alternative, adjust staffing or redirect guests. Then, when we're frantic, trying to figure out what just happened to us (and our swell plan) he would be "unavailable" to discuss things with us. Or worse, he would be available, but that just meant we'd get to see him smirking to himself about how he just screwed us and pretending he had no idea why we were upset, and had no recollection of agreeing to our agenda.

And the worst part was, he was really, really good at snowing the only people who truly mattered - the First Family.

Oh yes, he immediately established himself as Mr. Helpful, Mr.I-Am-Here-For-You, Mr.You-Can-Count-On-Me. He ingratiated himself with the Clintons so quickly and thoroughly that by the time some of us might have pointed out his real qualities, he knew too much to fire. The Ushers practically live with the family. They know an awful lot of what goes on in otherwise private moments. Of course, it would be the height of dishonor to reveal any of these secrets, but guess what - stuff happens.

At first when things went wrong I thought it must be my fault. After all, I was new to the White House, and there's a steep learning curve. They were the ones with all the experience. I respected his mandate to protect the House and care for the family. But I wasn't asking for help for myself, I was asking for help for something the President or First Lady wanted us to make happen. This is why we were all there to begin with - to do things the President and First Lady wanted - right?

But with Gary you'd think I was asking for my own, selfish purposes, out of nowhere. His constant response to our perfectly reasonable requests was, " Gosh, so sorry. No, we can't make that happen. Oh, no, absolutely not ... "

By the summer I was having my doubts about him. How could it be that almost everything we asked him to do was unreasonable? Can we run tours until he absolutely HAD to have the House empty to prepare for an event, set up a car fair on the South Lawn to showcase American industry (with a Presidential speech), run tours late when the President and First Lady weren't using the House ... ? No, no, and, um, no. These were things we knew the Clintons wanted - expected- us to do for them. Why were they all impossible or inappropriate to arrange? But he must be telling us the truth – right?

And then I started to collect and read old books about the White House, written by earlier butlers, ushers and First Ladies. I discovered the White House has ALWAYS been used exactly the way we wanted to. ALWAYS. There was nothing inappropriate about our planned events. Nothing impossible. The only thing inappropriate was his refusal to just get on board and help us implement the Clintons' wishes.

Most of the household staff was dedicated to serving the First Family in whatever official or personal need there was. They routinely put in eighteen to twenty-hour days with no complaints, eager and willing to serve. A loyal and devoted group of people, they loved the First Family and appreciated the honor of working in the White House. Some of the maids, butlers, plumbers, carpenters and electricians were the second generation of people in their families to serve there. They were wonderful people and we loved working with them.

Only the Chief Usher stood in our way, time after time.

Yes, it took a while for me to believe it was deliberate, but eventually I realized there was no other explanation for the way he consistently dug in his heels and opposed us (while always smiling and appearing helpful to the First Family). I wish I could tell you why he did this, but after eight years of coping with his relentless resistance, I left with no more understanding than when we started. Maybe it was just his personality. Maybe it was political. Maybe he was lazy. I still don't know why. I only know it was infuriating and frustrating - and completely unnecessary.

I can also assure you this wasn't my imagination. In June 1993, a former Director of the Visitors Office, who had worked for President Bush, came to visit us. It was kind of her to talk to me, and then separately to Robyn. We had lots of questions, and after she left I discovered we each asked her the same thing: "If you had it to do all over again, what's the most important thing you'd do differently?"

Without a moment's hesitation she said, "Fire Gary Walters."

I sat back, astonished. "You mean he was difficult for you to work with too?"

"Oh, yes," she nodded. "He dug in his heels and refused to help all the time."

"But I thought he made our lives miserable because he loved the Reagans and Bushes, and just didn't like the new family and the new administration. Or else he just doesn't like Democrats."

"No," she said. "It's not that. Whatever he's doing to screw you, I can assure you he did to us as well."

Damn. I was speechless.

"The thing is," she said, "by the time you all figure it out it's too late - he knows too much to fire."

When Robyn told me she had asked the same question and gotten the same answer, we sat staring at each other. If only we'd had this information months before, we'd have told Hillary and her Chief of Staff, Maggie Williams. But now it was too late. He did know too much to fire. (And, I'm not talking about anything unethical or immoral. Just the normal, family stuff anyone would want to stay private.)

I did take one positive thing away from my first meeting with Gary. As we sat in his tiny office, discussing our work, I kept calling the President "Bill". He smiled and firmly corrected me: "In this House, even people who have known the President all his life learn to call him, 'Mr. President.'" Point taken.

***

In early spring, 1993, when we were all still new at our work, my classmates from Georgetown and I were busy planning our upcoming college reunion. Thanks to Bill's (Mr. President's) kind offer to host, our dinner venue was, ta da!... the White House.

My friend, Tim Chorba, was a friend of Yousef Karsh, a world-famous photographer who had snapped every major political leader and celebrity for the last fifty years. Mr. Karsh was interested in the new, young President, and offered to photograph him and Mrs. Clinton. We'd give these photos as our class gifts to them.

Although it had nothing to do with tours or events, this little project became my responsibility because I was the class liaison to the White House for everything related to the reunion. I'd been up to my eyeballs with tours for months and had never run a Presidential "event" before. But, I'm thorough, and competent, and, how hard could this be, anyway?

We found a date to suited the President's schedule - which was harder than you'd think. Scheduling Bill Clinton was a truly impossible job that drove several people insane over the next eight years. A day or so before the shoot Mr. Karsh came to the White House to look at possible locations. He also offered to photograph Hillary and wanted to look at her clothes to pick an outfit. I greeted him in the East Reception Room. Mr. Karsh was in his eighties, but surprisingly spry and irresistibly charming. He was a small man, with wiry gray curls on the sides of his head, and an impish smile. He bowed over my hand and I admired his stylish gray bespoke European suit. (See - gray CAN be elegant!)

We walked over to the elevator and met Hillary's aide, who took us up to the Residence. My first time too, so I was just as excited and curious as Mr. Karsh. Even the little elevator was a revelation, paneled in rosewood and run by an usher. (For the First Family it's run by a butler in white tie and tails.) It opens onto a small lobby/hallway off the main living space. I was determined to see everything but didn't want to look as if I were a nosy tourist. After all, it's the most private space in the White House. Only family, invited friends, and the occasional visiting head of state get to see these rooms - just like at your house, right?

A large cross hall runs the length of the House, with sitting areas at each end. It's a beautiful, sunny, welcoming place, furnished with elegant antiques and some comfortable, family things. I saw an exquisite Mary Cassat painting in shades of blue, soft yellow, and pink, a grand piano, and flowers on most tables. Thanks to the talented people in the "flower shop" the White House has better flowers (way better) than Buckingham Palace, as I discovered on a visit there.)

Off the cross hall are the Lincoln bedroom, Queens' bedroom, President's study, Clintons' bedroom and the Yellow Oval Room, where First Ladies entertain privately. Many of these rooms

I'd come to know better, but this first trip my eyes were wide open. I kept reminding myself to close my mouth so I wouldn't look stupid.

Hillary's aide was in a hurry, so we got right to business. Next thing I knew I was standing in the closet of the First Lady, looking at dresses. I was surprised both at how small the closet was - like a closet in a small condo - and how little there was in it. My own small closet held twice as many clothes. Hillary was obviously not a clotheshorse. I liked her even better.

Mr. Karsh picked a gauzy white dress and said he wanted to photograph her in the cross hall, where there's plenty of natural light, "If Mrs. Clinton agrees, of course."

"I'm sure that will be fine. So, we'll see you tomorrow?"

He gave his trademark, courtly bow, she turned and left, and I took Mr. Karsh down in the elevator. We walked around the State floor, but he wasn't satisfied with any of those locations. We went down to the ground floor to look at those rooms and he decided on the Library for the President's photo shoot. It's less grand, and more intimate than the rooms above.

I had never arranged a Presidential or First Lady event, and had no template to work from, so I just wrote up a memo to the ushers, with all the information I had about the two photos - the time, location, details about what we'd be doing. Everything I thought I needed to cover. I ended by writing, "If there is anything else we need to be aware of for this event, please let me know as soon as possible."

I sent it up the next morning and didn't hear a thing. So I called them in the afternoon.

"Hey, did I cover it all? Did I miss anything you need to know, or we should know?"

"No, no, it's all fine, no problems, we'll see you tomorrow."

"Great, but be sure to let me know if anything changes. We never close ..." Silly me - I thought this meant we were good to go.

Hillary's photo shoot was fast and easy. She looked ethereal and lovely in the white gauze dress, with the sunlight behind her. Light makeup enhanced her lovely skin. Remember, this was a woman not known to spend a lot of time fussing about her looks, caring far more about her intellect and accomplishments. She was relaxed, glowing and animated, mostly at the conversation. Mr. Karsh made us all laugh with his stories of the other Presidents and First Ladies he had photographed, including Eleanor Roosevelt, Hillary's hero.

She patiently posed, chatted and seemed to be enjoying the moment. Mr. Karsh took a number of photos and then stopped. He thought for a minute then went over to Hillary and took her hand.

"Dear Mrs. Clinton," he said. "When I do a photo shoot I always - ALWAYS - use all the photographic plates I brought, just to be sure at least one of them captures the image I want. But today, for the first time, I know I've already got the perfect photo of you, and there's no point in taking any more. I hope this is all right with you?"

Hillary looked surprised, then pleased. "Of course, whatever you think will be fine."

Mr. Karsh's assistant also looked surprised, and whispered to me, "He's right - we never stop shooting until we've used every plate. He must think he has something really special already."

The next day Mr. Karsh arrived early to take the President's picture. Marc and I walked him over to the Ground Floor and into the Library. Just as you'd expect, the walls are covered with bookshelves filled with books. The only person I ever heard borrowed any of them was Chelsea, who occasionally found something to help with her homework in those days before Google. All the books, on law, history, science, biography, etc., are by American authors, and the story I heard said Mrs. Nixon asked a committee of famous American academics to make a list of the books they thought should be in the White House library. Each one came up with a completely different list. So, in the end, she just told the Curators to buy some books by American authors and put them on the shelves.

There's a round table in the center of the room, usually holding a large flower arrangement, and a suite of delicate looking Federal furniture, a fireplace on one side, with a beautiful painting above, and an unusual chandelier. Opposite the fireplace is the entrance to the only men's room in the White House public rooms.

There's none upstairs on the State Floor. No ladies' room up there either, but there is one across the hall off the Vermeil Room - the one filled with vermeil serving pieces and First Lady portraits. Every time I walked through on my way to the loo, I gave a little wave to Eleanor Roosevelt or Jackie Kennedy.

We looked at the furniture, and Mr. Karsh said he wanted to move things around. I called up to the ushers and reached Gary.

"Don't even think about moving anything in that room," he barked. "The President has an event up in the East Room, and in case he wants to use the men's room, the Library has to be in pristine order."

"But Gary, we're trying to set up for the **President's** photo shoot. Surely he won't mind if the furniture has been moved?"

"No. Absolutely not. He might need to go in there when the event is over, and we can't have it in a mess."

He refused to budge. I rolled my eyes at Marc and smiled apologetically at Mr.Karsh. We sat and waited. After about thirty minutes we heard the President's voice in the hall; he was on his way up to the event. Mr. Karsh stepped out of the Library just in time to catch the President's eye. He came over and greeted Mr. Karsh warmly, turning on the effortless, megawatt Clinton charm. The effect is like the sun coming out on a cloudy day.

"It's a pleasure to meet you. I looked at your book last night and the photos are beautiful. I'll be back later this afternoon - right?"

Then he headed for the stairs and his audience.

Since we weren't allowed to move the furniture, we just waited some more. Mr. Karsh was great company. He knew all the most famous people of the twentieth century, politicians, movie and opera stars, sportsmen - you name them and he had photographed them. And he had great stories about all of them, from Queen Elizabeth to Winston Churchill. We were utterly charmed.

Eventually, the event ended and the President went back to the Oval Office. I called Gary again. "Now, can we please move the furniture?"

"Certainly not. The only people who can touch the furniture in this House are my laborers. You wait and I'll send a team."

Well, OK with me, but I wondered why he hadn't told me this when I sent up my memo.

We waited for a while longer, Mr. Karsh now clearly anxious to get started. Eventually a couple of the House laborers, in their blue shirts and dark pants, walked in, carrying rolled up canvas and white gloves. They put down the canvas to protect the rugs and floor, then put on the gloves to handle the furniture. It made perfect sense, but why hadn't they told me this was the protocol?

Mr. Karsh pointed to the round table and asked them to move it next to the fireplace and take away the flowers. Then he headed for the bookshelves and almost - almost - touched a book to move it. Horrors!

"No! Wait!" the laborers said, and hustled over.

Mr. Karsh stopped in his tracks and smiled agreeably.

"Tell us which books you want, and we'll move them."
He pointed to a few he wanted on the table as props. Meanwhile, his assistant set up their worktable with all his equipment.

Mr. Karsh had now been with us for hours and looked parched. Remember, he was then in his eighties. He gently asked if he could please have something to drink. I was embarrassed not to have offered some refreshment, and I called the ushers again. "Please bring us a couple of sodas, some ice and water, for Mr. Karsh."

In a very grudging way Gary said, "OK."

In a few minutes a butler brought them, on a silver tray, with the little white paper napkins with the gold Presidential seal. He placed the tray on Karsh's worktable and left.

Now the President's valet brought a jacket and tie for the President to change into, and Mr. Karsh wasn't happy with them. The jacket, a black one, was all right, but the tie was not. He tried to explain to the valet what he wanted, but wasn't getting through.

I interrupted to say, "If you take me back up with you, I think I know what Mr. Karsh is looking for."

The valet shrugged, smiled at me, and gestured to the door. We went up in the elevator and the next thing I knew I was standing in the tie closet of the President of the United States. It was paneled in yellow pine and there appeared to be hundreds of ties hanging on pegs. Little did I know BC was just getting started on the world's largest tie collection.

I stood there, staring, trying not to look around too much or to listen to the voice in my head saying, *I'm in the PRESIDENT'S tie closet. Holy cow. I bet there's a camera hidden somewhere here, watching every move I make.* I mean, wouldn't there be?

There wasn't. Even Presidents get a little privacy in their home. The valet coughed, and I realized I had a job to do, so I looked around and found a tie with a navy blue background and embroidered eagles in white and red.

Just the thing. Very presidential.

Mr. Karsh now had the setting arranged as he wanted, so we sat back to wait for the President. For once, he didn't keep us waiting, but I soon wished he had. He was in a foul mood - impatient, cross, unfriendly. There was a scowl on his face and a nasty tone to his voice I'd never heard before.

I was horrified. How in the world would Mr. Karsh get a good photo out of a person in such a mood? It was going to be a disaster! I don't know what happened between the sunny mood of the morning and the pissed-off mood of the afternoon. Could have been nasty allergies (which all the Arkansans suffered from our first spring.) Could have been a missile crisis - who knows?

Mr. Karsh offered the jacket and tie.

The President looked at them and barked, "Oh, great. A black jacket and a blue tie – how's that supposed to work?!"

In his most soothing tones Karsh replied, "Actually, sir, with the kind of film I use we won't see a color difference, so it shouldn't be a problem. But if you prefer to wear something else I'm happy to defer to your choice."

"Never mind," the President snarled, grabbing the jacket and tie and heading for the men's room to change.

I stood by the worktable, frozen. *This is dreadful! How can Mr. Karsh get a good photo from a man in such a bad mood? And I'm the staff person in charge. I am so screwed ...*

I should have had more faith in Mr. Karsh. He had photographed all those famous people over the years - did I think they were all lovely, happy people? Of course not. He was well experienced in the art of jollying up impatient, cross VIPs.

When the President came out, Mr. Karsh asked to him to sit at the side of the round table with one arm on the books, all the while telling fascinating stories about the famous people he had known and photographed. When he mentioned JFK, the President's face changed. This was his hero, who was photographed here in the House where Bill was now President. He wanted to hear this story.

"Well, sir, as it happens, President Kennedy did not like the tie I picked for him either, but he did like mine. So I suggested we trade ties for the photo. We did, and then, I'm sorry to say, I remembered to give the President his tie back. How I wish I had kept his instead!"

As Karsh puttered around making adjustments, the President's mood started to improve. But then I spotted another problem. His right arm was leaning on the books, and on his wrist was the clunker sports watch he wore for jogging. All black plastic, it looked cheap. I whispered to the assistant, "Please tell Mr. Karsh, the watch spoils the picture. The President should take it off."

The assistant walked over and whispered in Mr. Karsh's ear. Mr. Karsh looked at the President and said, "Sir, it has been suggested," turned and, to my horror, looked at me, " you should remove your watch. It doesn't fit the picture."

Now the President looked totally pissed off again and I tried to shrink into the sofa and avoid his angry eyes. He took off the watch and practically threw it at Mr. Karsh, who pleasantly smiled and promised to return it shortly.

The President's aide, Andrew Friendly, looked at me and rolled his eyes.

I whispered to him, "Andrew! When you're in the car later with the President, please tell him the watch had to disappear for two reasons. One is it detracts from his hands, and he has beautiful hands. The other is the watch is completely 1993 technology, and the photo is for history. It would be a shame to anchor it in the past."

Andrew nodded. I didn't realize until later the LAST thing he or anyone wanted to do was remind the President of something that had put him in a bad mood earlier. Once his anger passed, he just moved on and forgot it and staff were wise to do the same.

So Mr. Karsh snapped away, and later, when we saw the finished photo, it was wonderful. The President looks handsome, thoughtful, and serious. And his hands look beautiful.

I thought, all things considered, it had gone reasonably well. But I underestimated Gary. A day or so later my son, Shiloh, who was an intern with us, was walking through the Ground Floor and heard two of the household staff talking - about me.

"Yeah, she's really stupid, and careless. Can you believe it - she put their drinks on the **antique tables.** The butler had to move them and wipe up the ring they left. And she moved furniture around by herself, without gloves! She'll never last long here," and they laughed. At me.

I was furious, but there was nothing I could do, except file it away to keep in mind every other time I had to deal with him. Like I said, a real snake

CHAPTER NINE ~ THE TOURISTS ARE COMING!

The White House is unique. It's the only residence of a head of state in the world that's open to the public for free, on a regular basis. It is "America's House," belonging both to the current occupants and to the American people – and they know it. Boy, do they know it. You'd be surprised at how emotional people get about visiting. I know I was.

It wasn't uncommon for people to burst into tears during a phone conversation if we couldn't arrange a tour for their group. This was usually parents, pleading for a child's class. I'm a mother, so I understand parental passion, but I thought it was ridiculous for the father of a fourth grader to say, "You don't understand – this is her ONLY chance to see the White House!"

I'd put on what we came to call my "psychiatrist's voice" to soothe them, while thinking, "Get a grip! The child is ten! Let's hope she has a long and interesting life, with many opportunities. It's the aging WWII vets who may only have this one, last chance to visit – before they DIE. And I'm gonna make sure they get it. Your kid can wait."

Of course, I could never say such a thing to anyone.

The National Park Service once ran a survey of visitors, and my favorite crazy lady wrote, "Access to the White House is too important to be restricted to just a few hours a day. Since the First Family has to live somewhere, and conduct official events somewhere, I think we should just build them another house, somewhere on the South grounds. Then the public can tour the White House itself all day long."

Sure!

One of our more ridiculous callers identified herself as a history teacher from Alabama. She wanted her class of middle-schoolers to come up to meet the President. Marc gently explained the President would love to meet her kids, but unfortunately his schedule would not allow it.

Then she asked, "Well, how about that Vice-President fella – Quayle? Can they meet him?"

Remember, she was a history teacher!

Marc responded, "Perhaps you're unaware there has been a change in administrations. The Vice President is Al Gore."

"OK, how about him, then?"

I rolled my eyes and let him talk her out of that idiocy as well. I thought later we should have noted her phone number, called the school, and reported her to the principal as an idiot who had no business in a history classroom.

Of course, there were also the ranters and ravers who made my work so interesting. One man called, sputtering with rage. He was in a long line at the NPS Visitors Center; there were "foreigners" in line with him, and he wanted me to assure him no "foreigners" were going to get tickets in front of "genuine Americans."

I gently explained the White House and the Park Service do not request information on a person's nationality for the public tour tickets, and it is (clearly) impossible to determine a person's nationality by his or her appearance or accent, and, anyway, he was just going to have to stand in the long line with everyone else. He was not a happy camper. I know it's bizarre to say so, but I always enjoyed interacting with these loonies. I liked using every trick I could think of to soothe them. Sometimes it worked, sometimes not, but it was a perverse kind of fun for me.

I also respected the passion and sense of ownership. I lived in Washington my entire life and never once thought of visiting the White House. When we had out-of-town visitors my parents took them for a drive downtown, passing the White House, but this drive-by was enough for all of us. It was the President's house, important events happened there, but I had no sense of being connected to her, and no deep desire to set foot in her halls. (And make no mistake, the White House has plenty of personality, filling her from the basements to the rafters, and is definitely a grand dame.) From my new vantage point I could see the joy and amazement on people's faces when they walked through her doors. I knew it meant we could never take our responsibilities lightly.

We hated to disappoint people, but there's just not room for everyone who wants to visit. The White House is not only a museum of American history. It's filled with world class nineteenth-century furniture, objects, textiles and art requiring study and careful preservation. We were astonished to learn, right up until the Kennedy years there was no law protecting White House furnishings. So, departing Presidents (Truman) might make off with, say, a mantle from the State Dining Room (now in the Truman library). Or, the incoming First Family might not like the "old fashioned" things they found there, so they'd have a yard sale to clear them out and raise money to buy new furniture. Thank God for Jackie Kennedy, who began the process of bringing these historic things back to the House, and Pat Nixon, who also worked tirelessly (and very successfully) to carry on the task.

There are a lot of competing demands on a house that's relatively small for the head of state of the most powerful country in the world. One minute you're ushering the last tourist of the day out the North Door, and the next you're frantically cleaning and setting up a luncheon in the Library for Yasser Arafat and Menachem Begin in the hope they will find a way to make peace.

One minute you stand in the East Room, telling a group of wide-eyed children about the sad days when President Lincoln's body lay there in state. An hour later the current President steps up to the mic for a press conference. Oh yes, it's quite a juggling act!

Visitors from overseas were often astounded they could get free tickets – or, for that matter, ANY tickets – to see the President's house. They knew they couldn't do this at home in Caracas, or Dublin, or Rome. They also realized it said something important about America, and our openness and democracy. It makes me sad now to know security concerns have caused tours to become very limited. It also says something about who we are and the realities of the world we live in.

We were still in our first summer when I got a call from the British Embassy asking me to meet with a representative of Buckingham Palace. Well, sure, send her right over. Who wouldn't want to meet someone who worked for the Queen?

A pleasant woman with an upper-class English accent sat on my love seat and said, "It's very kind of you to meet with me. I've been tasked with learning everything possible about how you are able to open the White House to the public; how tours work; how you schedule Presidential events in the House; and how you handle security."

I spent a happy couple of hours explaining everything I could think of. Then I called in Lt. Purdie to brief her on security. When the lady left, we grinned at each other, both thinking the same thing: "We should start planning our site visits to the Palace and Scotland Yard right away – surely they're going to need more advice. This is great! I see a trip to London in our future!"

Only two months later we were startled to read that, for the first time in history, the Queen was going to open Buckingham Palace to the public during the month of August, while she was away at Balmoral for her annual Scottish holiday. Disappointed (and annoyed), I called the Social Secretary at the British Embassy to laugh a little.

"Gosh Amanda, what happened? We were so sure the Queen's advisors would want more information from us, we had practically packed for our site visit."

She laughed too. "Well, you see, the Palace belongs entirely to Her Majesty. There was no committee involved in making the decision, just the Queen, and when she wants to make a decision, she does. So things there can move a lot faster than one would expect. So sorry about your trip ..."

This was funny, in unintentional ways, and most likely accurate. I already understood nothing similar could happen at the White House, where every little decision (much less the really big ones) had to go through endless layers of committees and advisors. God bless the Queen.

***

Meanwhile, we were now using the new tour tracking system with good results. When Republican Members of Congress whined about supposedly not getting any tours, we could look up the records and tell them they were wrong - they were getting a fair share (so shut up about it already).

I wanted the word to get out on the Hill – don't mess with

us. We're working hard to make the system work for all of you. If you need a special favor, feel free to call and ask. We'll do our best to help you. If I have to say "sorry, no" it will be because we really can't do it, not because we're not trying.

And, once they understood our integrity and good faith, we made a lot of friends for the President, on both sides of the aisle. This was really our mission – to keep the Members of Congress happy and off the President's back. The tours were simply our means to this goal. But, we still had a lot to learn about how important they were.

There is (or, at least, there was) a special tour in the mornings called the "Members' Tour" because the Member of Congress him/herself, or the spouse, or the chief of staff, had to personally accompany their guests to a different entry gate, then walk them into our reception room. There, I greeted them with a little speech, and sent them off with a tour officer. Unlike everyone else, they got to go out into the Jacqueline Kennedy garden and take photos. (No photos on regular tours.) The experience was very nice, and the guests were impressed with their unusual access.

But, as the peak summer tour season started to ramp up, we found our reception room, only about thirty feet square, often filled to bursting. People were packed in, standing shoulder to shoulder. With everyone talking at once it was very loud. We thought this was not a "special" experience at all. So, I decided to limit the number of guests on the tour, scheduling them first-come, first-served. Seemed fair to me.

Well, on the Hill the Members were instantly outraged. They wanted their tours, dammit! Soon the wife of a Congressman from Oklahoma asked for a meeting. She came to my office, where Robyn and I greeted her warmly but warily. She was a little agitated at first, and then got to the point: the Members' Tours.

"All of us on the Hill are very upset you've started to cut off access to the tour. I'm here to represent a lot of different offices. We believe if we're willing to get up at the crack of dawn to drive into Washington to meet our guests, and then drive them down to the White House, you've got to accommodate us!"

I tried to explain we'd been observing the tours and thought the overcrowding was awful, and the experience unpleasant. Then she said something that stuck with me for all eight years:

"You clearly don't understand. Access to these tours is more important to my husband's re-election than any speech he will ever give!"

Whoa! Robyn and I sat back to absorb this. "Well. Thank you so much for this advice. We'll certainly consider what you said and see what we can do about it. We appreciate your coming to share this with us."

After she left, we talked about it.

"She went to some trouble to come here," I said. "And I believe she does represent a number of Members. I guess the good-faith thing to do is to accommodate all their requests. It's my guess the crowded experience will be so unpleasant, the Members themselves will call us and say we have to cut back. Then it will be THEIR decision, not ours."

We did this, and the room and tours were packed throughout the summer. We thought it was terrible. But, I have to tell you, many Members called to thank us for helping them, and not one office called to complain about the quality of the experience. So, we learned another valuable lesson: it's all about the ACCESS; it's never about the quality of the experience.

There were many times over our eight years I yearned to offer tours with more time or information. After all, I had a museum background and was now working closely with the White House curators. We had lots of ideas for improving the tour experience. How about a tour that focuses on art, or the nineteenth century furnishings, or the architecture? There were so many interesting things to see and learn about.

In our first months I brought in the great White House historian, Bill Seale, to educate us. Bill started years ago, writing a monograph for the White House Historical Association, and it was so brilliant they told him to just keep writing. Many years, and thousands of pages later, he produced the definitive two-volume history of the House and its residents.

I gave him a microphone and sent him off to walk around the

House, just talking about anything he wanted – the architecture, the art, the antiques. Then we made multiple tapes for the Visitors Office, the Curators, and the USSS Tour Office, so we could all learn from this amazing man.

The Tour Officers benefited, because they all loved the House and its history, and loved sharing it with the people on guided tours. The Visitors Office benefited, because the really fun part of my day started with a phone call from the Oval Office, or the First Lady's Office:

"Melinda, the President just met with (name your favorite star here) and wants you to walk him (or her) around the House, please."

Or, "Melinda, Hillary just had tea with the Queen of Sweden, would you please walk her around the House now?"

So, the more I knew about the House, the more fun we could have with a tour. I listened to those tapes in my car and read every book I could get my hands on to learn as much as I could, as fast as I could.

But these kinds of tours were possible only for a few special individuals or small groups. No matter how much we would have liked to improve the tour experience for everyone, we always ran smack into the reality of our situation – the White House is a museum, yes, but unlike any other museum it is also a home to an active family, the site of official President and First Lady events, and a very busy office building.

Those other demands meant we could only run group and ticketed tours from 8:00 a.m. until about noon, or sometimes later if the President or First Lady were not using the House for a bill signing or press conference. We had only this small window of time. When we had to decide between a better experience for fewer visitors, or a worse experience for more visitors, we always came down on the side of more visitors. It was that simple. Americans love their House; they know it's THEIR house; and they care passionately about just setting foot in the door.

By updating the processes, and pushing all the resources of the House, we managed to accommodate 1.5 million visitors our first year – a record we were all proud of.

I later heard when the Bush II people learned about it, they were furious to think they'd have to admit all those common people into "their" House. In fact, in 2001 someone inside the Bush White House told me they had never wanted the public to have access at all, but they recognized they'd face a public relations disaster if they tried to limit the tours. So, when 9/11 happened, the excuse of "security" allowed them to do things they wanted to do from the beginning – cut way back on public access to "America's House."

In late spring, 2001, when the Bushes (II) had been in place for 6 months, I got a call at home from a reporter for the *New York Times*. She was doing a story about access to White House tours, and wanted to talk about how they work. It seems the Bush Visitors Office sent out a letter telling people in New York if they were coming to Washington to see the White House, it would be better not to go on a tour bus, or with a tour operator. What did I think about this?

"I'm surprised for several reasons," I said. "Obviously I don't know the Bushes, other than what I read about them, but it seems, unlike the Clintons, they lead very orderly, scheduled, quiet lives. If this is true, then the Visitors Office knows well in advance if are no official demands on the House on any given day. If they know this, they can extend tours until 3:00 in the afternoon, and make thousands of people happy during the peak season. Aren't they doing that?"

"No," she replied. "Tours in the Bush White House end every day promptly at noon, no matter what."

"But, why?"

"I've been told it's so the House can be properly cleaned and maintained."

"That makes no sense to me either," I said. "The White House employs large teams of people whose job it is to appear the moment the last tourist walks out the North Door, to clean and polish like nothing you've never seen. The White House is always kept in immaculate condition."

"No, **you** don't understand," she said. "I've been told Laura Bush is like Mamie Eisenhower – with Clorox!"

For those of you too young to get the reference, Mamie

Eisenhower was every bit as much a general, in her own, ladylike way, as her husband, General and President Dwight Eisenhower. She followed him around the world, setting up homes in post after post, as he fought to save America in World War II) and she ran the White House with an iron hand.

This comment was the kind of thing only a person inside the House would have said, and I wondered who her source was. Whoever it was – good for him!

I thought about it for a moment, and said, "The only explanation I can suggest is the Bushes just don't like having the public in their House – and I find that very sad. I'd also like to say, as a Democrat, I'm a big fan of small businesses, and I think those tour companies do a fine job of bringing people here. Also, as a Washingtonian, I think if thirty-five people are coming to town, I'd greatly prefer they all come on one bus, and not in twenty cars, to clog our streets and degrade our air."

This was my epiphany moment of understanding: all those clichés about (some!) Republicans being snobs, interested only in rich, successful people, are clichés because, at least in my experience, they are TRUE.

In spring, 2002, I received an invitation to come to the White House for the unveiling of the two Clinton official portraits. These portraits are always created after a President and First Lady have left office. I showed up on East Executive Avenue in my best summer suit, positively buzzing with excitement, both to see so many of my old friends and colleagues, and to get to set foot inside the beloved House. I have to say President Bush made very gracious welcoming remarks to all of us in the East Room, and Mrs. Bush stood in a receiving line with Bill and Hillary to smile and meet all of us. She was very kind to tolerate our jubilation on such a special day.

I didn't return to the White House again until 2008, when some friends and I visited on a brilliant June afternoon. It was a thrill to stand in those spaces and remember all our exciting times. As I looked around at rooms once so familiar to me, I realized the House looked exceptionally beautiful, and sparkling clean. So it seems

Mrs. Bush was a good steward of America's House. Credit where credit is due ...

And by the way, some years later I received an invitation to Gary Walters' retirement party. If I had not been living in Mexico then, I would have gone just to see the House, and reconnect with old friends. And to wave him good bye.

***

"President and Mrs. Madison" at Hillary's 1993 birthday party.

Chapter Ten ~ The Arkansans are Coming!

One problem I'm sure the Bush people (I or II) didn't have to deal with was the one that quickly became a thorn in our sides: the home folks from Arkansas.

Bill and Hillary Clinton come from a state with only two million inhabitants in the '90s. And, thanks to his sunny gregariousness, many of those people visited him in the Governor's office in Little Rock, passing the time and sitting in the Governor's chair, having their picture "made" as they oddly said. Or, if he was not in, they'd look at the office, sit in his governor's chair, spin around and pretend for a moment to be the one in charge.

So, why couldn't they do this now that he was President? They really did think they could either casually show up and immediately be ushered in to the Oval Office, or, if they called ahead, they could insist on a visit with the President or First Lady.

I guess during the campaign Bill kept telling people, "When I get to the White House, you all are invited to come see me in the Oval Office!" (The electioneering equivalent of, "Y'all come on down, now!")

And, soon enough, these hordes of visitors began to descend on us. Buses and carloads of people drove to Washington to "see Bill and Hillary." In 1998, my boyfriend, Steve, told me about seeing a car with Arkansas plates on the Beltway, sometime in 1993, the driver clearly confused and lost. He leaned out his window and yelled, "Are you looking for the White House?"

"Yes!" they all yelled with relief.

"Follow me, I'll take you there," he shouted back, and led them into town.

These visits were no burden to the President – he loves to meet and visit with people, from janitors to heads of state. All this pressing-the-flesh would exhaust some politicians, or be regarded as a necessary evil for election, but for Bill Clinton it's a way to recharge. These folks from back home knew they were welcome at the Governor's place. It may have been no problem in Little Rock, but it became a big problem for us in the White House, and letting these people down gently was a job that fell to me and Robyn.

In my first meeting with David Watkins and Janet Green I'd been smart enough to be happy about the Clintons choosing Robyn Dickey, an Arkansan, to be my Deputy Director. I figured even then she'd have plenty to do just taking care of the hometown crowd. I had no idea.

The requests came in by the boatload. They came to me first, with little notes on them saying this person was a friend since kindergarten, or that person had served with Hillary on the Hospital Board ... I quickly learned to hand these right over to Robyn. Maybe they were lifelong friends (in fact, they probably were) or maybe they weren't, but I was in no position to know. I brought expertise on Washington, the Hill, lobbyists, and the diplomatic corps, but I didn't know a thing about Arkansas.

Fortunately for us, Robyn did, and she was able to tell me who should have a tour scheduled, and who we should try to put on the POTUS or FLOTUS schedules. We knew the President and First Lady would probably love to see all these people, but they were no longer Governor and First Lady of a small state. Hello? They were President of the United States and First Lady, and their lives were now very different. We tried explaining this concept to the folks from back home,but they just wouldn't take "sorry, we can't" for an answer.

I had a conversation with the tour coordinator from an Arkansas congressional office and asked her how they handled the flood of requests.

She giggled and told me her new mantra: "We Arkansans have always known how wonderful they are. Now we have to share them with the world ... You'd be surprised how often it works."

"Thanks so much - I'll add your clever phrase to my repertoire of soothing things to say to irate petitioners."

Even my skill and affection for working with difficult people weren't always enough.

Those first few months in the Visitors Office trained me and all my staff in a whole new level of gently but effectively saying, "So sorry. No, we can't. Yes, I understand, but we still can't schedule your meeting/tour/photo..."

I got to be pretty good at it - but not as good as Robyn.

I'm direct and honest. If you ask me for help I will absolutely do my best to assist you, and if I have to tell you "no" it won't be for lack of trying. I'm not good at (have never been good at) subtlety and I can't even try to lie, because you'd see it in my face. (I like to think there are issues of personal morality to keep me from lying, but in any case, my face would immediately give me away.)

Robyn, however, has a way of talking to people in her sweet, southern accent, that makes them feel so happy they are out the door and down the hall, smiling, before they realize - they didn't get what they asked for. This is a fabulously useful talent!

When we had to say "no" we'd try to start out with me telling them, "So sorry, the President would love to see you but he just can't right now."

If they kept insisting, I'd refer them to Robyn, who spoke Arkansan (in both accent and content) and would also do her best to explain we simply couldn't do what they wanted. Surprisingly often they would get aggressive and rude, insisting, "He would want to see us!"

Or, "She told me to come see her when we got to Washington!"

I didn't doubt it. But there was still no darn way they were going to get a visit - good friends or not. As difficult as this was in the Visitors Office, I was left speechless after a conversation with another Arkansan who worked in the Residence. She told me she had to deal with a rumor in Arkansas that supposedly anyone who had an AR driver's license could call the White House and make a reservation to stay in the Lincoln bedroom. Good Lord!

As the requests began to flood in, we joked in the Visitors Office, "The Arkansas legislature must have passed a law REQUIRING everyone in the state to all come and visit – in the first six months. Thank God the state's so small. Maybe we can get a state-wide address book. Then we can cross out the names of everyone who comes to visit once, and not let them come back until the next term." At least, this was my fantasy.

But some of them wouldn't take "Sorry, no" for an answer. I well remember the scouts from a small Arkansas town who came with their mothers and the scout leader, a woman not to be trifled with. We gladly offered the girls a tour, then a special tour, but none of it was enough.

She told me, loudly and clearly, "During the campaign, Bill Clinton looked me in the eye and told me if he got to the White House I should bring these girls up here and he would meet with them. And now we're here, and we expect our meeting!"

OK, I believed her. And I knew he'd like nothing better than to welcome these folks from home into the Oval Office, handing out little souvenir boxes of M&Ms with the White House seal to the girls and taking photos with them. But he was about to leave the White House, on his way to his first overseas trip as President, and he was up to his eyeballs in briefings for this important event. I tried to explain it, but since I don't have an Arkansas accent, I wasn't credible to her.

I got Robyn to come out and talk to her, but even though she had the right accent, she was saying the wrong thing ("no"), and also got nowhere. She called the office of the Chief of Staff, Mack McLarty, the third highest-ranking Arkansan in the House, and pleaded for someone of, as we used to say, "a higher pay grade than mine," to please come to the gate and reason with this lady. Mack's assistant came out, but was equally unsuccessful.

The next thing I knew, the Chief of Staff to the President of the United States was at the tour gate, soothing an irate scout leader. At this point, all the children and their mothers were trying to disappear into the background, rolling their eyes and tugging on their leader's sleeves, but she was adamant. She didn't care about our excuses, and she didn't care how badly she behaved. She wanted what she had been promised, and she wasn't going to quit until she had it.

Finally, Mack, who I assume had a few more important things to deal with that day, (nuclear proliferation? Bilateral trade?) promised her, "When the President leaves the White House this afternoon, on his way to Air Force One, the motorcade and the limo will slow, the window will go down, and the President will wave at the girls. I know he'll be glad to see them."

I'm not sure if this satisfied her, or if she finally realized this was as good as it was going to get, but she grudgingly agreed. And so, I watched with amusement as the motorcade left by a different gate than normal (which is actually dangerous, but oh well) so the President could smile and wave at the scouts.

Over the years I had a lot of interactions with Arkansans, enjoying some, but not all of them. I was often amazed at how unpleasant people could be when pressing us for the favor of a visit or special tour. Eventually I developed a theory of behavior to explain this: People in Arkansas would plan a trip to Washington and tell all their friends, "We're going up to Washington to see Bill and Hillary."

Then they'd arrive and discover the disappointing truth: the best they could get was a tour. They weren't going to see the Clintons, or the Oval Office. Then they began to imagine what would happen when they got home. Friends would ask, "How is Bill? How is Hillary?" and they'd have to admit they hadn't actually seen them. No visit. It would be embarrassing.

But, being rude and pushy with us might get them the visit, and wouldn't embarrass them back home (who cared what they said to us?), so why not at least try it? After formulating my theory I asked Arkansans around the House if they liked my analysis, and they said it sounded right to them.

Don't get me wrong here. Bill and Hillary Clinton love Arkansas and Arkansans. There were many I worked with or came to know who I respected for their brilliance and dedication and loved for their commitment to the Clintons and their agenda. Some were just a little harder to love than others.

Chapter Eleven ~ Colleagues and Bosses

It didn't take me long to realize coordinating tours with competing uses of the House, like bill signings, press conferences, teas, receptions, etc., would be more challenging for us than for previous White House staffs. The Clintons are very different from the occupants of the previous twelve years. They're a generation younger, and have twice the energy and commitment of people half their age. They set ambitious schedules and pushed teams of people - hard - to make things happen. Then, just as you finally got things arranged for what you thought they wanted, they changed their minds at the very last minute and it was back to the drawing board to figure out how to do something completely different.

More than once I found myself welcoming a group of guests and briefing them on their event or tour, only to have a staffer come up and whisper in my ear - while I was talking – to say the President had changed his mind, or his schedule, so these plans were no longer operational.

Then I'd smile and tell the guests, "I know you were paying careful attention to my briefing, and now I'm going to tell you to forget everything we just told you because what we're really going to do is ... (something completely different!)"

On the inside I'd think, *What? He (or she) wants to do WHAT now? Oh gosh, how exactly are we gonna make **that** happen?*

But as long as I always **looked** calm and competent, people accepted this as simply a normal way to do business at the White House. And for the Clinton White House, it was normal.

Since this was my first experience at working for Bill (Mr. President) and Hillary, at first I thought this chaotic way of running their schedules and lives was a temporary circumstance. After all, they were as new to their positions as all of us on staff were to ours.

Surely, at some point they (and we) will settle into doing things in a more orderly and predictable way. Right? I mean, we can't keep going on like THIS, can we?

Ha!

I held on to this (erroneous) thought for the first six difficult months. Then one day I mentioned my theory to Ann McCoy, the pretty red-head who came from Arkansas to be Deputy Social Secretary. She looked up from the papers in her lap to stare at me incredulously, then sat me down for a serious talking to.

"Melinda! I don't know where you got such an idea, but it's completely wrong. This is not a temporary aberration. This is how they are. Their minds are constantly going at 1,000 miles per hour, and so their plans and schedules constantly change right up until the moment when they have to do something. Sometimes they want their flights changed while they're already on the way to the airport, or the event changed while guests are actually arriving. This is how they live and work, and it's our job to keep adjusting things to fit these changes. You have to adjust to this, or it will make you completely crazy and you won't last very long here."

Oh, my. Not what I expected. I'm a planner, myself, and like to stick to plans - at least when it makes sense to. But these two people are visionaries. Smarter than anyone else I ever met, and determined to change the world. Literally. Who wouldn't want to be part of changing the world, no matter how challenging it was?

I realized I'd have to change my expectations about how the Clinton White House would work, and change myself to find the best way to serve them. Where before I put all my time and energy into perfecting the plans for schedules we had, now I started making myself imagine all the possible ways the plans could change, and then figuring out what we'd do if/when they did. So, I always had a plan B in my pocket. Sometimes a plan C too. It wasn't easy, but eventually I came to realize how much smarter it made me to learn to adjust to changes on a daily, sometimes moment-to-moment basis - although I do have to say it never stopped being stressful.

The entity this was most difficult for was the U.S. Secret Service. They were accustomed to the organized, predictable schedules of the previous twelve years, and the full cooperation of the First Families. Things were different with the Clintons. The constant changes to their agendas meant security plans days or weeks in the making were suddenly inoperable, and new plans had to be created on a moment's notice. At first this made them all crazy, and I heard a lot of backstage grumbling. But after the first, rough year a senior officer admitted to me, having to learn to cope with these changes had actually improved their ability to protect the President. See, no one likes to have to change, but it often makes us stronger.

I also heard grumbling about the Clintons' supposed dislike for the USSS and their efforts to thwart security, which supposedly made it harder to protect them. I finally sat down with a senior officer and said, "You have to try to understand. Ronald and Nancy Reagan are an older couple who lead quiet, orderly lives and your presence didn't intrude. George H. W. Bush was Director of the CIA and Vice President before becoming President. He and Mrs. Bush, also a generation older, were long accustomed to being shadowed at every moment. Bill Clinton was Governor of Arkansas, for goodness' sake! He had a couple of State Troopers to drive him (and thank God for that, since he's a terrible driver with a real lead foot) and hang around the office. Nothing in his or Hillary's lives ever prepared them for this level of security. They find it smothering and bothersome. I think anybody would need a period of adjustment - just let them get used to it and I'm sure they'll come to appreciate what you do, and why, and will cooperate – more or less. You just have to give it time!"

It seemed to me this is what finally happened.

But the USSS were also capable of shooting themselves in the foot (metaphorically speaking, of course). In 1994 the Clintons hosted an event for Gay and Lesbian activists. The Uniformed Division officers, who staff entry security, check names off lists, and run the magnetometers everyone walks through, broke out plastic gloves to search bags or pat down any guest who set off an alarm. This was not standard procedure then (as it is now in airports), and the guests knew it. They were offended and upset. Hillary was furious and was overheard saying, "God Damn it! Are they doing this stuff to us deliberately? What were they thinking!"

Well, why shouldn't they know they had offended a lot of people?

But it pained me, because of my great affection and respect for many of these dedicated officers and the agents who shadowed

POTUS and FLOTUS. After all, they had pledged to put themselves in the line of fire, if necessary.

There were other divisions of the USSS we saw around the House, with interesting assignments. The men and women (mostly men) in black shirts and pants, with black baseball caps who work on the top of the White House are the "COUNTER-snipers." For God's sake, don't call them "snipers." Think of the PR disaster! No, they are COUNTER-snipers, up there to keep an eye out for any threats. And, if you're a Washington (or New York, or LA) hostess expecting the President to attend your party, there is nothing as thrilling as seeing your street blocked off with black SUVs and the counter-snipers stationed up on your roof!

Each of the different divisions creates patches and pins for their uniforms to reflect their mission. A Special Ops officer once brought me the design for a new patch the counter-snipers had created. It consisted of a human silhouette in the cross hairs of a scope. (!) Imagine how that would look sewn on to the already threatening-looking black uniforms. I could not believe my eyes. Fortunately, a phone call up to the USSS Director's office let wiser heads prevail.

The K-9 officers were especially happy in their work. The dogs, Belgian Malinois, are beautiful, intelligent, loyal, and love to work. One afternoon I was standing at the top of the South driveway with two K-9 officers and their dogs. One dog was out on the grass, his owner throwing a ball for him to retrieve, and pretty happy about it (the dog and the man). The other dog was in his van, jealously watching, and barking his unhappiness.

"Rocky sounds pretty unhappy about not getting out to play too," I observed to his officer.

"Yeah, well, he has to learn to deal with it!" he snapped back. After all, they are working dogs ...

And the happiest Secret Service officers I ever saw were the guys in EOD - Explosives Ordnance Division. Even though their mission is dangerous, and deadly serious, they LOVED their work. They invited me out to their training facility in the country for a demonstration of the kinds of threats they have to deal with. This meant they got to blow up a mailbox, a limo, a door, and assorted other common objects which can be turned into weapons. I enjoyed the BOOM! and BANG! of things blowing up, but not nearly as much as the guys doing it - they were grinning from ear to ear as they took us from one kind of explosive to another:

"Watch this! It's plastique explosive! Watch this! Explosive wire - it burns so fast you can't tell which end we light! And this one is ... " well, you get the picture.

As their finale, they pointed us towards a marshy area off to the side, and detonated a final, blinding charge. Well, guess what happens when you forcibly combine water and dirt? I'm no scientific genius, but I knew the answer: Mud! Yes, a small mushroom cloud of mud rose into the air, briefly hovered, and then, caught by a gust of wind, drifted right over to ... us! I ducked, and averted my face, but my white linen suit, white shoes ... everything was covered with tiny droplets of brown mud. I shook myself, tried to brush it off, and realized that only made things worse. *Better to let it dry. Then maybe I can dust it off. I'm going to look pretty funny back in the office.*

The EOD guys were laughing so hard they could hardly stand up.

***

In the early days the press made a big deal about how "young" Clinton staffers were, and how chaotic the House seemed. I thought this was silly. Many of the jobs paid little and required ridiculously long hours. Who was going to do a job like that - a thirty five-year old with a mortgage and children? No, it was the twenty-somethings who staffed the campaign and were happy to work eighteen hours a day in service to the Clinton agenda. Duh. And I bet it's the same in any administration where the President is younger than, say, seventy.

The House may have seemed chaotic, but I believe the Clintons accomplished more, faster, than anyone could have imagined. Every office I knew was constantly working at warp speed on the President's issues. People burned out pretty quickly at such a pace. We wore our exhaustion like a badge of honor: "I only got four hours of sleep last night."

"Really? I only got ... two! I hardly even know my own name any more ..."

My favorite expression of this came from Joyce Bonnet, briefly Deputy Social Secretary. We were standing at the back of the East Room watching an event unfold and comparing our levels of exhaustion and immersion into the work. She watched the President for a moment, turned to me and wearily said, "I don't know about you, but I'm now well into my husband's underwear drawer!" Oh yes, me too!

Most people lasted about eighteen months. They either couldn't take the pace any more or realized they didn't want a life of never seeing their kids, never taking a real vacation, or being far from home in a city they never had a chance to enjoy. These were a couple of the reasons I lasted all eight years - and am the first person in history to run the Visitors Office that long. My children were old enough to be off to college and didn't need me to tuck them in at night or make their dinner. My then-husband was self-employed (he's a brilliant designer) and was always out working, so he didn't miss me. We separated in 1994 and divorced three years later. And, I was born in Washington and lived there all my life, so I didn't have to pack up and move from somewhere else (like Arkansas, or California). I already had a life in DC, with friends, family and a familiar neighborhood. I had a deep understanding of how Washington works - at least enough to know the lovely invitations and friendships offered were almost all strictly about the job, not about the person. So, when you leave your cool job, those things disappear. Nothing personal. Literally.

In March, 1993, I attended a reception at a nice restaurant for the new Members of Congress. I brought Robyn with me. We were given name tags with only our names - no titles. We wandered around the lovely room, tasting from the elaborate buffet, drinking a little wine, and talking to each other - because no one else would talk to us. That
's right. The other guests were mostly men, and when they glanced at us and took in the nametags with just names, their eyes slid past and they kept walking.

After twenty minutes of this, I got a little irritated and said to Robyn, "This is the perfect time for me to show you how Washington really works. Please hand me your name tag." I headed for a table and turned my back to the room.

I took our tags out of the plastic holders, turned them over and wrote, "Melinda Bates, Director, White House Visitors Office," and "Robyn Dickey, Deputy Director ... " I put the tags back in the holders and held Robyn's out to her.

"Now, before we turn around, I want you to tell me how long you think it will be before someone talks to us."

Robyn looked puzzled, but game. "OK, I'm not sure what you're doing, but I'll guess, hmmm, 5 minutes."

"You're on. Now put on your tag and let's see what happens."

We turned back to the room and the guests, and I'm not kidding when I tell you no more than thirty seconds later some man glanced at us, glanced at our name tags, started to walk by and realized what they said. He stopped himself, flashed a big smile, held out his hand and said, "Hi, I'm so-and-so, from ... it looks like you ladies have interesting jobs."

And off we went, on our first conversation of the evening. Pretty soon we were the center of a knot of interested men. I kept looking at Robyn, who was having trouble keeping a straight face. When we left, I said, "I can't think of a better demonstration of how this town really operates. Without our titles and swell jobs we aren't worth talking to. If you can remember this, you'll keep a realistic balance in your life and you'll be OK when we leave."

Chapter Twelve ~ Parties! Festivities! Celebrations! Oh My!

There were plenty of people who had more challenging responsibilities and more impressive titles than I did, but who rarely got to walk around the White House as I did, rarely attended parties, rarely saw the President in more casual, festive moments. Being the Director of the Visitors Office was a big deal in Washington - overnight I became everybody's "best friend." My staff kept a running pool of guesses over how short the time would be between when I was introduced to someone and how quickly they asked me for a favor. The shortest ever was a man who heard my title as we were introduced, instantly registered what my job was, and asked me for tour tickets while still shaking my hand.

I laughed and said, "You know, there's usually a couple of minutes of socializing before I get asked for stuff. We pretend you're interested in more than what I can do for you. But since you're asking for your mother, sure, I'll be glad to help you."

He wasn't even embarrassed.

The administrative tasks were the unavoidable scut work of my job, but the events were my delight. The Visitors Office was the perfect place for me with my lifelong dedication to beauty and celebrations of every kind. We all like to think of ourselves as unique beings, but I've learned just how much I'm like generations of women in my mother's family. My Cuban grandmother died early, when my mom was only three, because she insisted on going out to dance at Carnival, shortly after giving birth. She caught a "chill" and passed away, leaving four small children. Such was her passion for parties.

My mother was a brilliant hostess, throwing dinner parties almost every week. She cooked, she decorated, and she and my dad presided over a table of great food and wine, interesting conversation and laughter. Early on, she let me cut flowers from the garden and arrange them for her. I learned to fold the napkins and set the silver and crystal. I was proud to assist the maid at serving dinner (serve from the left, pick up from the right), because it made me feel like a grown-up, and because I got to hear even more of the conversations.

This goes so deep in the bone. When I was no more than four years old I was already staging elaborate ceremonies. The excuse was usually the sad death of a tiny pet mouse or lizard. This was cause (excuse) for a very odd funeral procession. Apparently, in my childish mind, there was some confusion between funerals (I had never been to one) and weddings (nor to one of those). So, I got my mother to make me a white net veil I anchored in place with a wreath of flowers. I wore one of her silk slips and carried a blue velvet pillow (she made for me), with the matchbox coffin on top.

I bullied confused neighborhood children into lining up as my "attendants" and slowly marched us all out to the far corner of the garden, where "Mousie" was laid to rest.

This was followed by lemonade and cookies, with me presiding over my own table, just like Mom. Now, where do you think my passion came from? Has to be genetic, don't you think?

And, isn't it the joke of the universe that what seems to be frivolous - a love of parties, for goodness sake - took me all the way to the White House?

The Social Office, upstairs in the East Wing, ran events inside the House, like state dinners, and receptions. The Visitors Office coordinated the large, outside celebrations, like the Easter Egg Roll and July 4 fireworks watching, or the Hope, Arkansas, watermelon tasting. Of course, we all worked together on whatever needed doing. There are never enough hands for these projects, and I firmly believe in pitching in wherever there's a need. Early on, I told Ann Stock, the Social Secretary, she could count on all of us in the Visitors Office to help her in any way she needed. More bodies at the entrance gates? We'll be there. Welcoming guests inside the House? I'll be there. Helping put down the place cards for a large dinner? Sure, no problem. Just let me know.

Our first year, at the same time we were working our butts off to re-invent the tour system, we also faced our first Egg Roll - and David Watkins' words about how difficult it would be were ringing in my ears. We'd also heard the advice of an aide to Nancy

Reagan, who warned, "Until you've lived through a White House Easter Egg Hunt you don't know what hell is." Not exactly encouraging.

The minute Robyn arrived in Washington we sat down to talk about it.

"Do you have any experience with big events? This sounds really complicated and we're already getting calls from the performers who worked for the Bushes - but I really don't want to go there."

"Oh sure, I love this stuff. Back in Little Rock I coordinated our 'River Walk' and October Fest celebrations - tens of thousands of people downtown for performances, food, crafts, kids activities. It sounds like the Egg Roll is a lot like those fairs - what do you think?"

"I think I just died and went to heaven. You're perfect for this! You can be the White House Egg Lady while Marc and I are working on this tour stuff - it's tying us in knots. Just keep me informed and let me know what you need so I can get it for you. It's a First Lady event, so we'll need a plan to present to Hillary to make sure she likes what we're doing. I can't tell you how glad I am you're here!"

"Me too - I love this kind of event. Anything else?"

"Oh yeah, one last thing - no clowns. Please, no clowns," I said with a little shudder.

"OK with me, but why?"

"Well, for one thing, I think they're kinda creepy. But that's just me. And for another, they're making us crazy with their calls and letters. I don't think we have any obligation to bring back performers who worked for President Bush. I mean, there's a new sheriff in town now and people need to get a grip!"

The Egg Roll normally takes a year to organize, but Robyn worked miracles in only two months. The pressure was enormous. If you pull it off, it's a success for Hillary. If you screw up, it's an embarrassment for her - and there were plenty of people in Washington hoping for us to fail. Robyn organized entertainers, found cool children's books and got their authors and Cabinet

Secretaries to volunteer to read them. She designed decorations for the Lawn and came up with a theme. She worked with the Volunteer Office to bring in and supervise the hundreds of people who help little kids roll eggs, decorate eggs and play games. The sweetest touch was the hundreds of eggs we stamped with a little paw print and signed "Socks." They were a big hit.

There's always a breakfast reception early on Easter Monday for the sponsors of the event, and Robyn had thought about eggs in a different way: the Malcolm Forbes collection of Faberge Easter eggs. (Hey! Think big! Why not?) I don't know how she did it, but she got Christopher (Kit) Forbes, a charming man, to come to the White House with a fabulous jeweled egg once belonging to a Russian Czarina. He brought this priceless object down from New York on the train himself, with no body guards, in a small metal case. We had a problem getting it past security, because on the X-ray machine the egg looked exactly like a grenade, and the Secret Service insisted he unwrap it. I begged them to let it go, but they wouldn't. I stopped breathing and clutched my chest while they examined it. Suppose someone dropped this priceless object? Thank God it went back safely into its case.

When I had read the description of this egg, in the book Kit sent us, I learned there was a five carat yellow diamond on the bottom, so I borrowed a round mirror and glass dome from my neighborhood jewelers. We placed them in the middle of the table in the middle of the Blue Room, and everyone could see that gorgeous stone. The President and Hillary loved it.

Socks naps with Easter eggs

The 1993 White House Easter Egg Roll was a success all around, getting great reviews from the press and the families who participated.
"Clintons' First Easter Bash is a Smash" was my favorite headline.

But what I remember most clearly is a Presidential moment from which I learned an important lesson.

Robyn and I had worked closely with the Secret Service and promised them the Clintons would make remarks from the stage on the north end of the driveway, and then step down to shake hands with people crowded behind snow fence (the cheap, wooden slat stuff, with the wire in between. Works great for crowd control outside.) They'd walk down the grassy alley, maybe go as far as a little platform part of the way down the lawn, and then come back to the house. We were surprised the Secret Service were so nervous about a crowd of people who had all gone through magnetometers to get in, but they were, so we promised: no farther than the little platform.

As soon as the breakfast reception ended, we briefed the President and First Lady so they'd know what to do outside. Everything went as we planned - happy remarks and a huge crowd of people reaching out for a handshake with the Clintons, who slowly made their way along the grass to the platform. But when the President stepped up there he looked out to the south and saw, in a corner of the Lawn, the petting zoo Robyn had installed there. A man stood looking up with a huge eagle perched on his outstretched arm.

I was thinking, *Wow, how cool is that!* when I heard the President say, "Hey, look over there! I want to go down there!"

Oh no! The Secret Service will be furious if I let him go there - but who am I to stop the President from going where he wants?

I didn't know what to do and fumbled for the right words. I got as far as "Um, uh, Mr. President ..." when Robyn, thinking faster than I did, and more experienced at working for Bill Clinton, said smoothly, "Of course, if you want to, Mr. President. But you'll be responsible for killing and maiming a lot of little children if you do."

The President recoiled, looked at Robyn, smiling angelically, and said, "Oh. No, I guess I won't. Never mind."

"Well," I thought. "What a smart woman, and I just learned a great lesson. You can't say 'no' to the President, but you can redirect him away from a bad choice if you think fast and choose your words carefully."

On the way back up the grassy alley, still shaking hands and nodding to ecstatic visitors, the President heard an insistent little voice saying, "Mistah! Mistah!"

We all looked over and spotted a small boy, freckled face mashed flat against the snow fence, but wildly waving his arms. We all thought he wanted to meet the President. How sweet. But no.

"Mistah! Please move! You're in the way of the Easter Bunny"

I looked at the President, who raised his eyebrows at us, and gently stepped to the side. I could practically hear him thinking, *Well, I guess now I know MY place on the importance scale!*

The people who come to Egg Rolls are frantic to get the ultimate souvenir - a little, brightly-painted wooden Easter egg with a graphic of the White House and the stamped signatures of the President and First Lady. We doled these out only to the little children, although we were pretty sure the kids didn't care all that much. The parents were going to snatch it away the moment they exited the South Lawn.

***

During the 1992 campaign our classmate, Bill, made a promise to all the Georgetown classmates: If he were elected we'd celebrate our twenty-fifth reunion at his House in June, 1993. We were all excited, I more than most, because I got to be the White House person who interacted with the class committee and the Social

Office about all the arrangements.

Sometimes this meant I got to fill in my friends on the exciting plans for the dinner. Sometimes it meant I had to push back against energetic White House staff who expected me to show up for meetings during the reunion.

"Sorry," I had to say. "This is my reunion too, and I'll be at a polo game at 11am on Saturday. You'll have to muddle through with what I can give you on Friday - when I'm supposed to be on vacation but will be here working."

Thanks to the Clintons' generosity we celebrated at a dinner for over 1,500 people, in a tent on the South Lawn. You read the word "tent" and have some mental image of a tent you saw somewhere. Trust me. You never saw a tent like this. I can tell you how big it was - just imagine an airplane hangar. Got it? **That** big. But, by some miracle of physics I never understood, it stands with no internal supports, so it's easy to decorate any way you want, and we made it beautiful. Huge chandeliers of cascading lights hung from the ceiling, votive candles flickered on tables with white cloths and low arrangements of white, pink and rose flowers. Gold ballroom chairs sat on narrow legs on the grass of the lawn. It was magical. (I learned over time the White House does "magical" on a routine basis. It's in the mission statement.)

This was such a special night for me. I felt beautiful in a red silk Bill Blass, halter-top dress (from a local a discount store; I am a brilliant shopper), with black and white plaid trim. Kind of a '50s glam look. The full skirt swished over a stiff petticoat when I walked. I had black and white buttons made for my red silk heels and wore my mother's diamond and pearl earrings.

This was my first invitation to a dressy White House event, and I felt right at home. I was definitely born in the wrong era - I'd like to "dress" for dinner every night! When I was a child, I tore ads out of my

Dad's *New Yorker* showing willowy ladies in jewels and long gowns. "Mom, can you make this for me?"

"Where in the world would you wear such a dress?"

"I don't know. I just think it's beautiful ..."

Think I've seen too many old movies? Maybe so. My own mother once gave me a button reading, "I was born entitled" and that about sums it up. I used to wear it when we went shopping together.

At this dinner I was especially excited to be seated, not just at the President's table, with the college roommates (his closest friends) and their wives, but actually next to the President. This is a BIG honor. In all the photos I'm grinning from ear to ear. Someone suggested we pass around our programs and each sign them, so we did, and mine has my name on top and Bill's below. I also snagged his place card, with the beautiful calligraphy on heavy stock and the gold Presidential seal that reads, "The President." It's a pretty swell memento - and he wasn't going to need it again.

This was the moment when we finally presented the Karsh portraits to the President and Hillary, and Mr. Karsh was there as an additional treat. The President seemed truly surprised and delighted. I didn't have any of experience with photographic portraits before, and was amazed at how beautiful they were - the softness of the colors and shadows, the way the camera captured their character and spirit. The Clintons were very pleased.

My classmates gave me the honor of presenting our other class gift to our hosts - a set of china we designed for them, white with a dark blue border and gold edge, and the Georgetown and Presidential seals in gold. Very classy. I made a little speech about our college days and people laughed in all the right places. We knew Hillary wouldn't use the china for anything official, but hoped they'd find it useful up in the Residence. I guess now it's in the house in Chappaqua - or maybe the Clinton Library.

Chapter Thirteen ~ 1993 ~ History Marches On

Next to the Egg Rolls, our largest events were the fireworks viewings on the South Lawn on July 4. This instantly became my favorite annual event (well, after Christmas. God knows, I do love Christmas.) The calligraphers upstairs in the East Wing designed invitations we sent to all White House staff and some special guests of POTUS and FLOTUS. But, thank God, NO members of Congress.

I was astounded to learn the invites traditionally also went to the press who had White House passes. So, out on the lawn you might have a White House staffer with her family, sitting on a blanket, talking shop with a colleague nearby, while next to them, unbeknownst to them, was a reporter, listening in. Seemed crazy to me, and over the years I kept pushing to eliminate their access, but without success. The Press Secretaries always thought it was a terrible idea and they'd be mad at us and take it out on the President with bad stories. Hello? They were already writing nasty, untrue stories! What more could they do? We should just bite the bullet and pull the invites. But we never did.

Over the years issues like this baffled me. We caved in, repeatedly, to pressure in ways I thought didn't serve the President well, because we feared some potential negative reaction, from people who already didn't like us or wish us well. I thought we'd do far better to just take a stand, regardless of whether people liked it or not. The people who didn't like us would go right on hating us no matter what we did. And the people who liked us, even if they didn't like what we did, would at least respect us for doing what we believe in. I will always believe the President would have done better to act this way, but he (or senior advisors) so deeply believed in his ability to make friends out of just about everyone, they didn't want to risk "offending" anyone. Too bad. Americans respect strength and authenticity.

On July 4th my staff, volunteers and I dressed in red, white and blue, which for me was white linen pants and a campaign tee shirt. Clinton/Gore 1992! We stood out in the scorching heat at

Various gates and let in thousands and thousands (and THOUSANDS!) of staff and their guests. This took me back to my true visitor services roots - I love being out with the public. It's fun to meet colleagues' family and guests and see them in a relaxed setting.

On the lawn people set out their blankets and enjoyed the patriotic music of the Marine Band, playing above them on the Blue Room Portico. Just before 9:00 p.m. we shut the gates and hurried in to meet our own families and friends. When the fireworks started, the Marines packed up, and we switched to the radio feed of the National Symphony Orchestra, down on the Capitol lawn.

I gathered my own guests, waiting for me in the air conditioned hallway, and took them up the steps from the driveway to the Portico. We sat in splendor, on folding chairs, watching the bursts of stars over the trees to the south, lighting up the Washington Monument with red, blue, silver and green sparkles. I LOVE fireworks! It gave me chills to think I could be there, in America's most iconic place, celebrating our independence. The honor and emotion of it were overwhelming, and it reminded me of the sacred trust the public gave us. *What are you doing today, Melinda, to make people's lives better?*

***

In August I started a personal tradition of giving the President a tie for his birthday. I picked one to go with his favorite pale gray suit. He returned the favor by having me come over to the Oval to have a picture taken of us with him wearing it - a nice surprise for me. Once I gave him a tie in shades of soft green and red. A few weeks later I happened to look up at the television in my office and saw he was overseas at a NATO conference, giving a speech, wearing my tie. I'm glad he liked my taste!

The Vice President's office asked me to arrange a tour for the Grateful Dead. Turns out Al Gore had been a fan since he was in Viet Nam, and played their tapes endlessly over the camp PA system. Who knew? I was glad to do it, and welcomed the band members in my East Wing reception room. I'd never been a Dead Head, but I needed to say something nice, so I told Jerry Garcia, "I really like your ties." He seemed surprised to learn I knew he was an artist.

Then I introduced the Tour Officer, who said, "And I really like your ice cream!"

We all laughed, and Jerry said, "Of course I had nothing to do with it, but I can tell you the day Cherry Garcia came out was the happiest day in my lawyer's life!"

Off they went on their tour, and the plan was for them to "coincidentally run into" the VP as they walked through the House, so he could invite them over to his office, where Tipper was waiting. His staff didn't want the press to see the meeting on his schedule, so this was our work around.

The same day the Grateful Dead visited, we also welcomed the elegant and beautiful former Queen of Greece, and her adorable - and very well behaved - children. They all signed the guest book too. On the same page. I wish I had made a copy of those signatures! Now our guest book is at the Clinton Library, and someone would have to search hard to find it. But this was an entirely normal day for us: royalty in the morning, rock stars in the afternoon. Sooner or later, every interesting person on the planet made an appearance.

The next day, Dennis Alpert, the VP's senior aide came by the office. "The tour was great, Melinda, the Gores are very happy; thanks for arranging it. We appreciate your help. Now, next week we have another group coming who are important to the VP. We really need to accommodate them."

I reached for a notepad and pen. "OK, who are they, how many, and when do they want to come?"

"It's the heavy metal band, *Metallica*, and they have about 200 people with them," he said with a straight face.

I gulped, and bought it. "Um, gee, 200 ... wow, that's gonna be a challenge. But if the VP really wants it ..."

He enjoyed my discomfort for a minute, laughed and said,
"Gotcha! Ha!"

I laughed too. And began to plot my revenge.

A couple of days later I wrote up our normal memo for special group tours, which went to the Director of Oval Office Operations, the Chief of Staff, my boss, the Assistant for Management and Administration, the Chief Usher, and assorted other Very Important People. In it, I requested a special tour for the 200 guests of *Metallica,* requested by Dennis Alpert in the VP's office. Of course, I didn't actually send the memo to all those people. I only made **one** copy and sent it to Dennis in the morning through inter-office mail. Then I put my pager on my desk and went to lunch at the Mess, telling the staff if Dennis called, I was "out" and not reachable.

I had a leisurely lunch and took my time getting back to the office, where the staff were all in hysterics. "You've got to call and put him out of his misery! He's called here every 10 minutes for the last hour, your pager goes off every 5 minutes, and it sounds like he's afraid he's going to lose his job. He really thinks the Metallica request, with his name and the VP's, went to the Oval Office."

When I figured he had sweated enough, I called him on speakerphone, with Marc and the rest of the staff listening in. "Hey, Dennis," I said crisply, "I hear you've been trying to reach me? Looks like we're all set to go on your tour for Metallica. It is what you wanted, right?"

"Oh, Lord, Melinda. I thought you understood - it was just a joke. I can't believe you sent out this memo to everyone, including the Oval Office. I'm going to look like an idiot ..." now he was just mumbling in despair.

Marc and the girls were holding their hands to their mouths to stifle giggles. I couldn't help myself. I started to chuckle and it quickly became a big belly laugh.

"Oh, Dennis," I teased. "You can relax. You're the only one who got that memo. This time I got **you**! And I think I got you really good!" Then we all dissolved in laughter.

On the phone we heard him sputter and choke. He blurted out, "It's a JOKE? You didn't really send it out? Oh, Lord, you did it. You got me really good! And I sure am glad it was just a joke!"

Over the next few days I got a lot of emails and calls from people in the VP's office who all loved Dennis but were delighted this time HE was the one who got suckered. I was proud of myself, because I'm not really a practical joker. The only other time I ever carried one out was when I worked at Macy's, and it took careful planning. A few days before April Fool's Day, I snagged a piece of the store manager's stationery, and wrote an official-looking memo: "Our store has now been open for a year, and it's necessary to do some maintenance on the telephone system. In order to clear out the lines, at 8:30 a.m. on April 1, please remove your phone receivers from the base unit, and carefully place them into a trashcan. Air will be blown through the lines, and this will keep your workspace clean. Thank you, Store Manager."

I put a copy in every department manager's in-box the day before. Then, on the appointed morning, I walked around the store, astonished to see how many people had actually done it! The manager was furious but I never confessed, and they never suspected me - an advantage of appearing to be such a proper lady.

***

Some Presidential families live quieter, less stressful lives than the Clintons. They may use Camp David, or a family compound, or a fake ranch in Texas, to get away every weekend, giving themselves and the staff a break. Not Bill and Hillary. They didn't have any family home from before the White House, and they didn't care for Camp David much. Chelsea was soon a teenager; she wanted to stay in town to have fun with her friends. The result, for the staff, was a staggering, seven-day-a-week workload and level of exhaustion. 'Cause if **they** never go away, the staff don't either.

We began to anticipate, with weary glee, the First Family's summer vacation, which they'd take when Congress adjourned in August. But we knew them, so even when a date for their departure was announced, no one was sure they'd actually go. So, vacation morning, everyone I saw took a guess as to what time they'd leave - or even IF they'd leave. We kept checking our watches, and our own plans for a holiday.

Their helicopter departure was scheduled for 2:00 p.m., but I knew better than to stand in the ground floor hallway, waiting. I went right to the top - I called the Ushers and asked them to give me a heads up when the Clintons headed for the door. They finally came down, only a couple of hours late - practically on time, for them.

I saw them head out, watched the 'copter take off, and walked slowly back into the House. I stood in the ground floor hallway and shivered. *How odd. The House actually feels different - as if it knows they're gone. I know this isn't possible, but it sure feels like it. It's as if the air pressure changed when they left.*

In fact, the White House daily takes on the mood of the President and First Lady. You can feel their enthusiasm, joy, and satisfaction as well as their sorrow and discouragement. Their energy drives yours. You just "know" when the agenda is going well, and when it's a struggle, without having to look at CNN.

And something else changed when they went away - the expression of perpetual stress and concentration on everyone's faces. The forehead lines I carry to this day, the anxiousness around the eyes, the hunched shoulders reflecting our normal exhaustion and ceaseless worry that somehow, something urgent had been left undone ... for a few weeks each summer our faces relaxed, our shoulders loosened, we stood up straight, and we looked almost like ... normal people.

***

In September they returned, refreshed, and plunged immediately into two major events. On Monday, September 13, the Israeli - Palestinian Peace Accord Signing, and on September 14 a big NAFTA announcement.

The Peace signing had been agreed to on a Friday, giving everyone only the weekend to put together plans and guest lists. It was so hurried, the State Department didn't take the time to proof read the program, and it reads "Isreal." Oops! They weren't delivered 'til the morning of the event, so there was no time to correct, we just had to hand them out, hope no one noticed, and ask forgiveness.

The entry gates were a real mess, as so many diplomats from everywhere felt they HAD to be at the event, whether or not their names were on our lists. We had to scramble around for people who could help identify these folks. I ended up at my gate with Hannan Ashwari, the Palestinian spokeswoman, pointing at chosen individuals in the mob trying to get in. There was a lot of pushing and shoving. I thought we were about to be in the middle of a riot, and I think the Secret Service did too. "You're armed, right?" I gasped to the Officer running the gate.

"You bet," he said through clenched teeth, using a strong forearm to block the crowd and then push the gate closed. "And we're not having a riot on my watch." Well, thank goodness!

Marc and I finally approved the last guest and went to find chairs at the back. It was a dazzling September day, with clear, blue skies and warm sun. The grass at the White House is so green and lush, I always had to stop myself from taking off my shoes and running around barefoot. And I'm not normally a grass person. Give me flowers any time.

What a gorgeous place this is. What an incredible blessing.

And then, during the ceremony, I glanced over at the House and saw a rat, the size of a house cat, slink across the driveway, heading for the Andrew Jackson magnolia. I straightened up in my chair and looked around. *Oh, shoot! I sure hope none of the diplomats are looking over there! Damn tourists keep feeding the squirrels and whadda ya get - rats!*

I nudged Marc to look, and he echoed the horrified expression on my face. But no one else even seemed to notice.

After the event, I went into the House for my next assignment: controlling Barbara Walters. Yes, you heard me. Ms. Walters and a small crew were waiting in the ground floor Library, because she insisted Prime Minister Rabin had agreed to do a brief interview.

Did he? I have no idea. Now, Barbara Walters didn't get to be *Barbara Walters* by being shy and retiring. She was perfectly polite, but insistent. She wanted out of that Library so she could ambush whichever important person came into view. My job was to keep her IN the Library, and it wasn't easy.

I said all the gracious - and non-committal - things I could think of: "I'm sure your interview will happen, we just have to wait for Mr. Rabin to leave the Oval Office and come this way. Yes, I know it's urgent, but we'll just have to wait here. I'm sure you understand ..."

Still, I ended up standing in the Library doorway to physically block her from going out, her crew looking on in amusement. It was a funny dance between us, and I was holding my own, until we all heard an unmistakable voice in the hall. The President was walking by. We both stopped talking, and I could see an even more determined expression on her face. I looked at Ms. Walters and said, "Just give me a moment," left the room and closed the door behind me.

The President saw me and his eyes lit up. He was totally jazzed about the peace signing and his (all of our) hopes it would lead to true peace in the region. He strode over, practically lifted me off my feet in a hug, let me go, stood back, and high-fived me. Really. I had been hugged and kissed before, but now my first Presidential high-five. *Wow, he is REALLY excited about this.*

"Mr. President, Barbara Walters is in the Library with her crew and she's desperate to get a word with you. Can you give her a minute?"

"Sure I can," and he strode into the room, where he greeted her happily and did a 5-minute stand up.

I watched from the side and thought how impressive she was - and how happy with her Get. I bet ABC was the only network that night to have an interview with the President. Years later when I wrote this book and wanted to promote it on The View, I hoped she would remember and be grateful. Sadly, no.

During the afternoon I was in the House with my event program tucked into my pocket. I wouldn't normally have done this, but it was so historic ... so I asked each of the principals (Hillary, the President, PM Rabin, Mrs. Rabin, and Chairman Arafat) to sign my program. As far as I know it's the only document with all those signatures on it. It's a precious bit of White House and world history and I think belongs in a museum somewhere. If you know someone who'd like to buy it, let me know!

The next day, the President hosted former Presidents Bush (1), Ford and Carter at an event to push NAFTA through Congress. Bush and Carter spent the night in the House, but Ford stayed at the Willard Hotel. I asked the Curators, who keep the White House history, if there had ever been an event there with the current and three former presidents, and they said they couldn't find one. Hooray! We make history again!

Because of my long friendship with the President, and because of Hillary's great kindness to me, I had a kind of access most staff, at any level, did not. So I felt free to walk up to the State Floor for events like this, or press conferences, or out to the Lawn or Rose Garden to watch a ceremony honoring some football team, or teacher, or astronaut. I loved to stand at the back of the East Room, squinting in the glare of the television lights, watching the "pencil press" (reporters for print media) shuffle together on risers at the back of the room, the television press, shifting in their little gold chairs, sensing the tension in the room as everyone waited for the President, the hush that falls when the VOG (voice of God) announces, "Ladies and gentlemen, one minute," and then the little rustle of reporters straightening their suits, patting their hair and checking their notes as the President walks down the red carpet in the Cross Hall, steps up to the podium and stands at the lectern with the seal of the President of the United States.

It always gave me a thrill. In 1997 I was traveling in Saudi Arabia, in a tiny town in the back of the beyond, so close to the border with Iran all our escorts carried automatic weapons - and very nervous expressions. I checked into my room, turned on the television, and there was the President, on CNN, holding a press conference. Small world!

CHAPTER FOURTEEN ~

HOW MUCH FUN CAN ONE PERSON HAVE?

Most people don't' know it, but the White House has a birthday: October 13. Even though we hadn't even been there for a year yet, we all passionately loved her, and were honored to be among the chosen few who got to work there. I wanted to celebrate the birthday somehow. (Do you recognize a theme, here?)

The year before, 1992, was the 200th anniversary of the laying of the cornerstone (which no one can locate today). There were VIP events and academic discussions to honor the date. We couldn't - and didn't want to - compete with those.

So I decided to celebrate the way everyone does with a beloved relative - we'd have a party, with cake! Everyone loves cake, right? I asked the President's aide, Glenn Maes, to create a cake, and was stunned when I saw it. Four feet across, by three feet wide and five inches tall, it was AMAZING. The entire top was covered with a picture of the White House and gardens, executed in icing. He's an artist with butter cream!

The other Navy Mess Master Chiefs baked dozens and dozens of sheet cakes, iced with red, white and blue. Have I mentioned yet how glad we all were the Navy was in charge of feeding us? Nothing against the Army, Marines, Air Force and Coast Guard, but everyone knows the Navy serves the best food!

Early that morning we set up tables on the North Driveway, where the tourists come out from tours, with Glenn's amazing cake on display, and trays with squares of birthday cake. My staff and I, and the Mess staff put on the Navy's "Presidential Food Service" blue aprons, with the seal on the front. (I still have one.) We took turns offering cake to the visitors of the day as they walked out of the House on their way to the street. They were surprised and delighted to be included in the festivities.

"Cake? Yes, please! The White House birthday? How lovely!" And, always, "What an incredible cake! We've never seen anything so beautiful! Martha, come stand right there so I can get a photo ..."

Everyone took pictures - none of us had ever seen such a glorious cake before either - and ate cake. The USSS Tour Officers came out to watch us and eat cake. Some White House staff who had access to the Driveway came out too. We invited POTUS and FLOTUS, but they were too busy. I LOVED this little celebration. We did it every year, and the tourists got to expect it and specially request tours on October 13, so they could see Glenn's latest creation. They were different and beautiful every year.

***

Hillary's birthday is at the end of October, so her first one in the White House was a full-on, surprise, Halloween costume party. Robyn planned it, and everyone actually kept it a secret from the First Lady, which is harder than you'd think.

THE PRESIDENT & HILLARYLAND request the pleasure of your company at a

Surprise Halloween BIRTHDAY PARTY of The First Lady it's a surprise! on October 26, 1993 it's a surprise! at seven-thirty o'clock it's a surprise!

BOO!

RSVP Helen Dickey only 202-456-2103
Please enter through the VISITORS ENTRANCE
·COSTUME REQUIRED·

She had spent a serious and tiring day on the Hill, lobbying for the health care initiative. When her car pulled up to the South Portico, all the lights in the House were off. This never happens. She stumbled towards the door and was met by a figure cloaked completely in black (a young staffer) who wordlessly beckoned the First Lady into the Diplomatic Reception Room.

This was also dark, but there were light sticks on the floor, guiding them through the blacked-out hallway to the elevator, while Hillary giggled and asked, "What, exactly, is going on here?"

When they reached her bedroom, she found a costume of Dolley Madison laid out on the bed, and the President, too tall for the part by a foot, elegantly costumed as President Madison, in knee britches and a brocade coat. Once she was dressed, "the Madisons" descended the formal stairs to the State Floor, where a group of friends, staff and family, all in costume, shouted, "Surprise!" And she sure seemed to be.

The President escorted her into the East Room, where Jerry Jeff Walker, a wild 'n' crazy singer and musician in the style of Jerry Lee Lewis, banged out raucous rock 'n' roll on his piano. (NOT the state piano!) Robyn had to warn him, NO dancing on the piano or playing with your feet. Please! It's the White House!

I dressed as First Lady Edith Wilson, in my great grandmother's lace gown, diamond pin and flowered, straw hat. One of the President's best friends came in red and yellow, full jester regalia, including even the shoes with turned up toes and little bells - hysterical. After the party, he walked across Lafayette Park, in costume, to the bar at the very stuffy Hay-Adams Hotel. He sat for a moment, contemplating his twinkle toes, and before he could order the barman set a drink in front of him.

"What's this?"

"From the man at the table over there," he gestured. "He said to tell you, he doesn't know you, but he can tell from your suit you must be the new Clinton admin Secretary of the Treasury."

I had to laugh every time I saw Bruce Lindsay, the President's very serious friend and advisor. He was dressed as a nun. With his perpetual 5:00 shadow, solemn expression and dark hair he looked especially funny. I took a photo and sent him a copy later in the week, with a note: "Dear Bruce. I have the negative. Regards, Melinda."

One year Robyn decorated the House for Halloween, with spider webs and spiders on filament hanging between the marble columns of the Cross Hall. In the square planters the gardeners usually filled with small trees, she put dead trees, with bats stuck to bare branches. Candles flickered in Jack-O-Lanterns. Roland Meissner, the brilliant pastry chef who in 30 years never once duplicated a dessert for a head of state, made a volcano cake with smoke coming out the top.

Oh, it was fabulous and spooky. I believe the White House had never seen anything like it before. And the spoilsport Chief Usher was determined no one outside the party guests would see it either. He made all the laborers stay on duty until the party ended, so they could take down all the Halloween decor. God forbid the morning tourists see this!

But he hadn't counted on Hillary, and her sense of humor and delight. "What fun," she exclaimed. "I love it! Let's be sure to leave it up for the next few days so the visitors can see the White House dressed up for Halloween." Wonderful!

In November, the President pardoned his first turkey. Did you know the chosen farmer always brings TWO turkeys? It's just in case turkey #1 keels over from all the excitement. You can't have a dead turkey for a Presidential event – OMG, think of the symbolism! These turkeys are never served on anyone's Thanksgiving table. They all go off to a petting zoo. Since they're so top-heavy they can hardly stand, I wonder how long they last.

DAVID CROSBY WATCHES GRAHAM NASH PLAY AND SING "OUR HOUSE IS A VERY FINE HOUSE" ON THE PRESIDENTIAL PIANO IN THE FOYER. IT WAS A VERY SPECIAL MOMENT!

One Saturday I welcomed Graham Nash and David Crosby for an afternoon walk through the House. For people from my generation, this was the equivalent of, say, Sinatra for my parents, or Britney Spears for my kids. We were enjoying the history together when we got to the grand foyer, where the impressive Truman piano, with eagles for legs, sits waiting for the Marine band. Graham immediately sat, ran his hands over the keys to check the tuning, and began to play and sing, *Our House is a Very Very Very Fine House*. What song could be more perfect for the

White House? And for my generation? I was thrilled. And, did I mention? Graham Nash is **very** handsome.

***

We'd been warned: Christmas in the White House is overwhelming, non-stop, and exhausting. Too much on every level. But I love Christmas so much, I couldn't imagine "too much". As far as I was concerned, there was never enough of Christmas. That was about to change.

The month-long festivities take a year to plan. The First Lady selects a theme from several offered by the Social Secretary and the head of the WH Flower Shop. Once the decision is made, the chief floral designer starts working on designing and ordering all the elements and trees to fill the public and private rooms. Right after Thanksgiving she gathers her team and a large crew of volunteers who work twenty-hour days to set it all up.

There are literally dozens of trees, and more dozens of wreaths and mantle decorations to assemble. It's a logistical nightmare. Nowadays you can watch this happen, with time-lapse photography, on an HGTV special, *Christmas at the White House,* every December. It's fascinating. All the trees were real, except since President Clinton has bad allergies, the trees in the Oval Office and up in the Residence were artificial.

Once the decorations are up, the bell-ringers and carolers appear to make a joyful noise in every corner. Now, I really, truly love Christmas music, have been known to hum Christmas music all month, sometimes wear a Christmas bell on a red silk cord, frequently break out into spontaneous ho-ho-ho-ing. But after a couple of weeks of ding-dong, ding-donging, and fa-la-la-ing, I got to the point where I thought, *If I see just one more damn bell-ringer I'm afraid I'm going to have to slap him silly.*

And then there are the parties and special tours. First, the general public is frantic for tickets to see it all on morning tours. Then there are all the special groups who expect invitations to afternoon tours. We figured out once we had put 60,000 people through the House one December. Sixty thousand! In a House not all that big to begin with.

Throughout the month the Clintons endured (the only correct word) a marathon of parties, one after the other, night after night. The only way to accommodate everyone who wants, or expects, to come is to schedule like this: Reception A runs from 5:30 pm to 7:00 pm, and Reception B, from 7:30 pm to 9:00 on the same night. Fun for all, right? Except for the Clintons, who never got to actually enjoy the party, or the guests. How could they? The guests all want a photo of themselves, smiling and shaking hands with POTUS and FLOTUS in front of a White House Christmas tree. So the Clintons spent hour after hour standing in receiving lines, greeting guests and smiling for the camera.

Next to State Dinners, the most elegant party of the year is the Congressional Holiday Ball in early December. Don't be misled by the word "Ball." None of these politicians knows how to dance or cares to - it's all about the networking, and the photo. Over the years I used to gag at the sight of Representatives and Senators who hated the Clintons, constantly said awful things about them, routinely lied about them, standing in line at the White House to get a photo with them. The hypocrisy factor in Washington is truly staggering.

At the 1993 Ball, Darryl and I wandered around the State Floor looking at the incredible decorations - pure magic. I was in heaven. All my life I'd imagined dressing up and "going to the Ball," and now, here I was, actually AT a ball, at the White House. The only thing – the only thing! -that could have made it better would have been for Prince Charles to show up as my escort and whisper in my ear he wanted to take me home to meet the Queen. Darryl might not have been a prince, but he did look handsome in his dinner jacket, and I felt beautiful in my evening gown. Brown silk, with a pin shaped like a bow, made of glittery, gold stones. Unfortunately, our photo with the Clintons was taken at an awkward moment, and I look like Quasimodo. Damn!

Everywhere we looked, every corner was touched with Christmas (or "holiday") sparkle. It always amused me that Republicans refer to "Christmas" while Democrats prefer "holiday," As in "Christmas decorations" vs. "holiday decorations." I understand the cards (holiday cards) should be inclusive, but let's face it, the House is not decorated for Hannukkah or Eid - it's decorated for Christmas! However, this was an argument I could not win.

Another odd difference: Republican First Ladies use fake snow, and Democrats do not. Go figure.

Amid the multitude of trees, the largest and fanciest is the eighteen- footer filling the center of the Blue Room. They have to take out the chandelier to move it in. It was incredible.

I stood, staring at the thousands of glittering ornaments, each one a tiny piece of art from an American craftsperson, when behind me I heard Darryl saying, "Oh, Mr. Gingrich! It's wonderful to see you. My mom is from Atlanta and we're big fans!"

Now, in case you don't know it, Newt Gingrich was the opposition leader who truly HATED us all. So no, I was not a fan. And yes, I was in a mixed marriage.

Oh, Jeez, I thought. *Newt! I don't wanna meet Newt! I'm not even going to turn around. Maybe he'll just move on.*

Behind me I heard Newt making the polite noises politicians make when they've assessed you as "not important," they're not interested and just trying to move on. But Darryl would not be deterred.

"It's so exciting to meet you. And I'd really like you to meet my wife!"

I couldn't believe my ears. *In twenty years of marriage he NEVER remembers to introduce me to anyone, but now he just can't wait to bring me together with Newt Gingrich. Swell!*

I turned around and forced a smile.

Darryl proudly said, "And this is my wife, Melinda Bates."

Newt heard my name and his face changed instantly from bland politeness to intent interest. "Melinda Bates? You're Melinda Bates?"

Before I could even nod, he reached out with both hands, using one arm to shove Darryl out of the way to get in close and take my hand in both of his.

"I'm so happy to meet you! Your office does a wonderful job! You know, we thought we'd never get any tours for our constituents with a Democrat in the White House, and your folks have just been great - always cordial and professional. They're a delight to work with. Thank you so much for all your help."

I nodded and thanked him for the compliment, trying not to choke on the words while pulling my hand away from his.

I'm glad we've been able to help you," I said. "Our goal is to be fair to everyone."

As he walked away I rolled my eyes and turned to Darryl. "You OK? That was a pretty strong shove he gave you. I'm surprised you didn't land right in the tree!"

He grinned and rubbed his shoulder. "No, I'm fine. It was great to meet him. Wait 'til I tell my mom!"

Yep, the Members of Congress are no dummies - at least when it comes to sucking up to the people who can do them favors. At one DNC event I was introduced to Senator Carol Mosley Braun, who, hearing my name and title, actually curtsied to me. I couldn't believe it.

"Senator! Please get up," I hissed. "We're always happy to help you - just call me when you need something special."

I looked around quickly, hoping no one else had noticed our little meeting. I mean, really. I'm pretty sure we fought a war to keep from having to curtsey to anyone!

 At the beginning of December I told Hillary about the Washington tradition of the *Messiah Sing Along* at the Kennedy Center. For years I'd been leaving my house in the middle of a freezing December night to camp out in front of the Kennedy Center doors with a couple hundred other Handel lovers, to get two free tickets. Of course, I wasn't suggesting Hillary do this. The President has a swell box, with a lounge area, in each of the three theaters there. I just thought she might like to go. She loves music.

When I mentioned it to Robyn, thinking she might enjoy it too, she heard me out about the long wait in the cold wind off the Potomac and gave me an odd look. "Are you nuts? Why put yourself through such torture? Just ask for tickets to the President's box!"

Of course. It hadn't even occurred to me. Some staff were able to ask for tickets to performances there. Then if the President or a senior person didn't claim the seats, chances were good you could get them. It was exciting to sit in the box, with everyone in the theater looking up and wondering who the "important" people up there could be. And they were the best seats in the house.

I walked over to the West Wing to see Debi Schiff, the President's receptionist and keeper of the Kennedy Center access. "Sure, I'll put you on the list for two, but there's no guarantee until the morning of the event. You have to come see me then."

No problem. I'll wait and hope.

On December 23 I went to see if I had tickets. Debi smiled up at me. "They must really like you. I had a full list of requests for tonight, but Hillary decided she and Chelsea will go."

My heart sank. If the Clintons used the box, everyone else got bumped. Damn!

But Debi kept smiling. "... and they bumped everyone else on the list - except you! So, here are your two tickets. Here's the combination to the refrigerator with the champagne. Have fun."

I danced back to my office, thinking, *I bet if Hillary and Chelsea are going, the President will go too. This is gonna be great! I gotta call Darryl right away!*

When we got to the Kennedy Center, parking was impossible, so Darryl let me out. I saw a crowd filling the lobby outside the theater, and then saw the magnetometers - *the President must be coming. What fun!*

I battled my way through the crowds and handed my ticket to the ticket taker. "Box One" it read. She grabbed it – and tried to keep it! "Hey, please give me back my ticket stub."

"Um, no, I'm supposed to keep it." We each tugged at an end.

"No, you're not. How will I get past the usher upstairs without it? Do we need to call a manager over here?"

She finally handed it back. I guess she wanted it as a souvenir. Well, so did I!

It's one flight up to the box level and there I found a couple of Secret Service agents, who I didn't know, manning a small, roped-off perimeter outside the box door. I showed my ticket, and my WH ID, and they let me in. As I passed them, I said, "My husband, Darryl Bates, is also coming and has a ticket. Please let him in when he arrives."

They nodded and I went in to the lounge area adjacent to the box. The President, Hillary, and Chelsea were sitting there and smiled at me.

"Well, Melinda, you see I took your advice about coming to this event, and I brought Bill and Chelsea!"

"This is a wonderful Washington tradition, and I'm very glad you came. Now all your events for the month are done, I hope you get to relax and enjoy Christmas."

I picked up the songbooks from the lounge table. "Here, I'll turn down the corners of the pages for the pieces we'll sing. Whatever you do, don't listen to me sing. I'm not very good, so I just do my best to make a joyful noise."

After more chatting, I began to wonder where Darryl was. Eventually a staff person stuck her head in the door, "Are you expecting a Darryl Bates?"

"Yes," we all said. "Let him in."

I asked him later what kept him so long.

"The Secret Service. I couldn't argue my way past them. Finally they said, 'You don't understand, sir. A very important person is using the box tonight.' And I said, 'Yes, and it's my wife! So, when she comes out, please tell her I was here and you turned me away.' That got their attention and they finally let me in."

This was the Clintons' first Christmas in Washington, and everyone in the theater was excited and curious to see them. I was excited and honored Darryl and I got to be there with them. I'm not a great singer. Actually, I'm not any kind of singer. That's not why I went, year after year. I went because the music is so beautiful and uplifting.

At the intermission we all returned to the lounge and I asked, "How do you like the singing?"

Hillary laughed. "My voice is simply terrible. SO bad, in High School the only way I was allowed to participate in musicals was if I promised I'd only open my mouth, but not allow any sound to come out. So, I'm just faking it out there - and it's better for everyone that way"

The President looked at the music in his hand and then up at me. "It would be so much easier if they'd just give us the note first!"

I hadn't even thought about his being a musician - of course he wanted the note!

Before we went back out to sing (or not) again, I said to the President, "What a month! I'm exhausted, but at least I had a couple of nights off. You never did. I don't know how you're still standing!"

He nodded wearily. "Yep, my back sure feels it. We're looking forward to Hilton Head and some rest!"

And so ended our first year.

CHAPTER FIFTEEN ~ 1994 ~ WE HIT OUR STRIDE

With our first year under our belts, I thought maybe things would get a little easier. Ha. I can't speak for other administrations, but for us, NOTHING came easy. Ever.

In January, the President's beloved mother, Virginia, died. They were very close, and he was devastated. While he was leaving for the funeral in Little Rock, I watched Senator Dole, on CNN, make a nasty crack about the President, and thought, *for God's sake! Can't they just let the man go home to bury his mother? There will be plenty of time for political attacks next week, and all the weeks after. What a jerk.*

And, in fact, much later Dole did apologize.

At the funeral, the minister remembered Virginia by revealing she had once said to him, "Imagine what I could have done in my life if I'd been born with eyebrows!"

Oh, she was a pistol. In my opinion, she was a huge part of his success in life, as well as a reason he respected and enjoyed smart, capable women so much.

Later in January I attended the National Prayer Breakfast with the President and Hillary, and met Mother Teresa, the featured speaker. Now, the official reason for this event is for congress and invited guests to pray for the President. Maybe it worked like that when it started, back in the Paleolithic, but in today's world? What a quaint idea. Now it's a highly politicized pas de deux between the President and the opposition party.

Doug Coe, the event's organizer, has a sense of humor, and always seated me at an entirely Republican table - enemy territory. So, over the years, I found myself next to Wendy and Phil Gramm (ugh!), or Ed and Ursula Meese. I'd arrive late at the table (because I came in the motorcade with POTUS) and slip into my seat, smiling, holding out my hand, and saying my name. When they figured out where I came from, the atmosphere got chilly, fast. Remember, we were supposedly there to pray for the President.

Once breakfast ended, and the program began, I reached into my coat pocket for the small Bible I kept in my office and put it on the table in front of me. I naively thought we might want to, you know, read from the Bible at a prayer breakfast. Everyone else (**everyone** else) at the table looked from it to me in shock. You'd have thought I'd brought in a snake. They simply could not believe their eyes. I, a devil-worshiping Clintonite who undoubtedly was concealing horns under my hair, and a tail under my suit, had a Bible! And one clearly read a time or two. I had trouble keeping a straight face.

Mother Teresa spoke first, and it was just what you'd expect. She was a Catholic nun, for goodness' sake! About sixty percent of her talk was about the evil of abortion, which she called murder, and how her orphanages never give a child in adoption to a couple who'd had an abortion. Nothing shocking there. Catholic nun, remember? But another twenty five percent of her speech was about contraception, which she also equated to murder, adding, "We never give a child in adoption to a couple who have practiced contraception!"

I thought, *OK, well, there are plenty of people who agree with her about abortion. This is why it's such a passionate debate in America. But the contraception thing, well, even* **Catholics** *don't believe and follow that. It's a non-starter in political circles here. Won't it embarrass her supporters?*

Well, no, actually. They weren't embarrassed at all. That very same morning I watched various Republicans take to the floor of the House of Representatives to use Mother's remarks to attack the President, but not one of them had the nerve to quote her about contraception. Hypocrites!

When the President rose to make his remarks, there was an air of nasty tension in the room. People seemed to be waiting to hear him rebut Mother Teresa, as if the event were some kind of debate. It's not, and he'd never, ever do such a thing. Instead, he spoke, in humble and personal terms, about how difficult it is in public life, in Washington, to follow the ten commandments, and how important it is to keep trying. It was a lovely speech, but I don't know how many people really heard it.

***

Every day things happen at the White House to astonish and amaze. The scheduled events are wonderful enough, but the spontaneous things you could never plan or predict are often even more memorable. We called those a "White House moment." One of these moments happened to me one morning when I greeted a tour.

I've mentioned the morning "Members' tour" (for Members of Congress). On this tour, the Members (or spouse or Chief of Staff) must personally escort their guests through the gates of the White House and into the East Reception Room, just down the hall from the Visitors Office.

One of my favorite duties was to welcome these visitors each morning. During our first year I wrote a little speech, and stuck to it as the years went on, although I always tried to make it sound as if I'd never said it before. After all, it was new to the tourists of the day, if not to me and the Members. My goal was to make these guests feel honored and special.

I started off with, "Good morning! Ladies and gentlemen, I'm happy to welcome you to the White House on behalf of the President and Mrs. Clinton, who are delighted to have you in their home today."

Then I'd follow this with information about the tour. Most visitors were thrilled to be there, and the welcome made it even more exciting. *Wow! We're guests of the President and First Lady!*

But it was also fun to say it because of the pursed lips and squinted eyes of Republicans in the room, who just couldn't stand to acknowledge the Clintons belonged there. I so enjoyed reminding them of whose House it was.

One morning that spring there was an unusual group in the Reception Room. General Carl Mundy, Jr., our Commandant of Marines, was hosting a group of Marine Generals from around the world and escorted them to the Members' Tour himself. Since Marines played a prominent part in White House history, I thought it would be nice to recognize them in my greeting.

So I detoured from my regular speech to say "Ladies and

gentlemen, I'd like to offer a special welcome this morning to Marine Commandant Carl Mundy and his guests, also Marines, from around the world. I think it's only fair to point out it was British Marines who came to this House on a hot August night in 1814, and virtually burned it to the ground. There are still places here where you can see the black burn marks from the fire so long ago."

People laughed, and I continued, "Of course, we forgave them for it a long time ago, but there's a little more to the story. Because after doing their best to burn the White House, the British Marines headed for our Marine headquarters at 8th and I Streets. There they also set everything on fire **except** the Commandant's house, which we assume was a professional courtesy."

Again there was a laugh, but this time a handsome man in a fine British Marine General's uniform, with his cap under his arm, walked over and offered his hand. "How do you do?" he said. "I am General Ross, and you were just talking about my ancestor."

My jaw dropped. *His ancestor?* I spent many hours telling stories of White House history to guests, but never to a descendent of the story's long ago villain. And, did I mention, he was very handsome and spoke in a really cool British accent? And the great uniform ...

"I enjoyed your story," he said, "but you haven't got the end part right. Wouldn't you like to know what really happened?"

"Oh, yes, please, I would. We always do our best to get history right here." *And, you can talk to me as long as you like. I love British accents!*

"Well, as it happens, my ancestor was determined to burn the Commandant's house to the ground until his aide said, "Oh sir, you should reconsider! After all, where will YOU live?""

I thought about it for a moment and giggled. "Please excuse me for saying so, General, but he seems to have been a little ... optimistic."

"Indeed he was," the General agreed. "He was killed in battle three days later."

What could I say? "I'm sorry?" Well, not really. He probably would have gone on to lay waste to Washington. His death was a good thing for my city and country. I settled for a smile and a diplomatic response, "Thank you for telling me. I'm glad we've all forgiven each other. Enjoy your visit."

The next day I told the President about this visitor. He rolled his eyes, "His descendent? Really? Of the man who burned this House to the ground? I'm sorry I didn't get to meet him myself. Isn't this the most amazing place? Some days we make history, and some days we relive history. Sometimes on purpose, sometimes by accident, but it's always a privilege to be part of."

It would have been impossible to forget the importance of American Marines to the White House. Whenever the President was in the Oval Office, there was a smart-looking Marine in dress uniform at attention at the door to the West Wing. They must have selected them for height and appearance, as they were always well over six feet tall, very good looking, and shockingly young. Each year the Military Office, upstairs from me in the East Wing, celebrated the birthday of the Marine Corps with a cake and ceremony in my reception room. A handsome Marine would hand me his dress sword to cut the cake, and I'd get to give him a kiss - which always embarrassed both of us.

We had no trouble remembering the British Marines either, as there really are places back stairs, in non-public areas, where the scorched reminders of their visit are still visible. I loved to point them out to visitors on my special, private tours.

Gary Walters hated it when we walked people through the "backstage" areas, or through a room staff were cleaning, or setting up for an event. He wanted people to only see the House in pristine order. I understood and respected this, but I also saw how it delighted people, especially entertainers, familiar with "backstage," to get to walk through areas obviously not meant for public viewing. It made them feel like insiders, and they loved it.

On one visit I took Richard Karn, from *Home Improvement*, to the carpenters' shop, where he took photos with the guys, putting on one of their tool belts. I took almost every actor into the Mess kitchen, explaining the Master Chiefs were all Navy men and women, and could knock out a five-course meal on a submarine. Everyone loved to see the President's theater, a great place to watch a movie, or see the Razorbacks play, or practice for the State of the

Union speech. I also heard that sometimes a weary household staff person, or Secret Service officer with no time to go home between shifts, might be found in there, snoozing away in the President's oversized chair. But, I'd never tell.

Of course, I never took a head of state, or royalty through these areas. "Oh, your Majesty, look to your left and you'll see the White House recycling bins ..." Or, "We're very proud of the new floor polisher. Is this how you do your marble floors?" I don't think so!

***

Some of the best stories about White House families came from people who worked there for twenty or thirty years as butlers, waiters, cooks, electricians, plumbers, and every other kind of household staff. The White House Historical Association collected some of these remembrances in a video called, "Workers at the White House." My favorite story, and one I loved to share with visitors, was about the Kennedys:

Normally, the North and South fountains were turned off in the winter, for obvious reasons. Washington, as President Kennedy famously said, is "a city of Northern hospitality (and weather) and Southern efficiency".

But in January, 1961, when the Kennedys moved in, Mrs. Kennedy told the ushers she wanted the fountains on all the time. One frigid morning the First Lady looked out one of the Residence windows and saw the South fountain was not on. She called down to the ushers and asked them to fix it.

They dispatched a couple of plumbers down to the fountain, where they discovered it wasn't working because the jets were frozen. (Duh.) They stood around for a few minutes trying to figure out how to solve this problem, until some of the Park Service gardeners came by. "Hey, we have a small boat we use when we need to clean the fountain. Want us to bring it?"

The two plumbers got into the little boat and began to push themselves around the fountain, whacking at the frozen jets with an oar to free them from the ice.

Meanwhile, President Kennedy, not aware of Mrs. Kennedy's call, looked out a different White House window and observed the activity. After a moment of stunned silence he burst out, "My God. They are ice fishing in the South fountain!" After all, he was a Massachussets man.

***

In the summer of 1994, the Clintons decided it was finally time to host their first state visit. The diplomatic corps had been lobbying hard for this since the inauguration, but the President's first priority was domestic issues, so this had to wait. Now it was time, and they decided to go big, by welcoming the Emperor and Empress of Japan, at a white tie event. Not a lot of Emperors left in the world now, so just the sound of it is impressive.

The planning was fun and challenging. Thank goodness I had all those notes from Carol McCain. The Visitors Office invites guests to the Arrival Ceremonies, and coordinates with the Social Office and the Military on a thousand issues. We admitted almost 6,000 guests on a warm, cloudless morning. Hillary looked stunning in a pale pink suit and hat. The Empress was adorable in a white suit and tiny white hat perched at a jaunty angle. The Emperor is a small man, and it was amusing to watch him walk next to the over six-foot tall President.

The next day, Hillary sent a note of thanks for our hard work. I could almost feel the drop in tension around the House, as it was apparent to everyone her team knew how to pull off this complex, high-profile event.

Later that summer, we welcomed President Yeltsin of Russia, who appeared to spend the entire visit drunk. The State Department invited

Yeltsin's plane and lectern

me to be part of the official welcoming party at Andrews AFB, and our small group carefully lined up along the carpet to greet him as he left the plane. At least this was the plan. But Yeltsin staggered down the steps and blew right past us, angrily stomping into his limo and ignoring the assembled press as well. I didn't care. I wasn't impressed with Yeltsin. And I did get a nice photo of myself, standing at his lectern, with the Russian state plane in the background.

The Arrival Ceremony and State Dinner went well, but the next day I got an earful from the Secret Service.

Visiting heads of state and one or two of their close aides usually stay across the street from the White House at Blair House, a series of elegant, connected townhouses, set up to host Presidential guests. You may have heard of Blair House, but I bet you don't know WHY this guesthouse was created. The story I heard was that during WWII, Winston Churchill spent so much time with the Roosevelts the White House was his home for months at a time. Well, Winston loved brandy, and cigars, and kept very late hours. It seems one night Mrs. Roosevelt heard some noise very late, came out into the hallway of the Residence in her bathrobe and saw the British Prime Minister, staggering around, muttering to himself and waving his cigar and brandy bottle. Naked. The next morning she called the Chief Usher and said, "We need to find another place for our guests to stay." So they created Blair House.

The official entrance is a shiny, black door, up a flight of a dozen stairs above the street level. There's always a Secret Service Officer stationed at the foot of those stairs, even though they never open. Late the night of the Yeltsin State Dinner, the Officer on duty in front of the stairs heard a noise, turned, and saw one of the Russian men standing in his boxers and tee shirt, shouting, "Pizza! Pizza!" and clearly drunk.

The officer figures it's one of Yeltsin's overworked aides, takes pity on the guy and says, "Shhhh! OK, OK, but let's not make noise out here. Come with me," and takes him to the Blair House Secret Service command post.

Well, the room is dark, so they can watch all the security screens. The officers there sit the guy down, promising, "We'll order you a pizza - no problem. Just sit here for a minute."

And they call Domino's to order a pie, everyone very friendly although their guest doesn't speak any English. They all know what it's like when a President's schedule keeps them so busy they're desperate for a break. If the guy drank a little too much, well, the events are over, so who cares?

A few minutes later the Watch Commander comes into the command post, takes a look at the "aide" and realizes - it's President Yeltsin. Holy cow! Well, they're specialists in smoothing over any awkward international incidents. So he takes Yeltsin by the arm, and in his most soothing voice says, "Mr. President, we'll be happy to bring you your pizza when it comes, but I think you'll be happier eating it up in your official suite, don't you?" And off they go, with Yeltsin smiling and waving goodbye to his new friends, who are sitting, staring in shock.

**

In September, Darryl and I took a trip to Nantucket. On Monday morning I dragged myself out of bed at the crack of 9:00 a.m. and called the Visitors Office to participate in our regular, weekly meeting. Marc answered the phone.

"Hi, you can put me on speaker and get the meeting started, please."

"Oh. Well, we're not actually meeting now."

"You're not meeting? Why not?" I ask, while thinking, *great, I go away for a couple of days and already things are falling apart! What's up with that?"*

"I'm the only one here. Everyone else is out on the Lawn."

"Out on the Lawn? Why are they out there? I don't remember any event we're part of being scheduled for this morning."

"Oh, no, they're out there to look at the plane."

"Plane? What plane? What the heck are you talking about?"

"Melinda, have you seen the news this morning?"

"What? No, I haven't seen the news. I'm on vacation and I only got out of bed for the meeting. What is going on there?"

Marc laughed so hard it took him a moment to speak. "OK, let me fill you in. Early this morning some lunatic flew a plane up across the South Lawn and into the White House, just to the West of the Diplomatic Reception Room, near the President's doctor's office. The Secret Service thinks it wasn't an attack, just someone crazy or stoned, who probably thought he could land on the Lawn and be famous for a day. But there was a big event scheduled for out there, with chairs and Jumbotrons and a platform, and it was impossible to land. So he headed straight into the House. And it's just a small, light plane, so he died on impact. They've taken the body away, but the plane is still there. They have to finish investigating before they haul it off. It's been quite a morning."

No kidding.

Over the next week there was a big public discussion about why the USSS counter snipers hadn't somehow shot the plane down. What did they think? Those guys had rocket propelled grenades? Suppose they did, and fired one - where would it end up, in the heart of the city? Now, I guess they do have those weapons, and we all hope to God they never have to use them.

***

In December, the Visitors Office became the first and only department in the Executive Office of the President to win the Vice President's re-inventing government award. All our hard work on the tour systems paid off! We put 1.5 MILLION visitors through the House in our first year - a real record. I was very proud of us, and still am. I still drink my morning tea from the mug announcing our award. Somewhere in a box in my garage in Baja is the plaque, with a little hammer for breaking through bureaucratic red tape to make government more efficient and responsive.

One of my proudest achievements of all eight years was the installation, in December, of a removable wooden ramp to bypass the short stairway leading into the East Colonnade. The White House had been considered "accessible" because there's a wheelchair lift, in a back hallway. But guests had to self-identify as needing assistance and had to be escorted by a Secret Service Officer. Watching my own father's problems with walking, and his pride, I had come to understand some people just don't like to have to ask for help. But, the law provides exceptions for historic houses, so there was no discussion about doing anything else.

Even more serious was the need for access on our special Christmas (sorry - "Holiday") tour for terminally and chronically ill children. We set aside an afternoon in December each year for these children and their families, and it would break your heart to see them. Children in wheelchairs, using walkers, on gurneys pushed by hospital aides, or lying listlessly in their parent's arms.

Many of these little ones would not live to see another Christmas, and we knew the photos their families took would be precious memories forever. Some years Hillary had time to come to the State Floor and greet these guests, kissing babies and comforting families. I don't know how she did it. I'd watch for a while and then have to turn back into the Ushers' office to wipe away tears.

The first year I took Socks to see the children, I was surprised by the intensity of their response. They LOVED this kitty, pointing and grabbing. Thank goodness he's so patient and even-tempered. A parent, seeing my puzzlement, explained. "Many of these children have spent their entire lives in a hospital. They never go outside, never see any kind of animal. To be able to touch a cat, especially the PRESIDENT'S cat, may be the most exciting thing they've ever done. Thank you for bringing him."

Once I knew what it meant to them, I made sure to always take Socks along when we had sick or disabled children visiting. We also got a wonderful Santa Claus, with twinkly blue eyes and the most beautiful red velvet Santa suit you ever saw, who sat and gently talked to every child about their Christmas dreams.

We just wanted to make their visit a little easier, so I got the carpenters from the Park Service to build a removable wooden ramp they could all use to bypass the stone stairs.

Then we got the White House photographers to take pictures of these tiny guests using the ramp to come to the tour. I sent the photos to Hillary with a memo about how the families appreciated it. She sent a note back: "Wonderful! Maybe we can be an example for other historic houses."

It's a good thing I did that.

The ramp stayed in place all through December, but once the holidays ended, Gary Walters let me know it had to be taken away.

"But, why, Gary? Have you taken a look? It's useful on regular tours too. Not everyone with mobility difficulties wants to have to tell a USSS Officer they need help. It's a win-win, isn't it?"

I couldn't get him to tell me the real reason he didn't like it, and I suspect it was because it was MY idea. But I dug in my heels and said "No. The ramp should stay."

It wasn't really my place to say so - I had no authority over this kind of thing. But it was so clearly the right thing to do. I was furious at him.

Then Gary said it should be removed because if we didn't, "It will look as if the First Lady has altered the White House without working with the Historical Association, and she'd be the target of criticism for it." What a load of bull hockey!

For one thing, the White House belongs to the family who lives there as much as if they paid a mortgage on it. Any First Lady could make any changes she wanted, without needing anyone's permission. Of course, then she'd have to be willing to take the criticism she might get for it.

But, more importantly, the ramp wasn't "installed" in the sense of "attached." It wasn't bolted to the floor or the stairs. It was a stand-alone structure, merely resting on the floor, and able to be taken apart and removed. If that was "altering the White House," then so were the Christmas decorations. Give me a break!

We argued back and forth until, finally, Hillary's aide, Capricia Marshall (later the Social Secretary), said she'd hear us out and make a decision. We met in the Map Room, and Gary, slick as ever, made his case, framing it only as his intention to protect the First Lady. (I told you. He was so darn good at it!)

When it was my turn, I didn't even speak. I opened my folder and took out the memo from me to Hillary, with her comments on it, and the photos of the sick kids being wheeled up the ramp. I spread them in front of Capricia.

Well, she's no dummy. She took a look, turned to Gary and said, "It seems Mrs. Clinton has already voiced her approval for this, so we'll just leave it in place, for now. After all, it can always be disassembled, right?"

And so it stayed, for all the rest of our time there.

When we left the White House I worried about the ramp. The Bush II people made it clear they hated anything associated with President Clinton, no matter how successful. I figured they'd have the ramp taken away on principle. But they didn't. And then they began to need it even more than we had, as they welcomed hundreds of wounded service members from the Iraq and Afganistan wars being treated at Walter Reed. I last saw it during the Obama years, a really nice, fancy – and very permanent looking - version.

So, I'm still proud of the ramp, and proud of Hillary too.

CHAPTER SIXTEEN ~ 1995

THE REPUBLICANS ARE COMING!

THE REPUBLICANS ARE COMING!

And now I get to tell you about one of only TWO times in all eight years that I said something, uh, *inappropriate*, to a guest in the White House.

The unpleasant – for us - reality of the Congressional election of 1994 was a large influx of new Republicans in 1995, taking the places of many of our favorite Democrats on the Hill.

On the morning of their January swearing-in, we offered special tours for the new Members, their friends and family. Might as well start off trying to be friendly!

I didn't normally show up in the State rooms during tours, but I thought it would be a smart idea for me to get a few moments of face time with them. It's difficult to be angry with someone you know, even a little. Well, at least it's hard for me. For Republicans that truly makes no difference. Take someone like Representative Jack Kingston of Georgia - a lovely man who introduced me to his wife, sent me thank you notes, always behaved like a gentleman in person. Then routinely went to the floor of the House to say the most awful, untrue things about the President. Sadly, that's just how it works. We used to marvel over how Republicans enforced the party message so ruthlessly. Deviate from what the leaders tell you to say, and you'll never appear on *Meet the Press* again. We could NEVER do that with Democrats. Sigh.

So, for this special tour I stationed myself on the State Floor in the Foyer, to smile at guests as they walked out the North door and thank them for coming. I stood at the foot of the stairs that go up to the Residence floors. You've seen this on television - it's where Presidents and First Ladies stand with their international guests for State Dinner receiving lines. Hanging in the stairwell behind me was the portrait of President Reagan, with his genial smile and iconic dark hair.

It became apparent early in the morning that most of our visitors were Republicans. They smiled at me, and I said, "Thank you for coming," smiled back and nodded, expecting them to keep walking to the door. But I hadn't counted on the portrait of "Ronnie." People did smile and nod, but their gaze traveled past my left shoulder to the picture, and I began to hear:

"Oh, look! It's President Reagan!"

"Oh, look, doesn't President Reagan look great!"

"Oh, there's Ronnie!"

I freely confess I found this very annoying. But, my job was not about what I liked or didn't like, so for a couple of hours I stood there, now smiling through clenched teeth, and farewelling the guests. Until the end of the morning, when an attractive young couple walked up to me and smiled.

"Thanks for coming," I said. "Enjoy the rest of your special day."

That almost worked, but no, they looked past me to the portrait and the man said, "Oh, honey, look - it's the King!"

"The King?" I said, whipping my head around to look. "The King? Oh, no, sir. That's not Elvis - that's Ronald Reagan."

They looked at me in stunned silence, then at each other. The husband blurted out, "Well, you know, I meant, like, the King of our party."

I was just barely able to refrain from saying, "OK, that's one pretty significant difference between Republicans and Democrats right there."

Later that day I was talking to the President, who was pretty glum himself about the new majority on the Hill. "Mr. President, I need to confess. I said something today, to a guest in your House, that I shouldn't have."

"What could you possibly have said?"

I told him the story, and ended with, "I'm confessing, but I am NOT sorry. They had it coming."

"Elvis? You really said that? Elvis?"

"Yes, and if you take another look at that picture, and squint just a little, it's not an unreasonable resemblance."

"I will never," he said, "be able to look at that portrait again without thinking of this story."

***

In March we hosted a State Visit for King Hassan of Morocco. We were now experts on these complex events and looked forward to them. For Moroccans, the King is a spiritual as well as national leader, and we had a lot of guests who were so excited to be on the Lawn of the White House, in the presence of this holy man, they did that trilling, ululation thing - it sounds so eerie and makes all the hair stand up on your arms.

A few weeks later I received a large box from Morocco, opened it and found a red and blue hand-made rug, with a note from the King: "Thank you for your hard work in making my visit with the President such a success."

Well, my mother brought me up right, so I sat down to write a note of my own, on White House note paper. It began, "How kind of His Majesty to think of me ..." Then I sat back and stared at what I'd written.

Well, look at that. "How kind of His Majesty ...?" What's next? Glass slippers and a coach? Ain't life grand?

***

In the spring I was asked to give a tour to Larry Hagman (JR of *Dallas*) and Sharon Stone, and then take them to the Oval to meet POTUS. By this time I was used to the constant celebrity parade, and enjoyed meeting stars and their families. But this tour took an unusual turn.

Larry and I were standing in the East Room, looking at the famous portrait of George Washington. Sharon and her sister were off looking at the picture of Martha Washington. There was a pause in the conversation, I looked over at Larry and said, "Oh, Mr. Hagman, what a colorful tie. But, what's the design? I can't quite make it out." (Children, close your eyes and ears here!)

"It's ducks fucking," he casually replied.

That's not a word I've ever heard on the State Floor before. Surely I misheard? I choked and blurted out, "What?"

"It's ducks fucking," he repeated.

I leaned in for a closer look, looked up at his face, smiled weakly and said, "Why, so it is. I didn't know Donald and Daisy could, uh, uh…!"

Good grief. What kind of man wears a tie like that to the White House and then says something like that to a woman he doesn't know?

But I already knew "stars" are different from you and me, so I dropped the subject and soon walked these guests over to the West Wing for a brief visit.

The President was happy to meet them all, and they chatted for a few minutes. As the visit wound down I said, "Mr. President, whatever you do, don't look too closely at Larry's tie."

Well, of course, he did glance at it just as I had, and said, "Oh, it's a Disney tie. I have bunches of those - but my advisors won't let me wear them." Then he stopped and looked more closely, got a little red in the face and said, "Oh, wait. What's going on there? You've got Disney meets the Kama Sutra."

Everyone in the room fell out laughing. And, soon after, I became good friends with Larry and his wife Mai, who lived in a spectacular house in the beautiful mountains of Ojai, California, and were very kind to me. We spent the night there once, and slept in the Mary Martin suite, on butter yellow linen sheets. Oh my. But I still think that tie was a very odd choice to wear to the White House!

***

In July I told the President I'd like to travel with him to an event outside Washington, to experience the different vibe I'd seen watching these on television. He invited me to fly with him on Air Force One to a conference in Tennessee, hosted by the VP. Beyond excited, I called everyone I knew who'd been on the plane. "What's the best part? What should I know in advance?"

Turns out, the coolest part is the phone system. Who knew? In the staff cabin there are two phones at each comfy recliner, and the plane's attendants explain one is the "regular" phone, and one is the "secure" phone. I wasn't planning to make any secure calls (although I did have top secret clearance) but I learned if you call someone from the plane, it goes through operators, who announce to the person you call, "I have a call for you from Air Force One."

Well, this sure sounded like fun to me! Too bad I had been married such a long time and didn't have any old boyfriends I could call and torment! So I called my friend, Lansing Lee III, a partner at Patton Boggs. He was out of the office, and his assistant was so addled by the announcement, (I have a call for Mr. Lee from Air Force One ...) she kept shouting into the phone, "Who? What? Air Force One? Air Force ONE?"

After a few minutes of this the operator turned the call over to me, and I simply said, "Please tell Lansing, Melinda called." I'd accomplished my purpose - everyone on his floor heard her shouting, "Air Force One?"

There are actually two identical planes to carry POTUS, so one is always available while the other is being serviced. You can tell by looking at the outside they clean it with toothbrushes and fanatical attention - every inch gleams. When you travel on the plane the first time, the Air Force personnel who staff it take you around for a tour. At the front is the President's cabin, with two sofas that make up into full beds, and a television screen covered by a southwestern tapestry hanging. The Reagans ordered these planes in the 1980s, and Mrs. Reagan selected a desert theme for the colors, so shades of tan, caramel, brick red and cream predominate.

Next to the front cabin is the President's bathroom, in white and shiny chrome, with a full shower. Then the President's office cabin, with a large, dark wood desk and cabinets for books and CDs.

There's a black leather portfolio on the desk with the Presidential seal in gold. A dark blue bomber jacket, with "The President" embroidered over the right breast, hangs on the back of the desk chair.

Moving to the back, you come to the conference room, with a large, dark wood table, and screens high on the front wall, showing CNN or c-span at all times, and clocks with world times.

There's a medical room, with full operating and dental capacity. Everything but the central table folds cleverly into the walls.

All of these cabins are on the right side of the plane, taking up three quarters of the space. There's a hallway running the length of these cabins and on the opposite side, below the windows, are sofas, end tables, and lamps. It's comfortable and elegant.

AIR FORCE ONE

Thurgood Marshall Jr and me, staff cabin

Senior staff, ambassadors and the like have a posh cabin, and staff like me have one slightly less so, but still the equivalent of first class on any other plane (at least back then). There are tables at each seat, and the front edges fold up for work or down if you want to stretch out and relax. Screens face each set of seats, and a menu at every place lists the flight's meals and available movies.

Further back are the press seats, laid out like a normal plane, and the office workers and equipment (fax, operators, etc.) that enable the President and staff to keep working. Just like in Harrison Ford's excellent movie.

The plane rides were amazing. I was so excited I carefully

saved EVERYTHING with the AF1 logo on it - including the little paper napkin that came with the orange juice. I had these, and the photos I took, put together in a big frame for a collage in my office.

Then two weeks later I got an envelope from "Air Force One support." It clearly held a bill.

Oh my God! They're billing me for the flight! I can't afford to pay for the flight! I didn't know they were gonna charge me to fly. Oh no! Oh no!

I opened the bill and found a balance due of $7.50 for the breakfast I consumed.

As I'm writing this update to the book–in 2018, I've read President Trump wants the new AF1s the Air Force is ordering to have bigger beds, and a more, shall we say, colorful (garish) paint job. It would be such a shame to throw away the classic sky blue, white and gold design that has graced every plane since the very first one, representing the United States of America around the world. I hope they don't make any substantive changes. It takes so long to build these planes Mr. Trump wouldn't get to enjoy the new ones anyway and it would be, in my opinion, a mistake to turn the fabulous planes into something commercial.

***

The Easter Egg Roll went off well, and I was getting good at doing the morning stand-ups with Al Roker of *Today*, Brian Lamb of C-SPAN and Tony Snow, then the weatherman from the local Fox station. He was the most important interview for me, as parents in the DC area watched the show to hear me talk about the weather (how to dress their children), the activities and the availability of tickets (whether it made sense to come down to the White House and try to get in).

This year our producer, Gary Jacob, brought us the actress who played Marcia Brady in the new *Brady Bunch* movie. Tony opened the interview with me, then quickly turned to the actress and began a lengthy conversation. I stood waiting impatiently. Families out there needed information they weren't getting!

Finally, I interrupted, "Marcia, Marcia, Marcia! Doesn't anyone care about anything other than Marcia?"

Tony, startled, couldn't stop himself from snorting. The camera and sound guys burst out laughing. Even the actress giggled. Everyone remembered this line from the television show, and it worked perfectly here. Tony composed himself, turned to me and asked the logistical questions everyone needed to hear.

***

Someone asked me to take Oliver Stone, Anthony Hopkins and James Woods around, to help them in pre-production of *Nixon*. I'm not a big fan of Mr. Stone. I like history, and I like fiction, and I think we're all better off if we don't mix the two. But who cares what I think, and I am a big fan of Mr. Hopkins, so I was glad to meet him.

As we walked through the House, Mr. Hopkins BECAME Richard Nixon. No props, no make up, just his incredible acting ability. It was startling - and creepy.

They were excited to be in the White House, and when we got to the East Room they turned to each other and began a conversation about Nixon's farewell speech to his staff. I broke in to say, "I remember that speech really well. He thanked everyone - EVERYONE - including his sainted mother, and never mentioned his poor wife, standing next to him, who had suffered through everything with him. What an awful man."

All three men burst out laughing.

"What's so funny?" I asked.

"It's not you. Don't be offended. It's just, every time we mention this speech to a woman of a certain age, that's the moment she remembers. He really upset a lot of you."

"Well, it's even worse than you know. My elderly mother is in a nursing home. She had a stroke and is just coming out of a coma. She's not even fully awake yet. The other day, standing over her bed with my Dad, one of us mentioned the speech (God knows why). And my mother, still in a coma, said, 'Yes, the one where he didn't thank his wife.' True story."

I used to really dislike this about Nixon, as if one needed another reason to dislike Nixon. In fact, I'm one who would like to visit his grave - to make sure he's still dead. When I think of what that cursed war did to the families of my generation ... A friend tells me there's an Indian tribe in Ohio who "celebrate" the birthday of General George Custer each year by sending its braves to pee on his grave. I guess it's a good thing I'm not equipped to do that.

However, a few days later I told this story to Rex Scouten, the Chief Curator, and once again learned I didn't know everything I thought I knew. Rex had been at the White House for decades, first as a Secret Service Officer, later an Usher. In the 1980s he tried to retire, but the Reagans liked him so much they insisted he un-retire and made him Chief Curator (and named their dog after him). He didn't have the academic credentials for the position, but he was a walking encyclopedia of White House history he had personally lived. And, he was the nicest man. A perfect joy to work with.

Rex told me he was an Usher during the Nixon years, and was in the elevator with the family as they went down from the Residence for the speech on the State Floor. As you can imagine, the Nixons were all very upset and tense, and Mrs. Nixon said, "Dick, whatever you do, please don't mention me in your remarks. I will lose my composure completely, and I couldn't bear for that to happen in front of everyone."

So, it turns out his not mentioning his wife was actually a kindness to her. It makes me like him the teeniest bit more. But I'd still like to visit that grave ... I'm one of many who thought President Clinton was waaaay too kind in his remarks at the Nixon funeral. I guess he was thinking of what will be said at his own funeral by whoever is President then.

CHAPTER SEVENTEEN ~ 1995 ~
WHO'S COMING?

In June I met a new friend, Mark Erwin, a longtime friend and supporter of the Clintons, and a true Southern gentleman. He was also a friend to Senator Strom Thurmond of South Carolina. I have no idea why. I had recently lunched with the Senator, and before leaving the White House I asked my friends in Congressional Affairs for a briefing. You don't want to look stupid when you represent the President, even at lunch. Every single person I spoke to said the same thing: "Watch your back."

"Huh?" (I was a little slow.)

"Watch your back. He likes to pinch ladies backsides."

Let's remember this is a man who, when he was 60-something, had a political opponent who said Thurmond was "too old" to continue as Senator. Thurmond's response was to marry a woman forty-three years younger and father his first child with her at age sixty-eight.

I enjoyed lunch with the Senator, and he behaved perfectly - which was something of a disappointment. Was I not young enough to flirt with? He was ninety years old and I was not yet fifty!

When I met Mark, this story came up, and then he told me about his own most memorable encounter with Strom: Senator Thurmond was an overnight guest in his house. In the morning when they awoke, Mark's wife, Joan, said, "Gosh, how funny, it sounds as if there's a television on downstairs, but I know we turned everything off before we came up last night."

They headed for the stairs with their little daughters, Jennifer and Missy, all three ladies complete Southern belles. When they reached the foot of the stairs, they could tell the television in the den was, indeed, on, tuned to an exercise program.

And there, exercising in front of it, was Senator Thurmond. Naked. Yep, naked. Try to get that mental image out of your mind now! A ninety-year-old man, exercising naked. Mark hustled the ladies back upstairs, returned to the doorway of the den and encouraged the Senator to get dressed.

I thought this story was hilarious, and couldn't wait to tell the President, just before he left the Oval Office for a reception on the State Floor. Bill Clinton routinely does three or four things at a time, and still never misses anything. He was looking at papers in his hand, while an aide waited for some decision, and didn't appear to be paying much attention to me or the story until I said the word "naked!" At this his head whipped around, his eyes got big and he demanded, "Is that true? Mark Erwin told you that? Oh, my Lord. Strom Thurmond. Naked ... "

Everyone in the room was in hysterics as we tried to shake this unfortunate mental image out of our heads. About a month later I saw Mark at another party and asked him, "When you went through the receiving line at the reception last month, did the President say anything surprising to you?"

"Yes, and it was the strangest thing. He took one look at me, grabbed me by the arm and said, 'Mark! Is it true? Strom Thurmond, naked? Does Hillary know?' and then he dragged me over to tell her. They laughed 'til they cried. How did he even know that story?" Oh, a little bird, I imagine…

In July, Tom Hanks came to town for the presentation of the Presidential Medal to Commander Lovell, hero of the Apollo 13 mission, and a joint press conference. Tom had been to the White House once before, and Marc walked him around on a Saturday. He met the President and they got along. So when we heard about the events, Marc called to invite Tom to breakfast with us in the Mess. What a delightful man!

Tom came with his son, Colin. We met in the reception room and headed over to the Mess. As we entered the West Colonnade, I could see the President ahead of us, just entering the Oval. As soon as the maitre 'd seated us at a large, round table, I excused myself, went to the phone and dialed the Oval Office.

"Betty, I haven't seen his schedule yet for today, but I know he likes Tom Hanks, and wanted to let you know Tom is here in the Mess with us for the next hour or so." (In the White House, "he/his/him are always shorthand for "the President", just as "she/her/hers are shorthand for the First Lady)

"I'll tell him," she replied. "There may be time for a visit."

I went back to our breakfast, which was fun because Tom is fascinating, and because everyone else in the Mess could see I'M HAVING BREAKFAST WITH TOM HANKS. There were lots of startled looks from behind the morning papers. Celebrities didn't usually come for breakfast.

Neither did the President, but I looked up from my eggs to see him striding over to our table. We all stood. You do that when the President comes in the room. In fact, whenever the President called me, in the office, or even at home, I always stood up to talk to him. It just seemed right.

He was happy to see Tom, and they had an enthusiastic discussion about the Apollo 13 movie. The President said it was so popular it actually boosted the public's interest in and support for the space program. Tom was pleased to hear this. Colin looked thrilled.

After breakfast Marc and I took Tom and Colin all over the White House. Public rooms, private rooms, backstage nooks and crannies, and the theater where the President screened the movie. They were interested in it all, and it's certainly fun to share with such charming people.

After the tour we went off to the National Press Club for the Hanks/Lovell press conference, and then back to the White House in Tom's limo. When we approached the security check point, the driver got nervous. "How'm I going to get in there? I don't think I can – they will turn me away. What should I do?"

"No problem," I said, and took my staff pass out of my handbag. "Just wave this at the Officer. It'll be fine."

He took my pass, with a doubtful frown, but, just as I said, the officer looked at it, looked at me, looked at TOM, and waved us right in. Now Marc took charge of Tom and Colin, while I went to walk Commander Lovell around. It was an honor. It always seemed amazing to me that the most extraordinary people often appear completely ordinary. Lovell was an older man with thinning gray hair. You'd never look twice if you passed him on the street. So, heroism doesn't mark people on the outside. Courage and determination are interior qualities and stay hidden when not needed.

At the end of the tour I brought him to the Oval for the medal ceremony, then ran back to the East Wing to escort some Members of Congress who'd been invited to participate. We were just able to squeeze them into the Oval, which is not at all a large space, and I assumed there was no room for me. As I turned to leave, an aide grabbed my arm.

"Don't go," he whispered. "There's room for you too. Just stand at the back by the cameras and watch - it'll be historic!"

The President came in and spoke about heroism and inspiration. There wasn't a dry eye in the room. After the ceremony, I was walking Tom and Colin back to their limo on the East Side, and we passed a celebration in the Map Room, a birthday party for Nancy Hernreich, Director of Oval Office Operations. The guests saw who was with me, ran out into the hall and begged Tom to come in for just a minute. How could he say no? So in we went to a raucous welcome, and Tom kissed the birthday girl.

Of course, when the celebrity portion of my day ended, around 5:00 p.m., there were still piles of paperwork that had accumulated on my desk while I was out with the stars. I worked until 10:00 p.m. to get it all done. And this was my typical day.

***

In October I became the first Director of the White House Visitors Office to be promoted to Special Assistant to the President. Hooray for me! No raise, but I loved my impressive new title. I ordered new business cards right away. I was excited, and grateful to Jodie Torkelson, my boss, for promoting me. But a week later we had a conversation that dampened my joy considerably.

"Melinda, I want you to stop talking about your promotion. It's annoying people."

"Annoying people? How could my promotion annoy people?" I was baffled.

"I heard you told someone in the Mess she could now 'kiss your ring' to acknowledge your new status. That's not cool."

I took a moment to calm myself, before saying, "Of course, if I said that it was a joke. I thought my colleagues here would share my happiness about the promotion. I see I was wrong."

"Look, I'm glad I gave it to you - you deserved it. But now, just shut up about it."

I left her office thinking, *I've just learned an important lesson about how other people operate. I've always been happy to share anyone's good news - a success at work, an engagement, a new baby. I assumed everyone was like me. Well, now I know better, and I won't make the mistake of talking about my successes again.*

MELINDA NAUMANN BATES
SPECIAL ASSISTANT TO THE PRESIDENT AND
DIRECTOR, VISITORS OFFICE

THE WHITE HOUSE   (202) 456-2322

And now, here is the second time in eight years I said something inappropriate to a visitor – this time completely inadvertently!

The then Queen of Sweden came for tea with Hillary and I was asked to walk her around. Queen Sylvia is a beautiful woman who was a commoner until she married the King. (They met at an Olympics.) She listened politely and seemed to be enjoying the tour. Remember how short our history is to people from Europe or Asia - 220 years was barely a hiccup in their world. In the State Dining Room I told the story of British marines and the fire of 1814. Their commanding officer, Admiral Cockburn, forbade the Marines to loot, but they were allowed to take a small memento, to prove they had been at the burning of the President's House. The admiral himself took a seat cushion from a dining chair, because he said he wanted to be able to make rude remarks - about Dolley Madison's bottom. I'd told this story dozens of times, and it always made people laugh.

Well, the Queen and her Lady in Waiting were nodding and smiling with interest until I uttered the words, "Dolley Madison's bottom."

The minute those words left my lips the Queen's face froze. The Lady in Waiting froze. We stood there in awkward silence for what felt like an age until the LinW said, "Oh, dear, look at the time. Your Majesty, we really must be going."

They were out the door in a minute and a half. I'd never seen anything like it. Apparently, it's a diplomatic faux pas to say "bottom" to a Queen. Who knew?

***

At the end of October we celebrated Hillary's birthday with a surprise down home square dance, complete with a tractor, pumpkins, corn stalks and hay bales on the State Floor. The guests all came in jeans, skirts and boots, and we did some "boot scootin" across the East Room floor. Roland created a birthday cake in the shape of a barn and bales of hay. The things that man can do with spun sugar ...

Hillary's outfit was a red checked skirt, white blouse and Dolly Parton blond wig, with a black cowboy hat perched on top. She looked amazing. You had to smile when you saw her. The President wore black jeans and a plaid shirt, and all the ladies of Hillaryland wore white blouses and black/white checked skirts.

CHAPTER EIGHTEEN ~ 1996

A RIPPLE OF SCANDAL AND MORE INTERESTING VISITORS

In February 1996, the Clintons hosted the President of France at a State Visit. You may remember the movie *The American President*, starring Michael Douglas and Annette Benning. At the movie White House they hosted the President of France. So, Hillary invited Michael to the morning Arrival Ceremony and the State Dinner the night we honored the real French President.

The day before the visit I got a call from the Social Office: "Melinda, Michael Douglas is coming to the Ceremony tomorrow morning, and we're a little concerned that other guests may bug him for autographs or photos. We'd like you to escort him, you know, stay with him, and just make sure he enjoys his visit. OK?"

Well, what was I going to say? "Sorry, no, I'm too busy for Michael Douglas?"

Of course not. Of course I accepted my assignment happily. In the morning Michael enjoyed the bands, the troops, and the two Presidents making remarks. By the way, those remarks always follow this format: " ... honored to be here in the heart of America ... yada, yada, yada, George Washington ... yada, yada, yada, Thomas Jefferson ... yada, yada, yada ... our long friendship, yada ... " Always.

When the event ended I walked Michael to the driveway and stopped for a moment to get up my nerve. I didn't usually do this, but really, why not? I took a breath and blurted out, "Michael, I know you went all over the White House in preparation for your movie, but I'm guessing there's one experience you haven't had here."

"Really? What?"

"Lunch in the White House staff Mess. Would you like to have lunch there with me today?"

"Hey, sure, that sounds great. I have some things to do now, but I'll come back at noon. See you then!"

The minute he left I raced for the phone, called the Mess and asked for the Chief Steward. "Chief, I need not just one, but two big favors from you today. I hope you can help me."

"Sure, Ms. Bates. What can we do for you?"

"OK, well, first is I need a table for two, today, when I know you're already fully booked. And, second is, it can't just be any table. My lunch guest is Michael Douglas, and I need a table where everyone can see I'M HAVING LUNCH WITH MICHAEL DOUGLAS. In fact, if you want to seat us in the entryway, so everyone will have to walk around us, that will be fine with me. Can you do it?"

He laughed, "I promise to take care of you. See you at noon."

And when we got to the Mess, we did have a great table, in the main dining room, and everyone saw I was having lunch with Michael Douglas. It was a delightful hour. Michael was just back from Africa, filming the movie about the man-killing lion, so he'd been out of touch with the rest of the world for months. I got to fill him in on the news of the day - the air we breathe at the White House. As we got to dessert and coffee a Steward brought a phone to the table. I assumed the call was for me and reached for it.

"No, Ms. Bates, the call is for Mr. Douglas."

We both looked surprised, and Michael picked up the receiver with a shrug that said, "no one knows I'm here".

"Hello Michael, this is Hillary. I hear you're enjoying lunch in the Mess with Melinda - I'm so glad. I won't see you until dinner

 tonight, but I'd consider it a great favor if you have time to visit my office and say 'hello' to my staff. Melinda can walk you over."

For the rest of the afternoon I got emails from people all over the complex: "I saw you, having lunch with MICHAEL DOUGLAS! How cool!"

***

Almost a year before, Robyn and I had gone to Hillary with a suggestion that we create a for-sale version of the famous wooden Easter eggs we gave away at each Egg Roll. We'd use the graphic from each year's artist, but the for-sale ones would have a little star to differentiate them from the event eggs. The Park Service Visitor Center could sell them with the other White House souvenirs they carry. And, they'd only cost $3, so they'd be affordable to grandparents wanting multiples for the grand kids, or children on an allowance. Isn't this a clever idea? Hillary thought so. We thought so. Surely the folks at the White House Historical Association would jump on board with this swell plan. Um ... No.

WHHA didn't want to have anything to do with selling $3 wooden eggs. That's not up to their standards. Now, if we wanted to design and sell a $25 crystal egg, then great, full steam ahead! But a wooden egg? Not so much.

Of course, it would be impolitic for them to come out and say this, especially since the First Lady made it clear she was an enthusiastic supporter of the project. So, they played the timeless bureaucratic game of confuse and delay, confuse and delay. They scheduled meetings we weren't allowed to attend, discussed the plan at those meetings, then came back to tell us questions were raised they couldn't answer (but WE could have) so the issue would have to wait for the next meeting, a few months from now.

Clearly, we were supposed to roll over and give up. At one point they used the argument that Easter eggs weren't associated with the White House, so they shouldn't sell them in their gift shop. Really? I inconveniently pointed out there'd been an Egg Roll at the White House since Rutherford and Lucy Hayes, which sure gave the impression of a connection. And if Easter eggs weren't connected, how come they were selling Christmas ornaments every year, a big money maker for them? We didn't get an answer.

What really made me mad was the fact that Hillary had raised millions and millions of dollars - $10 million by the time she left the White House - for the Historical Association. You'd think this might make them a little, oh, grateful? Nope.

Finally, we faced reality and gave up on the Historical Association and the Visitor Center. But we learned the kiosk on the Ellipse, that also sold souvenirs to tourists, was run independently. We found a company to make the eggs with this year's graphic, and had them delivered to the kiosk a couple of days before the '96 Egg Roll. When I heard they had arrived, I dropped everything to walk down there, so I could be the FIRST person to buy some. I got a set for Hillary, and some for my staff. The salesperson told me as soon as she opened a Park Service Ranger came and tried to buy 25 eggs to re-sell in the Visitor Center. Those people have NO shame. "Did you sell them the eggs?" "Nope! I saved the first ones for you all!"

Over the years the for-sale eggs were very popular. In 2001, Mrs. Bush, in the Bush II purge of all things Clintonian, stopped offering them. But there must have been a fuss about it, as the following year they were back.

***

The President was up for reelection, but it didn't change my life much. I didn't travel, didn't campaign, and didn't fund raise - despite what you heard about us all. The only way I could help was to accommodate tour requests from people who offered other kinds of support and help, mostly Members of Congress also facing reelection. This we all did, pushing the House, and the staff, to welcome unprecedented numbers of visitors.

In the spring, my boss, Jodie, called. "Hey, I need you to take Robin Williams to lunch in the Mess tomorrow and keep him busy and happy through the afternoon. He's the headliner at tomorrow night's big DNC fund-raiser."

"Wow. Robin Williams? No kidding? No problem!"

Robin was one of the most interesting people I ever met. He showed up wearing a baggy, pale green suit with a tie that looked (literally). like a clown tie. In private he was shy, very smart, and as intense as you'd imagine. His mind went 'round a mile a minute, and it NEVER stopped. It was like being in the middle of a tornado, all afternoon.

I walked over to the Mess, and into the Ward Room, a private dining room I rarely entered. Robin was accompanied by Walter Shorenstein, the billionaire from San Francisco who supported Democratic causes, and Walter's lady friend, a sleek blond in a designer suit and serious jewelry - the kind of jewelry we rarely saw in our Democratic White House. The kind of jewelry I bet they see in Republican administrations, where billionaires are more frequent guests.

Lunch was a riot. Robin kept the conversation going at a breakneck pace but also asked a lot of political questions. I told him Senator Phil Gramm (the "genius" who predicted the President's 1993 budget would send us into a depression - how'd that work out, again?) was running for President by saying in his speeches, "Ah failed the first, fifth, seventh and ninth grades."

"You're making that up!" Robin exclaimed.

"No, I swear, he says it himself."

"But why would he say such a thing? It's crazy."

"I guess he's making the point that if you work hard, even if you're a stupid tool like he is, you can still get ahead. You know, 'Look at me, I are a United States Senator ... '"

Robin sat back to consider this, then went on to some other topic his brain had clicked into. When lunch ended, we left the Ward Room and stepped to the Maitre'd's stand on our way out. The Chief Steward was checking names off his reservation list. A long line of guests stood waiting eagerly for their tables. Robin took a bunch of menus in his hand and gently pushed the Captain aside. The people in line looked up in disbelief. They were already pretty excited to be having lunch in the White House with their relative or friend, but now Robin Williams was beckoning them to a table? The folks back home were never gonna believe this!

Walter and his friend went off to a meeting, and I then spent the afternoon escorting Robin around to all the public and behind-the-scenes spaces. As we walked down the ground floor hallway we saw someone familiar walking towards us - Dan Ackroyd was visiting the House with some other staffer the same day. These men were old friends, and greeted each other happily, but it was just another day at work for me, as you can see by my smile.

As we walked around, Robin kept trying out political jokes on me, asking, "What do you think? Am I going too far with this one?"

"Oh, you're asking the wrong person that question. It ALL works for me - the more cutting the better. I despise those hypocrites on the Hill. Say whatever you want!"

That night, at the DNC event, Robin told a lot of jokes, including one about Phil Gramm and his failures at school. I sat, beaming and told my friends, *this is so great! Now I'm a writer for Robin Williams!*

***

On April 3, tragedy. Commerce Secretary Ron Brown and thirty-four of our friends and colleagues died when their plane crashed on a mountainside in Croatia. Everyone I knew in the White House knew someone on that plane. One man had insisted on taking the place of a colleague with a wife and child. He knew (they all knew) how dangerous the trip was. We were shocked and heartbroken. We sat, weeping at our desks, watching the news trickle in and comforting each other as the names were released.

A day later, we heard from the Oval Office the President wanted a memorial service staff could attend. I scrambled to arrange it at St. John's Episcopal Church, just a block from the White House. I'd come to know the pastor through my work on the Pageant of Peace, and he kindly agreed to open the church and speak. By coincidence, that morning we had arranged a tour for a special gospel choir from a Southern university. (I'm so sorry I don't remember the name.) Marc and I thought of them at the same time, looked at each other and went running to the State Floor. We caught them just before they walked out the door.

We were so winded I had to hold up a hand to ask them to wait a moment while we bent over, wheezing, and caught our breath. They patiently stood, with puzzled looks. When we could speak, I explained the service now scheduled for an hour later, and asked the director if they could possibly come to the church and sing for the grieving President and White House staff? They very kindly agreed. Oh, their voices were angelic and added so much to the service. When it ended, the President and Hillary stood outside the church to hug every sorrowful staffer as we slowly filed out.

***

In June, I looked up from my desk and saw on my television the Treasury building, just a few steps across East Executive Avenue from the East Wing, was on fire. Horrified, I went outside to look, standing under the portico. Huge clouds of thick, black smoke billowed up from the roof. As I watched, Leon Panetta, Chief of Staff to the President, came and stood next to me. I didn't know what to say, ("Sorry the government is burning?") so I nodded in respect and he nodded back. We stood, side by side, in silence for a few minutes, until he sighed, shook his head and said,

"What's next? Locusts?" Then he turned and walked back into the House. Guess he had a rough month.

***

The crackpot scandal-mongering about FBI files on Bush I administration staffers was now building steam. It was infuriating for those of us who knew how things really work at the White House and knew there was no misuse of private information. Craig Livingstone was not the sharpest tool in the shed, and he was no spy master. He was a guy in over his head, dealing with an antiquated system.

How do I know?

Well, I know because the very first Easter, 1993, Hillary asked us to send a wooden Easter egg to every person on the White House staff. I figured I'd just ask for a staff list, with names and the office each person worked in. How difficult could it be? After all, it's not exactly easy to enter the White House complex. If you're on staff you've been through an extensive clearance process with the FBI, and the Secret Service issues you an electronic pass. So, there'd have to be an accurate staff list - or so we thought, and I sent Craig a memo requesting it.

A day or so later we received a thick envelope with page after page of name, title and office. It seemed rather long to me, so I sat down to review it, then couldn't believe what I found. "Hey, Marc, come in here. Look at these names - James Baker, Brent Scowcroft, Marlin Fitzwater - those are all Bush staff. How come their names are still on a current WH staff list? Please call Craig and straighten this out. Clearly, he sent us the wrong list."

Marc came back to me in a few minutes, shaking his head. "You're not gonna believe this. I know I have trouble believing this. But Craig says the Secret Service is barely functional with computers, and they simply don't have a way to keep up with staff changes. Old staff leave, but their names don't get purged. And new staff arrive, but their names don't get added. He says he knows it's crazy, but this list is the best he has. We're going to have to figure out some other way to do it."

We didn't know we were dealing with a potential scandal. How I wish we had - I would have saved that list! Marc and I just thought we were dealing with an inefficient bureaucracy. We shrugged our shoulders and set to finding a solution to the egg distribution problem. We decided to send memos to the heads of every office (a list we were reasonably certain was up to date) asking them to send us their staff lists. But we also started work on a computerized staff list we called "Bunny Base" (for Easter, get it?). Over the next few years we refined this list and used it for all kinds of things - invitations to July 4th fireworks viewing, or Christmas (sorry - "Holiday") tours, things like that.

When our enemies on the Hill - and make no mistake, they were implacable enemies - got hold of this supposed scandal, they ran with it, hard. Supposedly, Craig, and, by implication, somehow, Hillary, had kept these staff lists to violate the privacy of the individuals. How it violated their privacy to have their names and **public** service jobs printed on a list, I do not know.

The worst of it came when the top brass of the United States Secret Service went up to the Hill to testify before the powerful and evil men running the investigations. I was watching the hearing and couldn't believe my eyes. These senior officers testified that, without question, they always provided up to date and accurate staff lists to the White House.

I called Marc into my office - "Come watch this, you won't believe it."

We sat in stunned silence, staring at the television.

"What do you think?" I said. "There are only a couple of possible explanations for what we just saw. Either they're lying, and know they're lying, to appease the people who provide their appropriation. Or, they're incompetent, and don't even know they're lying. Or, the people who should have found the truth and reported it didn't tell them, and they don't know they're lying. I don't know which is worse. What a mess. Hey, the way to disprove this junk would be to show them that old list - do you have a copy somewhere? Please tell me you kept a copy somewhere!"

He looked at me, shook his head. "Who saves a bad list? I tossed it when we saw we couldn't use it. Damn."

***

In July, the Crown Prince of Nepal came by, after graduating from one of our fine, ivy-league universities. He was surprisingly dim and dull, not like any of the other random royals I'd met. Not really interested in the House, or the history, he almost appeared to be drugged. Five years later he went on a murderous rampage in the Royal Palace in Kathmandu, killing his entire family and himself. I shivered when I heard the news, remembering how strange he'd been.

***

This was the year all of us in the leading edge of the Baby Boomer generation turned fifty, the President in August, then me in September. I was looking forward to it - I figured the President would do something special, host a little get-together, have me come over for cake, a photo and a hug - something. In 1994, when I was in Nantucket for my birthday, Marc bought a cake and took it over to the Oval, where the President welcomed my staff for a photo with signs wishing me a Happy Birthday. The President was called away at the last minute, but I have a great photo of my staff, gathered around the Resolute desk. Surely, for this big number birthday, there'd be a celebration?

But I screwed up. I should have sent a note to the President's staff about it, but I just don't like self-promotion. Since someone always reminded him of my birthday, I figured they'd notice the number. Nope.

I put on my favorite dress and nice jewelry, had my hair done, and worked in the office expecting my surprise. Late in the afternoon Marc and Ann McCoy (now my Deputy Director) and the staff came in with a cake and sang Happy Birthday. I smiled and looked pleased, but I kept thinking, and finally blurted out, "Is that it? You didn't even invite any of my friends here to come over for a few minutes for my fiftieth birthday? Not even Robyn? For my fiftieth birthday? You didn't tell the President?"

They looked surprised, mumbled "Um, no, we didn't think to do that."

When they left, I called Robyn, now upstairs in the Social Office, almost weeping: "Did no one even tell you today's my fiftieth birthday? No one called you?"

"Oh, Melinda, I am so sorry! You know I would've come if I'd known. I just lost track of the date and no one called. You must be so disappointed!"

Well, yes, I was disappointed, and hurt, and then I got mad. *I've just learned an important lesson. I foolishly allowed myself to think of the people I work with as "friends." They're not "friends." They are professional colleagues who don't care about my life outside the office, so I better stop caring about theirs. Be a **boss**, not a friend. And let them know not to expect me to be the same as I was. Next time I won't be hurt by their thoughtlessness, because I won't expect any better.*

For a couple of days I stomped around the office, like a total bitch. I mean, it was my FIFTIETH BIRTHDAY. It's never gonna happen again. I was brusque, cold and demanding. Actually, I behaved the way **male** bosses behave all the time, and no one says a thing. But it was so different from the collegial, happy mood I worked to create in the office that people were shocked and didn't know how to respond.

After a few days, Marc and Ann came and stood in front of my desk.

"What?" I snapped.

"Melinda, we're truly sorry to have disappointed you about your birthday, but we've come to ask you to please stop being so awful to everyone. You are making it difficult for all of us to work for you, and really, we all work for the President here, not for ourselves. Please get over being mad. This is a great office, and you're a wonderful boss, and we need you back the way you were. Can you please do that?"

"I'll think about it," I snarled.

I knew they were right, and I had to change my behavior, but it was hard. And it got harder at the end of the next week when the President hosted a nice get-together in the Blue Room to celebrate ROBYN"S fiftieth birthday. Ouch! But I smiled and celebrated with her - why should my unhappiness spoil her happiness?

CHAPTER NINETEEN ~

EVEN PRESIDENTS HAVE TROUBLE LETTING GO

During the transition of 1992-93 the press was in a frenzy to cover every aspect of the new First Family. Although Chelsea grew up in the Governor's mansion, ("public housing") the Clintons always managed to protect her from the glare of public life, and the press in Arkansas had cooperated. After all, she was just a little girl, not a public person. Going into the transition, the national press was generally cooperative too, with a couple of major exceptions. The *LA Times* printed a hideous cartoon depicting Chelsea as an ugly teenager with bad hair, braces and a big nose. What were they thinking? She was a CHILD. Is there a parent anywhere who wouldn't have been furious?

Then Rush Limbaugh started referring to Chelsea as the "First Dog." What else could you possibly need to know about the despicable Mr. Limbaugh?

It reminds me of the old joke, "What's the difference between Rush Limbaugh and the Hindenberg? One is a disastrous Nazi gas bag, the other was a German air ship ..." Even some Republicans were dismayed. Friends and White House staff were furious.

Once they got to the White House, the Clintons made sure everyone knew Chelsea's life was off limits, and the press, perhaps embarrassed by the earlier lapses, cooperated. Of course, it helped that, unlike the Bush twins who followed her, Chelsea led a model life – smart, studious, well behaved, respectful, down to earth, and charming. There are no photos of Chelsea engaged in underage drinking, or smoking, or bar hopping, or sticking her tongue out at the press. The Clintons had done a great job raising a terrific kid. Hey - maybe it does take a village.

At Sidwell Friends, the Quaker school Chelsea attended, privacy was a personal as well as security concern, as I learned from an impeccable source. In the spring of 1993, I attended a luncheon and was seated next to Celeste Helms, wife of Richard Helms, who had been Director of the CIA for Presidents Nixon and Johnson.

"I'm very impressed with the new President," she said. "I first met him years ago at a reception and we chatted briefly. Then we were recently invited to the White House, and I couldn't believe it - in the receiving line he not only remembered me, he told me about a book he had read he thought I'd be interested in because of our conversation years ago. He has an incredible memory - not to mention the charm. It must be exciting to work for him."

Oh, yeah. When you think of the thousands and thousands of people he met over the years, his ability to focus on each one and truly remember was astonishing.

Mrs. Helms also told me her grandson was in Chelsea's class at Sidwell Friends. She was talking to him after school one day, in a general, grandmotherly way, and asked about his famous classmate.

"How is Chelsea doing? Does she seem to like the school? Does she have friends?"

"Grandma," her grandson, all of fourteen, solemnly replied, "Chelsea is a private person and we do not discuss her! Now, may I please have some milk and cookies?"

We both laughed, and I couldn't wait to tell the President and Hillary. When I returned to the White House I walked over to the Oval to see if he was free for a moment. Betty and I peered through the peep-hole in the door and he wasn't in a conversation or on the phone. She knocked, opened the door, and he looked up from his desk.

"Mr. President, do you have a moment for a sweet story?" I asked.

"Sure," he replied, and got up from the desk to stretch. "What's up?"

I told him about the luncheon and Mrs. Helms remarks about him. He nodded and smiled. Then I told him about her conversation with her very protective grandson, and he started to laugh.

"Has Hillary heard this story yet?"

"No, sir, I just got back from the event."

"Oh, I can't wait to tell her. It's just wonderful. Bless their hearts."

As Chelsea ended her junior year, she began to think about college, and made repeated trips to different schools around the country. People talked about her choices and this new stage in her family's life. Both the President and Hillary spoke and wrote about the upcoming transition they were dreading. It was a difficult time for them. The three of them were very close – much closer than many parents are with their teenagers.

The Clintons always worked hard to arrange their schedules around Chelsea. They often spent hours greeting guests at receptions on the State Floor (after exhausting days of work) before slipping upstairs to the Residence to have a quiet family dinner. After dinner Chelsea was likely to bring her math homework to her dad for help. They spent every precious moment together they could.

So, in 1996, the President and Hillary knew their baby girl was really growing up and would soon be leaving the White House for college. This "letting-go" period is difficult for all parents, but would be so much harder for them. The White House is a kind of cocoon, because it's often the only place the First Family can truly relax and be themselves. Some first families, like the Clintons, grow closer in that cocoon, and some are driven apart.

The Reagans, for example, had a very hard time with some of their children, who really hated the White House and their father's position. They openly took policies that challenged his, and it was hurtful to him and Mrs. Reagan. Thank goodness they had their deep love for each other, from which they both drew strength.

And, of course, the world is a far more dangerous place for a President's daughter than for her less famous friends, even with Secret Service protection. Imagine having to worry about random lunatics stalking your child. Also, for good or ill her parents' lives would continue to be front page news, and she wouldn't be at home to hear them discuss the issues first.

Aside from these uniquely Presidential issues, the most difficult thing for all parents is the hollow feeling you get when thinking about how much you love them, and how desperately you will miss them. You wonder, "Did I teach her everything I meant to, everything she needs to know to face the world?"

And, no matter how great you were as a parent, the answer is always "No! I'm not done yet! There was so much more I meant to do/teach/show them!"

I know this from my own experience when my older son, Shiloh, joined the Army Reserves. All his life we planned for him to go off to college at the right time. I've been to college myself, so I was mentally and emotionally ready for that transition. We were certainly proud, but his desire to join the Reserves took us by surprise. A week after he graduated from high school, at 5:00 in the morning, the recruiter came to take my baby off to boot camp - where I just knew they would be mean to him. I hadn't spent years preparing myself for it and was devastated. This one thought, "But I'm not finished yet! There is still so much I wanted to teach him!" haunted me.

I cried my eyes out the first day he was gone, and it took quite a while to get used to not having him at home – or just someplace I could easily reach him. Even understanding his pride and excitement at this new phase of his life didn't make it any easier to bear my heartache and loneliness. But, over time you adjust and encourage them in their independence, which is pretty much the whole point of raising them, isn't it?

As they struggled with their sadness at their only child's impending departure, the President and Hillary also tried hard to share her joy at this important life change. Chelsea was a very good student and had her pick of colleges. Her father strongly suggested his alma mater, Georgetown, not only because he loved it so, but because it would keep her close to them. Anyone who has ever been on the receiving end of a Bill Clinton "sell" knows you come away thinking it was the smartest thing you ever heard, and you'd be honored to go along with whatever he proposed.

He'd never try to talk Chelsea into a decision she didn't want, but still, he was completely invested in her choice. Hillary tried to be more hands-off, letting Chelsea find her own way, but it was tough. No parent is ever really ready for this stage in his child's life.

I'm not revealing any secrets here. They both wrote and talked about this transition and what it meant to all of them.

So I knew the President was dealing with his sadness about her looming departure when I saw him one day at Betty's desk outside the Oval. I meant to be comforting when I said,

"Mr. President, I know you're sad about Chelsea going away, but it's very important that she do this, and you all will survive it. I know from experience."

He gave me a thoughtful look and said, "Well, I've been thinking about it and I finally figured out what we will do and I'm going to tell her tonight."

I was a little surprised and truly puzzled. "Really, what are you planning?"

"I've decided she can go anywhere she wants - but we're going with her!"

Gosh, I didn't see that coming. I laughed, then blurted out, "You know, Mr. President, the way this works is, no matter how much they love you, they don't want you to go to college with them!"

He did his Presidential thing – stuck his jaw out and narrowed his eyes, looking down at me - the look he gets when anyone tries to tell him "no." The only things missing were his finger wagging in my face, the raised voice and red face we saw when he was truly angry.

"I don't care" he said, through clenched teeth. "I'm the President of the United States and I can go anywhere I want!"

I had to stifle another laugh and said, "OK, well, Mr. President, let me know how it works out for you! And, of course, if you go, we'll come right along to make sure you have everything you need."

He laughed too, but I don't think he was completely kidding. Even if he wasn't, I was pretty sure Hillary would talk him out of it. And, to be sure, if that was what he really wanted to do, all of us on staff would have followed him anywhere necessary to support him. I just couldn't imagine a California White House going over very well with the Congress or the public.

In the end, Chelsea chose to go as far away as she could in the continental U.S. – she chose Stanford, and they did not follow along – although they did take a lot of trips to California in the following four years.

CHAPTER TWENTY ~ THE PRESIDENT IS RE-ELECTED

In August 1996, I worked on my first political convention. What a great experience! I had attended a couple of events at the New York convention in 1992, but as a guest. And of course I had watched conventions of both parties since I was old enough to barely understand. My father, Oscar Naumann, was the Washington Bureau Chief of the *New York Journal of Commerce* for most of my life. I ingested a love of news with my daily cereal. Politics and civic responsibility were part of every dinner table conversation. My father's family has deep (VERY deep) Republican roots. My great-great-grandfather, Louis Naumann, ran for coroner of New York in 1860 and 1864, on the same ticket as Abraham Lincoln. I have his silver badge, and two of the campaign announcements, hanging on my wall in Baja. My grandmother was Josephine Ridder, of the Ridder newspapers, later Knight-Ridder, now, sadly, all dissolved. But it's a tradition I'm proud of.

Through most of my life my father, a wonderful, but very serious man, viewed my lifelong fascination with events as frivolous. He knew I was smart, he sent me to Georgetown, and then all I seemed to want to do was host parties or run celebrations as a career. He just didn't get it. And when my lifetime of experience with events and customer service paid off with a fabulous job at the White House, of all places, well, he was stunned. Proud, but stunned. My mother, from whom I got my love of festivities, always understood how important they are to public as well as private lives.

Once I got to the White House, there were many, many qualities I inherited from them that combined to make me successful at my work. Her imagination, creativity, love of beauty and warmth. His responsibility, dedication, and interest in mastering new, difficult things. What great gifts they gave to me, my sister and brother, and our children.

My mother had a stroke in October 1994 and lingered four long, difficult years. My father passed away on December 17, 1994. Yes, it was a very hard time and I'll never forget Hillary's thoughtful notes and the President's phone calls that were so comforting.

I loved my parents deeply and think of them often. I believe in Heaven, so I think they watch and cheer us on. The Bible tells me so.

***

Throughout the summer the President traveled non-stop, and the campaign seemed to be going well. I enjoyed watching it all, just like everyone else, on television. But then the word went out, some staff would get to attend the convention - under strict rules. First, we had to take vacation time to go and work there. The American people don't pay the salaries of White House staff to participate in partisan political events. And, second, many of us had to pay our own way for travel and accommodations. The DNC never had the financial resources of the fat-cat Republicans. Oh well.

I was happy to go under these conditions. Heck, I probably would have paid them for the privilege of participating! It was an incredible experience.

A friend arranged a bed for me with a woman who lived just a block off Lake Michigan. It was my first trip to Chicago, and I knew the minute I set foot in the campaign office I'd be sucked into a never-ending maelstrom of twenty-hour days. I didn't mind. I was used to it. But I did want to take just a couple of hours to see the city first, so I called in to say, "Hey, I'm here, and I'll be in the office later today."

"Oh, great, but we really need you right away! Can't you come in now?"

"No, sorry, I'm going to take a double-decker bus tour of Chicago first, so I get to see something while we're here. As soon as it's over, I'll be there, and then I'm all yours."

I'm so glad I did it. Those two hours were the ONLY time in five days I saw anything at all of this great American city. Chicago was fabulous! The city shone, all decked out in flowers and new trees for our enjoyment. My big regret was not being able to walk along Michigan Avenue, *the Miracle Mile*, and SHOP. I left for work so early, and returned, exhausted, so late, I never set foot in a single store. But I did see the city from my cab every morning, and loved it.

I told my colleagues, "If you see a headline saying, 'Presidential aide found floating in canal ...' and it's me, it most likely wasn't foul play. It was just me being so fascinated by the architecture that I went around looking up all the time, pointing and mumbling, 'will you look at THAT' and simply fell over a guardrail!"

My assignment was the usual: Clinton friends and family. A good fit for me. I knew most of those people now, and they were happy to see me too. The closest Georgetown friends came, the President and Hillary's families and friends, political friends and supporters ... it was like a great reunion at a series of fantastic venues.

We kept careful lists and distributed exclusive invitations to swell events all over the city. That meant a few times I got to go out too, enjoying Chicago's great restaurants and elegant private homes. But the most precious ticket was a credential to view the convention from the President's box. You're nobody at a convention if you don't have the right credentials hanging around your neck. We had to issue these in shifts to take care of everyone. Some nights I was there myself, both to work and to witness this important part of American history. It was exhilarating.

The final night, when the President spoke, his inspiring words made me even more proud to be part of his administration. Some of us actually appreciate "brilliant and engaged" in our leaders. Oh, and, I loved the balloon and confetti drop.

***

Back in Washington, work resumed at an even more hectic pace, but we were all optimistic. Senator Dole ran a dismal campaign. And, let's face it, the time for his generation of leadership had passed.

Once again I got to volunteer my vacation time and pay for my own travel, this time to Little Rock for the election night celebrations. Once again my assignment was Presidential friends and family - and let's face it, Little Rock was FULL of friends and family.

The most exclusive event was the party at the *Excelsior Hotel* to follow the election night speeches. Everyone wanted in, but there wasn't room for them all. So once again we had a tightly controlled guest list.

I was staffing the check-in desk at the afternoon reception when a man from Little Rock, whose name was not on my lists, brushed past me to enter the event. No harm there, the restrictions were all for that night. But I knew he wouldn't be able to get into the after-party without the credentials we controlled. I could have let it go and let him deal with his problem himself, but that's not like me. Remember, I LOVE customer service.

I went to considerable trouble to get an additional credential, and then walked around the crowded ballroom looking for him. When I found him, I tapped him on the shoulder and said, with a smile, "Hello, again. You're going to need this credential for tonight's party, and I'm happy to have gotten one for you."

Wouldn't you think the response to that would be gratitude? Nope.

He snatched the badge from my hand, looked down his nose and sneered at me. In a deep Arkansas twang he asked, "Where are you from? I can tell you're not from around here, are you?"

"Why, no, I'm not," I smiled again. "I'm from Washington DC. Happy to be in your city."

"Well, how long have you known the President?" he demanded.

"Let's see ... since 1964 when we were both freshmen at Georgetown. That's a while, isn't it? And, how long have YOU known the President?"

His face fell. Only Arkansans were supposed to be such long time friends of Bill Clinton. Some of them apparently thought he got to be President just with Arkansas help and support. I'd run into this before, a time or two, and tried not to let it bother me.

"Uh, oh, I guess since the 1980s" he muttered, knowing he was trumped.

"Wonderful! And, isn't he just the best friend?" It was my turn to look smug, and I did.

1996
Presidential Election Night

OLD STATE HOUSE
LITTLE ROCK, ARKANSAS
NOVEMBER 5, 1996

HONORED GUEST
LAWN ACCESS

Paid for by Clinton/Gore '96 General Election Committee

№ 2875

That night our careful plans for VIP access to the lawn in front of the Old State House were all for naught. The crowd was huge and ecstatic. Too huge and ecstatic for the Secret Service and State Troopers to control. They overran our area, despite our pleas to security to "maintain the perimeter," we had all agreed on. No luck. Those guys all knew it wouldn't take much to turn a crowd of happy supporters into an angry mob. No thanks. We shrugged our shoulders and gave up, determined to enjoy the historic moment ourselves.

You've heard the phrase, "delirious with joy." That about sums it up. Another four years! America approved of the job the President was doing, even after we failed with health care and lost the '94 Congressional elections.

Sometimes, when you're working your ass off, day after day and month after month, you lose touch with the big picture. At least I do. I focus in on the tasks at hand and forget all about the larger goals ahead. But at the White House, as hard as the work may be, the things you do make a difference in people's lives, and it's about the most exciting thing I can imagine. I got used to "doing good," and, to my surprise, found it addicting. I was part of a team that was changing our country and the world. Even my small part was damn exciting. Now we had another four years to keep working.

***

Back at the White House, we'd all been told it's common for Presidents to change their staffs after re-election. Maybe we'd all go, maybe some would stay, nobody knew. My people were anxious

- hell, I was anxious - wondering if they'd have jobs after the inauguration. I went to see my boss, Jodie Torkelson, and she didn't seem to know, but she warned me, no job was secure. Allrighty!

I knew the President might want to give my job to some other supporter who deserved a chance with a great White House position. I'm sure their advisors reviewed every job and urged him to make those changes. And I knew I had enemies in the House, who wanted me gone for their own reasons. Maybe so they could put a friend into the Visitors Office. Or maybe they just didn't like me, or were jealous of my long friendship with POTUS. But they didn't know how loyal Bill and Hillary Clinton are to their friends, and those who work tirelessly to advance the agenda. They were pleased with my work and my team. In fact, not once in eight years did anyone from either of their offices suggest a change to my staff. They let me do the job I needed to do, with the people I choose to help me. They were generous with their thanks, and I loved them for it.

In one of life's little ironies, I and my entire team stayed, while Jodie, who had often made my life miserable, lost her job. The story I heard said Erskine Bowles, at the time the Deputy Chief of Staff, had asked Jodie to assign him a car. A government car and driver. You know, to pick him up in the morning and take him home at night. Now, Erskine is a very rich man who could easily afford to hire his own car and driver, but it wouldn't be the same. He wanted the White House car with the Army driver. It's a status thing.

Jodie, in her infinite wisdom, wouldn't let him have it. Apparently, Erskine was annoyed. And then, whadda ya know, in December '96, Erskine became Chief of Staff to the President. Oops! I guess he remembered about the car, 'cause Jodie left soon after. At least, that's the story I heard.

I used to tell this little tale to my younger staff members, as an example.

"See, you should always be courteous and helpful to everyone around you, from the highest level to the lowest. I hope you'd do it because it's the right thing to do, but if that doesn't motivate you, just remember, you never know when the person at the bottom may end up at the top, and in a position to help you or make your life miserable."

Chapter Twenty One ~ 1997 ~ We Begin Again

It's hard to say whether the President's second Inauguration was more exciting than his first. In 1993 I was giddy with amazement and a kind of disbelief that a man I'd known so long, and counted as a friend, was now going to be the most important person in the world. In 1997, we were used to his being President, and used to being part of the whirlwind of the Clinton White House. His re-election was a vindication by the people, in the face of relentless attacks by political enemies who never accepted his election in the first place and were determined to un-do it by endless "investigations" and hearings.

We watched the reviewing stands go up on Pennsylvania Avenue with joy and excitement. Four more years. Four more years to work on their agendas for America, agendas I believed in heart and soul and was honored to be part of. And, I was thrilled I'd get to stay in my swell job, the most amazing thing I'd ever done. We still had work to do in the Visitors Office to improve our systems and continue to run fabulous events.

And, I'll confess, I had a petty reason for being happy. I thought about all those stupid bureaucrats who had stalled and blocked us, assuming (hoping!) we'd soon be gone. What a rude shock for them - another four years of Clintonites! Now they'd have to cooperate, wouldn't they?

Well, sorta.

In a bureaucrat's life, our four years was just a blip to sleep through. If they didn't like our ideas, they'd just continue stonewalling until we gave up. I think they really didn't understand we weren't interested in giving up. We were there to make a difference, and they could get on board or get out of the way. It did make us weary, but I knew we'd only have this one chance, so forget being tired and get busy about the people's business!

***

The year rolled along without major issues for the Visitors Office. The Egg Roll, high demand for tours, working around the Clintons' frantic schedules - all familiar challenges. I did have some unusual fun at this year's July 4 celebration. Our job was to invite and then admit hundreds of White House staff and press, and their families and guests. Sometimes as many as 14,000 altogether, spread out their blankets on the soft, green grass of the South Lawn, enjoying sodas, ice cream, Presidential re-enactors and bands.

"Mr. Jefferson, sir, it's an honor to meet you. Thank you for coming up from Monticello to visit the White House once more ..." I LOVED those guys.

Once the gates closed, I ran inside to make sure the President was on his way down from the Residence. He always made remarks to the crowds from the Blue Room porch. But he wasn't in the Blue Room, or in the Ushers Office. I looked at my watch. The spectacular Washington fireworks start at 9:10 p.m., and it was now 9:00. Where was he?

I went to the phone in the Ushers' office and called upstairs. "Mr. President, we're all hoping you'll come down and speak to the guests on the Lawn, but time is getting tight here. Will you come now?"

"Yes, yes, I'm coming, just give me a minute." He sounded distracted, but hey, he's the President - who knows what issues he's dealing with today.

I went back to the Blue Room to wait. At least it was nice and cool in there, as opposed to the staggering heat and humidity of the July night out on the Lawn. My friend, Howard, calls this our "annual humidity festival." Another couple of minutes ticked away. I fiddled with the flowers on the center table.

Where does Nancy get these huge chrysanthemums. They're gorgeous ... Gosh, it's getting so late. Should I call him again? He hates to be nagged ...

I heard the elevator ding, and thought *thank God, he's just made it. Time to cue the sound guys.*

The President, in khakis and an open-neck sport shirt, came running into the room, holding a long, narrow strip of paper in his hands, and looking really jazzed about something.

"Melinda, come take a look at this! It's incredible!" He held out the strip of paper, which turned out to be a series of slender photographs, in color.

I'm thinking, *what the heck, you're really late and if you want to talk you better get out there - now.*

"These photos are from Mars! The Mars lander sent them back just a little while ago, and now we're the first people to see them - it's incredible."

It took me a minute to register what I was seeing, photographs of a red and yellow desert landscape, and the little feet of the lander. *Mars? These photos came from MARS? Holy cow.*

The President grinned, took the strip of photos and ran out to the microphone, where he greeted all the guests and waved it in the air as he announced what he had. I heard a big roar of excitement and shivered. A chilling phrase took root in my head: *Open the pod bay door, Hal ...*

The next day those photos were on the front cover of every news magazine and newspaper in the world. But I had seen them first. From Mars to NASA. From NASA to the White House Science Advisor. From the Science Advisor to the President of the United States. And, from the President to ... me! When people ask me what was my most memorable experience – THIS!

***

In October, the President of China came for a State Visit that presented new challenges. There's room for 130 people at round tables in the State Dining Room, no more. This was plenty of room for the Bush II events, as they were not as eager to share the House with guests. But it was never enough for the Clintons' guest lists (or later the Obamas). You can squeeze in a few more tables if you move dinner to the East Room, but this presents its own difficulties, as it's harder for the kitchen to deliver the food hot, and, where can you stage the after-dinner entertainment?

The Chinese dinner was clearly going to be a big draw, so the Social Office had to find a different solution. They decided on a tent, to be set up under the trees on a flat bit of the south lawn, near the fountain. Everyone thought this was a great solution, until the nice people in the Protocol Office at State advised us we had a little problem: to the Chinese, a "tent" is a structure associated with a disaster. As in, "Tents were provided to the villagers after the floods destroyed their homes."

It was unthinkable that the President of the United States would welcome the Chinese Premier in a "tent." But still, it was the only way we'd have enough room. The solution nicely finessed the issue. The same structure was set up, but we were all instructed to call it a pavilion." Yes, a "pavilion" is a happy, celebratory place appropriate for this high-level dinner. The word "tent" was banished from our speech, and diplomacy saved the day.

***

My celebrity list grew as Roger Moore, the original 007, and Andy Garcia visited. Gorgeous men. But my favorite visitor ever was Tom Selleck, who came with his wife and adorable daughter in 1998. "I'm happy to welcome you and walk you around today. But, I know you've done lots of events for Republican presidents, so, haven't you already seen everything here?"

"No, actually, I haven't. When I came here those other times I waited in a holding room until they called me out to speak, and when the event ended I left. So, I don't know the White House at all."

I was shocked at this lack of hospitality, but grateful, as it gave me an excuse to spend the entire afternoon walking the

Sellecks around. He is the handsomest man on the planet. I swear. I went weak in the knees when he smiled. And one of the nicest. We went all over the House and had a great time. All the Secret Service officers we passed asked for a photo with him, which is unusual. They've seen everybody. And, did I mention, he's THE HANDSOMEST MAN ON THE PLANET? (My boyfriend got very tired of hearing this.)

The next day he sent me two dozen white roses, with a nice card. When they died, I hung them in my kitchen to dry and kept them a long time. What a great guy!

Then Tracy Ullman's assistant called. I'm a big fan, but I told her Tracy could only visit if she promised not to show up as the sexist Pakistani cab driver, Queen Elizabeth, or the repressed bank teller. She laughed and agreed, so I welcomed a surprisingly normal looking comedienne and her sweet and well-behaved daughter. I love the British!

***

You may think since I met all the most interesting people in the world at my job, at some point I'd meet a smart, attractive man who'd be interested in me. Nope. Never happened. What a disappointment. At this point, I'd been divorced for years, and was desperately lonely. I spent a lot of Saturday nights at home, organizing the Tupperware (literally) and watching C-Span. I had a social life, because of invitations to many of Washington's nicest events, but I always went alone, and went home alone.

After a year of this, my internal clock said, *Enough! No more organizing! I've worked on myself and my "nest" enough. Now it's time to venture out into the world all alone and find out who I am and what I want in life.*

OK, fine, but what should I do with my time? How about French classes? I love speaking French, and you never know when it could be useful ... Or art? I'm creative, but I'm not an artist, maybe I could learn ...

This went on for a few weeks, and then one day I saw a letter to the editor of the Washington Post, about dances at *Glen Echo Park*. I'd been there as a child, when it was an amusement park, but didn't remember a dance hall. *Maybe I should go check that out.*

I was afraid to go by myself on a Saturday night, but there was a waltz afternoon on Sunday, so I put on a dress and heels, and drove myself to Maryland.

Glen Echo Ballroom is a large, beautiful dance hall dating back to the 1940s, with the best wood dance floor on the East coast. I immediately fell in love with its genteel shabbiness. I couldn't believe I'd never heard of it before. From the sidelines I watched a couple give a beginner class in waltz, too nervous to join in. A man came over and asked me to dance.

"Thank you, but I don't know how."

"That's alright. I'll teach you."

I reluctantly gave him my hand and stepped into his arms as he counted for me, "One, two, three, one, two, three ..."

Off we went, slowly twirling around the floor, first to recorded music, then to the sounds of a string ensemble. I made lots of mistakes, but he was patient, and I was persistent. By the end of the afternoon, I was hooked. I picked up brochures listing class schedules, and went home, thinking, *I LOVE this. It's such fun to move to the music, and to be held in a man's arms, even if it is a stranger, and only for a few minutes ... and, it's so different from anything I do in the rest of my life. Guess I know what I'm gonna do with my spare time now ...*

This was the beginning of my love affair with dancing.

***

For Christmas, Hillary chose the theme, *the Twelve Days of Christmas*. Artists and craftspeople from around the country made gorgeous ornaments of lords leaping, partridges and pear trees. The first event of December was always a reception for the press, to unveil the decorations. I was standing in the Blue Room, admiring the eighteen-foot tree and the glass, metal, paper, wood and fabric ornaments that were really tiny sculptures.

My eye paused at an opening in the branches, and I thought, *Surely I'm not seeing what I think I see?*

I reached in and gently lifted out a piece made of what looked like five gold-wrapped condoms. *Five golden rings? No!* And next to it, a hypodermic needle with a message about drug abuse. Charming. Who had hung these? Was it deliberate, to embarrass the Clintons? Or an oversight by exhausted decorators? The Ushers supervise all the decorating ...

I took the two "ornaments" and marched to the Ushers' Office, laying them on Gary's desk. "I think the First Lady would be shocked to see these on the White House Christmas tree. Please put them away - or throw them away - so no one, especially the press who are entering as we speak - can see them."

Every State Visit begins with an Arrival Ceremony on the South Lawn, weather permitting, and they are splendid.

CHAPTER TWENTY TWO ~

1998 ~ THE TROUBLES BEGIN

In January 1998, I had dental problems I'd put off for too long. Four - count 'em, four! - wisdom teeth were pulled. I don't remember much about it, until waking up in my own bed, seriously drugged out and feeling no pain. I was so zoned out the television was on, the program I woke to was HOCKEY, the remote was lying next to me on the bed, and I could not move my hand two inches to pick it up and change the channel. (I am not a hockey fan.) All I could do was fall back onto the pillows and slip gratefully back into oblivion as quickly as possible.

An hour or so later I awoke again, this time to a news report, saying the "independent" counsel, Mr. Kenneth Starr, was accusing the President of an inappropriate sexual relationship with an "intern," Monica Lewinsky. My fogged-out brain considered this for a moment, and groggily decided, *I must be hallucinating. Man, those are some STRONG pain-killers.* I gave myself up again to a virtual coma.

Another hour passed, unconscious, but when I awoke for the third time to the sound of the television, I heard the same news report. My head cleared a little. I peeled one eye open and squinted at the screen, barely able to take in the news in a semi-rational state. I blinked, hard, tried to shake my head, immediately regretted it, settled back, and made myself listen.

I heard the report. I heard the detested Mr. Starr's name. He was well known all over the White House, both for the inexcusable and illegal leaks from his investigation, appearing daily on the front page of the Post, and for the steady march of his subpoenas. They landed on the desk of every Director with relentless, and depressing regularity. At least once a week I opened a tan inter-office envelope to find a memo from my boss, the Assistant to the President for Management and Administration. The Independent Counsel, Mr. Starr, or Senator (ack ack!) Alphonse D'Amato, or some other Republican slimeball, requested documents related to issue XYZ.

The law required us to drop everything important we were doing (you know, to make people's lives better!) to search our records to find anything mentioning whatever he was searching for, make copies of it/them, and send them back to my boss, who would review them and send them to WH Counsel, who would review them and send them to Mr. Starr.

I don't know what documents any other office found, but time after time the Visitors Office found absolutely nothing - after spending hours looking. And, of course, they were only partly hoping to find something they could use against us. The other (fun - for them) part of the equation was tying us up in knots so we couldn't do our REAL work. God knows, we detested them all.

So just hearing Mr. Starr's name was like fingernails on a blackboard. He'd been hounding the President and Hillary for years now, spending millions of your tax dollars to investigate non-existent "crimes" and "scandals." But the truth, hobbled and gagged as it was, kept trying to break through, and nothing he accused them of had traction.

I hope you realize the major "scandal" he pursued, Whitewater, was no more than a failed land deal in which the Clintons LOST money, years before he ran for President. There never was any wrongdoing, and Starr knew it after simple preliminary inquiries. Everything else - EVERYTHING - was political. And, in fact, it still goes on, supported by your lazy-ass mainstream press who love nothing better than to regularly trot out the "Clinton scandals." Getting them to say what exactly those were is a fool's errand.

But now this accusation about Monica was a whole different thing. My stomach lurched. *Maybe it's the meds again? No, it's the NEWS.* I was startled and appalled, but only for a minute. Because that's exactly how long it took my brain to say, *Wait! If THIS is where Starr's going, it means he hasn't gotten any other damn thing to stick. He's got nothing from all his efforts. He's doing this out of desperation. He's got to produce something for his Republican masters, who hate the Clintons and have spent years trying to destroy his Presidency. And, he's got to somehow justify all those millions of dollars spent pursuing them. So now he's going here. Good God.*

And then it took only about one more minute to think, *Well, if I could figure this out, I bet it will take the American people only just as long to figure it out as well. They'll know he's got nothing else. They'll know how despicable he and his "investigation" are, and they'll hate him for it.*

Holding tight to that thought, I gave in to the drugs again, fell back on the pillow, and passed out.

***

It's technically true that Monica was an intern, but it depends on the meaning of "was." She was an intern in 1995, when she met the President. Later she was hired in the office of Congressional Correspondence, so she was on staff. Lots of offices had interns. There were always one or two assigned to the Visitors Office, and we needed and valued their help. There are never enough hands for the tasks at the White House. Our interns did the scut work (answering phones, filing) that makes any office work. But they also got to help us with President and First Lady events and to be up close with the day's celebrity visitors, who were always graciously willing to pause for a photo. They were even happy to go for coffee, because it gave them a chance to walk over to the West Wing and maybe see the President on his way to the Oval.

Socks the cat spent a lot of time in our suite, because he liked the down-filled cushion on the love seat in my office, and he liked to be off his halter to roam around and graciously allow us all to dote on him. The interns all loved him and thought it was fun to take a photo with the Presidential pet. One young man got so excited to play with Socks he forgot he was allergic to cats! Hello! Marc noticed he was turning red and his head had blown up to the size of a large melon.

"John - are you OK?"

John looked up from tickling Socks' tummy. "Oh, um, I just remembered I'm **allergic to cats** and shouldn't be around one, much less play with one ... "

Marc dragged him to his car and made a quick drive to the George Washington Hospital emergency room.

***

So in 1995 Monica was part of the intern program, working in Congressional Affairs, just down the hall from us in the East Wing. I didn't know her in 1996, when she met the President. Newt Gingrich had forced a budget showdown with the President, and the government shut down. You remember, all those Republicans told the American public government was their enemy, so shutting it down should have been no big deal - right?

Well, it turns out people wanting or needing to travel found it useful to have a passport, which they now couldn't get. People receiving government checks found them pretty useful too and got kind of unhappy when they stopped coming. Museums and public monuments, including the White House, shut down for tours, and that upset quite a few people. Turns out, government does a lot of things people rather like, or need, and shutting it down was a big mistake Newt made. Big mistake.

But, in the meantime, everyone in the Visitors Office, including me, and almost all the rest of the White House staff were sent home. Only "essential" staff were supposed to work, a very small group over in the West Wing. But interns, being unpaid, weren't "staff" so they could come in and work, and most of them did. Monica was asked to deliver a pizza to the President, in the Oval Office and this is how they met. I never did understand it. I mean, it's not as if the Navy Mess Stewards who took care of the President weren't at work. They would've been happy to MAKE a pizza for the President ... I guess someone thought it would be a nice change for him.

And, unfortunately, it was. She was a pretty girl, with shiny black hair, lively eyes, fair skin, a much nicer wardrobe than most interns, and a very flirtatious attitude. Apparently the President noticed her right away (hell, I read she flipped up her skirt to show him her thong! What guy wouldn't have noticed that? And she referred to this as "flirting." Boy am I a geezer...) and began his appalling "relationship" with this woman.

But I didn't know anything about all this, either at the time, or in 1998 when the news broke. I only knew Monica was now on staff in Congressional Correspondence, in a tiny, two-room office right next door to the Visitors Office. She and another woman were responsible for dealing with letters from Members of Congress who wrote to the President, by routing them to the appropriate people to answer. I'd run into her in the hallway, or pass by their open door, and say "hello." She was attractive in a sleek, pampered kind of way that was very unlike other staff - even the young ones. She could have stepped from the pages of a *Glamour* photo shoot, with bright red lips and lots of mascara. Most people at the White House are too broke - or too sleep-deprived - to achieve that look.

What I didn't know about Monica, until Holly told me, was that everyone else in the White House knew she was stalking the President.

"She's infatuated! She makes up excuses to go over to the Oval Office, or show up at Presidential events, like bill signings, where she had no business being. I know I've seen her and wondered what the heck she was doing on the State Floor. She begs the other people in Congressional Affairs to give her any papers to be delivered to the West Wing, and then casually walks by the Oval Office. She chats with the officer by the door, so the President can hear her voice and invite her in... It's ridiculous! My gosh, WE all knew it - how could this happen?"

Behind the scenes some people were trying to deal with it. Nancy Hernreich, the classy and beautiful head of Oval Office Operations, had been with the President forever. She understood the problem. Evelyn Lieberman, the plain-spoken and talented woman who had been Hillary's Deputy Chief of Staff, then Deputy Press Secretary, and was now Deputy Chief of Staff to the President, was lobbying to move Monica out of the White House.

But by the time they transferred her to the Defense Department it was too late. And, she wouldn't stay gone! She was lovesick and miserable there, missing both the President and the excitement of working at the White House. She kept calling him, and dropping by or trying to drop by. You know, it's not actually possible to "drop by" anyone in the White House, especially the President. You have to be "cleared" by the Secret Service. You must provide your name and date of birth and Social Security number in advance. And then the USSS has a record of who visited. So, who cleared Monica in to see him? Who put through the phone calls? Betty Currie, his administrative assistant.

Betty is a kind and unflappable woman who in every other way was the perfect assistant. But this was like offering candy to a diabetic. It was very wrong. It was incomprehensible to me. I heard her say once the reason she did it was she was simply a career government employee, not an old Arkansas friend, and she didn't think it was her place to say "no" to the President of the United States.

Well, OK, you can understand that, but she didn't have to say "no" to him. She only had to tell Nancy Hernreich, who for damn sure would have said "no" to the President and would likely have told Hillary there was a problem. But, as the whole world knows, this never happened.

Or Evelyn. To give you an idea of just how plain-spoken Evelyn was, I wandered into her office one day when she was Deputy Press Secretary, just to say "hi." When I saw there were a dozen people in the room, I tried to quietly back out. Evelyn looked up, saw me and waved me in with a smile.

"Everybody!" she barked. "This is Melinda Bates, Director of the Visitors Office. Don't fuck with her!"

"Gosh, thanks, Evelyn. You can introduce me any time!" I never did know who those people were, but I bet they remember me!

I liked and respected Evelyn very much. You never had to guess what she was thinking (see above), and she was really smart. I was thrilled when she and Maria Echaverria were named the first women Deputy Chiefs of Staff to the President.

Her strengths were perfect for such a demanding job. In fact, she did her darnest to get the Monica problem under control, but she was too late.

And, look, obviously it's absurd to even say the President had this particular problem and the staff needed to help him control it. There's no getting around the fact that it was his problem, and he should have dealt with it. All I know is, the older I get, the less I expect people to be perfect. I love and respect Bill Clinton for his brilliance, his life of service, and his commitment to making people's lives better. Those things seem noble and important to me. If he had trouble with attraction to women besides Hillary, that's just sad - for him and for his family. But lots of people have problems they deal with and don't give in to.

I think Bill's failure was rooted in this fundamental belief from childhood: he's special. So special that if he occasionally does something wrong, he will surely be forgiven. So I guess he thought, *Oh, I'm working so hard, and I'm so tired, I can do this, and no one will know, it's just a little fun, I work so hard - don't I deserve a little fun?*

This is just my own, completely unprofessional psychological analysis, for which I have no training at all. So you can take it for what it's worth - but it does fit the man I know pretty well.

For any man, much less a man so smart (intellectually, anyway) to think he could keep this a secret in Washington is just crazy. You can't spend any time in Washington and not know: sooner or later EVERYTHING comes out. And how much more unlikely was it Monica would keep this secret? Duh! She was a lovesick girl with the emotional maturity of a twelve-year-old! She was having sex with the President of the United States - you think she wasn't going to talk about it?

And I should say here, to me what they did is certainly sex. Although, to my great discomfort, when the news came out there were a number of men I only knew professionally, who took the time to tell me they too didn't regard this as "sex." Just fooling around - which is exactly what Monica said to the odious Linda Tripp, and what the President meant when he said he " ... did not have sex with that woman, Ms. Lewinsky." So, at least they did tell the truth - as they saw it. I'm pretty sure that's a minority view, though.

Just to be fair, let's be sure we acknowledge there's NO way he was the first President to do this. The names of Roosevelt, Eisenhower, JFK, and Bush I all come to mind here. He was just, unfortunately, the first one to be caught, exposed and hounded by a rabid, lunatic prude of a special counsel, who probably thought this transgression between two consenting adults was WORSE than the crimes they accused the Clintons of (and they were ultimately cleared of.)

Not only did I not know any of this at the time of the accusations, I also was convinced the President was innocent, and these were simply more (and more disgusting) baseless charges brought by Mr. Starr. I agreed with Hillary. I couldn't believe it. For one thing, the Bill I knew in college had been serially monogamous. He wasn't a playboy. I thought since he'd been like that at college in the 1960s, when no one would have cared if he fooled around, then how could he possibly have been unfaithful in his marriage? How could he betray Hillary and all of us? It was outside my ability to imagine.

OK, of course I'd heard all the other accusations, but I didn't believe them - and it's not just that I had drunk the Kool Aid. Gennifer Flowers, for example, claimed he had met her for sex in a hotel that did not exist at the time. She also claimed he and Hillary had MURDERED people. Can you say, "credibility problem"? Eventually Bill admitted to one encounter with her, but at that point, her other accusations were so outlandish, who cared?

And one of the uglier rumors (put out by a disgruntled FBI agent!) said the President was slipping out of the White House at night, hidden in Bruce Lindsay's car, for assignations with women in a DC hotel. Bruce is an old and dear FOB, and was Counselor to the President. Know what kind of car he drove? No? No reason you should - except it was a MAZDA MIATA. I'd like to know where exactly a six foot, two inch man would have hidden in a Mazda Miata? But you never heard about that from the press, did you?

Even more important, I couldn't bring myself to believe he would put in jeopardy everything he and Hillary and all of us had worked our butts off to accomplish. This was really it for me. The sacrifices we made, the sacrifices our families made, the trust the public gave him, not once but twice. Surely, surely he was too smart, too decent and too principled to throw it all away for a little fun. Right? So, for most of 1998 I believed his assurances of innocence. I simply hated Mr. Starr even more - and I wouldn't have guessed this was possible.

In the Visitors Office we tried not to talk about it, but this was hard. I wouldn't discuss it with the staff, nor with my peers. The television was always on in my office, and the staff constantly monitored the news online at their desks. Everyone knew what was happening. If they talked among themselves, I didn't hear about it, as they knew I wouldn't (couldn't) allow it. To this day I don't know who believed the President's denials, and who didn't. We went around in shock, with grim, determined faces. Some days I'd look up to see some new, infuriating story, get up, close the doors to my office, lay my head on my desk and weep.

But only for five minutes. Five minutes was all I allowed myself. After five minutes I'd fix my face, plaster on a smile, and reopen for business. I watched the dignity Hillary showed, and her determination to stay focused and keep going. I tried my best to follow her example. I remembered what she and the President said at that first staff meeting in 1993 about reaching inside ourselves to find more strength, more compassion, more patience, more wisdom and dedication than we ever imagined ourselves having.

I thought I'd tapped into this well before, but now I had to dig extra deep. You work so hard at the White House. You're always at the office. You rarely see your family and it's almost impossible to have a social life. You never get enough sleep, but you have to perform at top efficiency no matter how exhausted you are. Even in the best of times you figure half the people around you are functioning as zombies. You make these sacrifices gladly, because it's such an honor to work for the President, in the White House. That's what makes it all worthwhile. Now the President's honor, and ours, was under attack. You don't hear a lot about "honor" these days, but it still matters. How can you trust a spouse, a colleague, a business associate, if you judge them to be without honor? I just could not believe he would betray us all and hurt Hillary so much.

At every Visitors Office meeting I said something like, "I know the news of the day (or week) is very distressing, BUT, the American people are depending on us to do our jobs for them. Even when we're discouraged, or dismayed - or enraged, -we still have a job to do for them, and we're going to do it, by God, no matter what. We can't allow ourselves to be distracted, no matter how upsetting the news is. We have important tasks to focus on, and I'm counting on all of you to keep going."

I hope they found it encouraging. I know they all continued to work hard, to get the jobs done. I could imagine their conversations at home and with their friends, because I knew what mine were like. People who weren't real friends either asked rude questions or kept an uneasy silence. I answered the rude questions with a cold stare, and appreciated any kind of silence. Real friends talked about anything BUT the President's problems and I was grateful to them. We were so proud to work for this President, and now, no matter what happened, all his accomplishments and all our work were tarnished forever.

Around the White House we didn't talk about it, and we avoided looking each other in the eye. I noticed the President didn't look anyone in the eye either. For months I thought it was because he was so embarrassed at the charges. Eventually, of course, I realized it was because he was guilty of this inexcusable "relationship" and was torn in pieces about what to do about it.

Years later, a major Democratic philanthropist in LA asked me why the White House staff had not all resigned in disgust at what the President did.

"I can only speak for myself," I said, "and I thought the entire 'independent counsel' operation was thoroughly corrupt and un-American. The President was targeted in a fundamentally unfair way, as no President had ever been targeted before, by ruthless people who were determined to undo an election they viewed as illegitimate and destroy a President. To abandon him would have given them a victory that would hurt America."

So, as disgusted as I was with him, I was even more outraged at Mr. Starr and his crew of Javerts, relentlessly pursuing the Clintons over nothing - nothing at all - until they trapped him in his one area of weakness.

My favorite comment of all, in those unhappy days, came from the comedian Chris Rock, who talked about the President's troubles this way (please excuse the language):

"OK, so he lied about sex. Fuck, everybody lies about sex. Fuck, most of us lie DURING sex. I mean, it's not as if he lied about ... where the BOMBS are..."

This really stuck in my head, and was especially relevant in 2003, don't you think? I mean, if they could impeach a President for lying about consensual sex between two adults, what should be done to a President who lies to lead his country into an unprovoked, unnecessary and disastrous war?

Also a year later, when the truth came out, my boyfriend Steve kept asking, "How could this happen? Clinton is a Yale-trained lawyer, one of the smartest men in the country. Why the hell didn't he just tell them, 'You ask me whatever you want about the so-called scandals and I'll answer. But I'm not answering anything about my private life. So take me to court if you want, but I'm not going down that road.' He would have paid a political price for it, but, for God's sake, look at the price he paid for lying!" And, he's right.

***

Another good reason for us not to talk to each other was the ever-present threat of being hauled in for your very own chat with the FBI. Then they'd ask you about every conversation you ever had with anyone at work about the "troubles" and if you had, even the most casual conversation, then that person would be hauled in too.

And, my God, it was unbelievably expensive for those who were. I heard Maggie Williams, who had been Hillary's Chief of Staff for our first few years, had legal bills in excess of $100,000. For goodness sake, how was a person on a government salary supposed to pay THAT? She would be indebted forever. People disappeared from their offices in the middle of the day, for hours at a time, and no one asked why. We knew why. They were undergoing their own interrogation du jour.

One colleague told me she had been questioned by the same two FBI agents so many times, covering the same ground over and over, that the last time they called her in, she went without her lawyer, who she could no longer afford. They sat and stared at her across the table, looking frustrated and annoyed. She calmly stared back. They had tried so hard, for over a year, to get her to say something - anything - that would incriminate the President or senior staff in some way, and it hadn't happened.

Finally they asked, "Ma'am, is there anything we **should have asked you** about White House operations or the President that we didn't ask?"

She shrugged her shoulders, lifted her hands in the universal sign of, "I can't help you," and replied, "No, there's not."

"Anything you should tell us we haven't heard yet?"

"No, honestly, we've covered it all."

"OK then, you can go. We're done." And they waved her away for the last time.

And on a lighter note, NASCAR pays a visit:

CHAPTER TWENTY THREE ~

THE "SCANDALS" CONTINUE

Here's how these Washington "scandals" really work: the investigators for Mr. Starr, or some Congressional committee call you in for an interview. They make you answer questions about some event from years ago, and a transcript is made - but you don't get a copy. Then you go away, months pass, and you forget all about it (which they're counting on). Then suddenly they call you back in. They ask the same questions again, and if your answers are the tiniest bit different (the TINIEST bit different) they charge you with "perjury." Never mind that now a year or more has passed since your first answers, and God knows how long since the events they're interested in. No, you must remember every little detail in exactly the same way, in exactly the same order, or you are a LIAR, and your life is about to become a hideous maze of lawyers and committee hearings, just like Alice down the rabbit hole (or the old Soviet Union).

There's never any acknowledgment -never!- that in the real world truthful people may remember things differently from one another, or differently after some time passes. No, you must be lying. Oh, it's a fine system for tying decent people into knots and destroying their lives. Mr. Starr and his cronies indicted people who refused to lie about the President and Hillary for him. He gave immunity to people who lied or committed other crimes, like Linda Tripp and her despicable - and illegal - recordings of Monica's phone calls. He actually threatened to revoke the adoption of an orphan from Romania, when the mother wouldn't lie for him. All this in the name of upholding "morality." What a twisted, depraved man. And I mean it in the truest sense of the words.

Later in the year, I had my own up-front-and-personal experience with the investigation.

Mr. Starr and his Republican Congressional cronies were convinced to the core we were ALL corrupt, and if they just kept the pressure on, just kept asking all of us the right questions, sooner or later, by God, they'd lift up the right rock and uncover the squirmy mess of Clinton scandals they just knew were lurking. They couldn't imagine we weren't all guilty of SOMETHING they needed to expose to embarrass the Clintons even more and discredit his entire Presidency. And, since their Republican masters in the Hill leadership believed all this even more fervently, the pressure was on Starr to produce the evidence to bring us all down.

Just think about it - suppose your whole career hung on your ability to remember exactly where you were on a specific day three years, or eight years ago, who was with you and what you said or did. Could you answer questions like that? No? Well, welcome to the club. Because any inability to answer simply HAD to be evidence of wrong doing or a cover-up. No other possibility existed in their twisted, narrow minds.

So, you'd think we'd all be hyper-aware of the danger looming over us, and I'm sure my colleagues were. But I was busy with my own responsibilities, keeping my head down and not thinking about any danger to me when the FBI called. You may be surprised to hear it was 10:00 at night, and I'd just gotten home from work when the phone rang.

"Ms. Bates?"

"Yes?"

"This is Agent X from the FBI calling. We'd like to meet with you to ask a few questions."

I thought, *OK, my time has finally come. Damn. I was really hoping to escape this...* I said, "All right, when would you like to meet?"

"How about tomorrow night, your house, at this time?"

"Well now, just a minute. I assume the questions you want to ask are related to my official duties, right?"

"Yes, they are."

"Then why do you want to come to my home late at night? That doesn't seem right."

In a very pleasant and soothing voice he explained, "We know all you folks at the White House work incredibly long hours, and White House counsel has told us we are not allowed to come to see people at their jobs, so late in the evening is usually the only time people have available for us."

I thought *No, this still doesn't sound right*, and said to the agent, "Please give me your phone number and I'll call you from the office tomorrow."

The next day I called my friend, Lansing Lee, a partner at Patton Boggs, and FOB from way back. "Lansing, I got a call from the FBI last night. They want to meet me at home tonight. I'm supposed to call them back this afternoon. Do you think I need a lawyer?"

He practically exploded on the other end of the phone. "Melinda, stay right there at your desk, do not go anywhere, and I'll call you right back!"

He was so emphatic I did just that, and a couple of minutes later the phone rang. "Melinda, I'm in Tom Boggs' office with him and Mitch Berger, a partner here."

"Hi, Tom, how are you? How do you do, Mitch?"

Tom Boggs was one of the most important unelected men in Washington. Actually, he was a lot more important than many who are elected. I'd gotten to know him during the '92 campaign over the course of many events. He was a big, handsome, roguish guy who pretty much invented the lobbying game in Washington. Mr. Berger was new to me.

"Hi, Melinda," Tom said with a charming hint of his Louisiana roots in his voice. "We think it's imperative you have representation. Mitch here will be your lawyer, and you should do whatever he says - he's a smart and experienced man."

"Tom, thanks so much. I knew you'd know what to do. I promise to be a model client."

Tom and Lansing got off the phone and I began to talk to my new lawyer. He asked for the phone number of the agent and said he would call him. We agreed to meet soon.

When we hung up, I called the Office of White House Counsel and asked them, "Is it really true you told the FBI they can't come to our offices for their interrogations? That's what they told me last night."

"Of course it's not true. We told them they can see anyone here whenever they make an appointment, **as long as we're advised**

they are in the complex."

OK, so they are lying to me from the start. Something to keep in mind. And, hey! I thought they only did that with "criminals." I'm no criminal! I'm an upstanding citizen - don't they have to play fair with me?

Words cannot express how naive this is.

Over the next few weeks Mitch helped me prepare to answer whatever questions we could imagine them asking, and to assemble any papers they might ask to see. Then we met with the two agents - not at my home, and not at 10:00 at night. We met in a conference room at Patton Boggs, in the middle of the day. I have to say these two were not the brightest bulbs in the lamp. They seemed to be confused by the word "Visitors" in the title of our office. They interpreted this to mean I must be in charge of visitors coming to see the President - which I hope you now realize wasn't at all what I did. (It reminded me of the joke the Secret Service tells about the FBI: If they're so freakin' "special" –as in "special agent" Jones – how come there are so many of them?)

They also thought I had something to do with the "coffees" hosted for contributors, who then got a briefing from senior staff or a cabinet secretary. Sorry - the Social Office, not us. So they kept asking me about people who might have met with the President, and what did I know about them. Not much, actually - unless they were celebrities who wanted a tour of the White House.

They weren't happy with my answers, so they tried reading names from a list.

"No. No. No, never heard of him. Never saw her..."

Finally they offered up the name of Johnny Chung, and my eyes lit up. Mr. Chung raised a lot of money for the President and was known around the House as a high-maintenance supporter.

"I did talk to Mr. Chung, once. He called the White House on a Saturday in July and was so insistent the operators forwarded the call to me at home. I was in a bathing suit, sweating and working in my garden. He asked me to come in to the White House right away to walk him and his important friends around. I told him I was sorry but couldn't do that.

'Do you know who I am?' he demanded.

"Oh, yes, I do, Mr. Chung, and we're all very grateful for your support, but unfortunately I'm here with guests (so, I lied) and I'm not able to leave, so next time just give us a little notice and we'll be happy to take care of your friends."

"No, I really need you to come in now!"

"I'm so sorry, I'd love to help you next time ... yes, I know, I'm so sorry I just can't do this for you today ..."

We went back and forth with this for about ten minutes before he finally believed me - I was NOT going to drop what I was doing to come help him. I guess that never happened to him before.

Over the years I had a lot of experience dealing with people who wanted something we couldn't do for them, and it seemed to me that while many people felt free to get really ugly about it, (which, by the way, never worked with me) most people from Eastern cultures just kept repeating their demand, over and over, in the apparent belief that if they made it often enough I'd give up and give in and do what they wanted. This didn't work either.

I'm sure there were White House people who would have left their homes to do this favor. I wasn't one of them. I had no intention of dropping my trowel, taking a shower, dressing in office clothes and driving downtown. In the end, he just gave up, but not without letting me know how unhappy he was.

The agents listened to my story, with grim faces and narrowed eyes, but I swear one of them was starting to laugh when the other one kicked his leg. We went around the same ground a few more times, and my truthful answers - I didn't know anything about the things they were asking - finally penetrated. They reluctantly told us they were finished but might call me in again sometime for further questions.

"Sure, any time," I assured them (as if it were up to me).

After they left, I turned to Mitch and said, "This has been a very interesting experience. When I was young and "foolish" in the late 1960s, I had a very poor impression of law enforcement, especially the FBI. When I got older, married, and had children, I became more socially conservative and very supportive of the "authorities." Now, here I am in my fifties, and it turns out the assessment I made when I was nineteen is more accurate than anything I learned as an adult. I'm shocked!"

As the whole world knows, after months of denials, in August the President finally told the truth. He told it first, finally, to Hillary and Chelsea, and I'm sure he broke their hearts - as well as his own.

I heard many people publicly say she "had to have known" and "her reaction now is all fake." But a friend was up in the Residence that day, helping Hillary get ready to leave on their vacation. She came down and sat in my office, wiping her eyes with trembling hands. Just looking at her brought me close to tears too, as she struggled for composure. I got up and closed the door to give us some privacy.

"Melinda, this is so painful, so awful. Hillary is broken, devastated by this betrayal on so many levels she couldn't even comprehend it all. My heart is breaking for her - and for Bill and Chelsea. I didn't even know what to say to her."

There's no way this was faked for one old friend.

Then it was my turn to witness their pain. You'll remember I was responsible for the helicopter departures, and this one, taking the Clintons off to vacation in Martha's Vineyard, was one I wanted to be damn sure was as private as I could make it. The last thing the Clintons needed was to have some visitors they'd have to smile at or talk to.

Unfortunately, I didn't control the press, so they were out in their usual stakeout spot on the West side of the driveway. I was standing in the Diplomatic Reception Room when the Clintons came through, Hillary barely holding herself together in her deceptively cheery turquoise jacket, the President looking beaten (there's no other word) and Chelsea between them, holding her parents' hands for dear life.

I stood back out of the way so they wouldn't have to speak to me, and watched this sad little group walk by. Their pain was palpable. I know heartbreak when I see it. Then they had to square their shoulders just before they went out the door to walk to the helicopter. The minute the Usher opened the door for them, the press began to shout questions. Thank God for the noise of the 'copter rotors. Some of the reporters, I noticed, were silent and just watched. But not many. A story is a story, I guess. Never mind the humanity.

The Clintons stared straight ahead and marched to the 'copter. Then Marine One took them away.

I shook my head, dashed the tears from my eyes, and walked slowly back to my office. I know a thing or two about heartache in marriage. My husband - ex-husband since 1994 - was a good man, but after many years of struggling in our marriage he just gave up. It had broken me. Coping with the pain was the hardest thing I'd done in life. But at least I got to do my grieving and recovering in private. I tried to imagine what it felt like to be humiliated in front of the whole world, but I couldn't. I tried to imagine if they would ever be able to rebuild their love and trust, but I couldn't. The only thing I could think to do was pray for them, and I did.

And in the end, to the surprise of a lot of people who didn't really know them, they rebuilt their love and trust in each other. It took a lot of hard work but they came through the pain stronger and with a better marriage. People ask me all the time if the Clintons really love each other or if it's a marriage built on politics. Of course I am only an outsider, and not a very close one any more, but it sure seems to me their love for each other is deep and real, and their commitment is stronger than it ever was. I can tell you for sure that when Hillary ran for President, Bill was more anxious about her success than for any of his own elections over the years.

During the years immediately after the "troubles" I found it fascinating – and completely hypocritical – to see people on the right, who claimed to represent the "family values" party, criticize Hillary for deciding to stay with Bill. They seemed to really want her to divorce him, but she said publicly, in explaining her decision, "I made vows. One of them was 'for better or for worse' and this sure is 'worse.' So I am keeping my sacred vow." You'd think people would respect that, wouldn't you?

There was one funny story out of all this misery. After Monica left her office, the other staff from Congressional Affairs went in to clean up. There was a small refrigerator in the corner, the kind people use for soda and their lunches. When they opened the door of the refrigerator to defrost it, a pile of unopened envelopes fell out. Huh? What are these? Why, these are letters. Lots and lots of letters: correspondence from Members of Congress who had written to the President or senior staff about some issue. Monica's job was to direct these to the appropriate office, or to help draft answers, but that would have been too much like real work for her, so she simply "disappeared" them, into a place no one would look. I'll never forget the incredulous expressions on the faces of those staffers ... what a bimbo!

I understand in today's environment people are more likely to view Monica as a victim. People think, "She was young, he took advantage..." But my direct experience of her and how she stalked him without any thought of the consequences of her actions, makes me far less charitable than others may be. This in no way excuses the President, but he certainly paid a terrible price for his failings.

***

Here in the East Reception Room I welcomed Mikhail Baryshnikov, the Crown Prince of Nepal, the Queen of Sweden, Michael Douglas, and the Grateful Dead. Not all at once.

Chapter Twenty Four ~ 1998 ~

The Rest of the Story

I don't want you to think all we did that year was obsess and grieve over the President's troubles. Life, even at the White House, goes on, even in bad times, and there were still plenty of opportunities for fun. We needed them more than ever, and I was determined to do all the partying I could. I'd been divorced for several years and was lonely. But, I've learned the way the universe works is, the more desperately you want something, the less likely you are to get it. It's only when you let go and surrender that it can come to you. I don't understand this, and I'd like to have a serious talk about it with the universe. But since this seems unlikely to happen, I just have to accept it.

The turn for me came in December of 1997, when I made a deep, heartfelt decision to move on with my personal life and do things differently in the new year. I wasn't expecting anything else to change; I just determined **I** would change. I might well have to live without love in my life (statistics said I was more likely to be struck by lightening than to find a mate at my advanced age). I'd just have to find a way to have a rich and fulfilling life without it. I didn't reach this decision gladly, but sometimes you just have to make a decision anyway. I bowed to the universe.

Can you believe it - on January 1, 1998 (the FIRST day of the new year, new decision), I met a man I really liked at a dance party I was invited to and he crashed. I was smitten by his twinkling blue/green eyes, his long legs, and his ability to dance - which was important to me. It didn't hurt that he was 6'2" with broad shoulders and narrow hips. The hair was starting to go, but it didn't bother me. He kept coming back to me to talk and dance, but he didn't ask for my phone number, and I didn't offer it. When he left, I thought, "Oh well," and put him out of my mind.

Then in February, at a weekly tango event, I looked up and saw him standing in the door. I sort of remembered him (I really had put him out of my mind), so I went over to say "hello." Tango is a difficult dance, and men are a precious resource. I wanted him to feel welcome.

"Hello, I'm Melinda, welcome to tango. Haven't we met before? Do you remember me?"

"Sure, I do," he said, with a slow smile. "I'm Steve Ense and it's nice to see you again."

I took one look at those eyes and remembered exactly when and where we met. It wasn't until months later I learned he'd come there specifically to find me. Turns out he was smitten too, and had talked about me with his friends every day for the last five weeks. They got so tired of it they told him, "Give it up! You didn't even get this woman's phone number! You'll never find her."

But he knew exactly how to find me: just go to a tango event. I didn't know this at the time, and I didn't know he was there not just to learn tango, but to observe me and see what my character was. Lots of people go to dances just for the social life. Lots of people go home with a new person, or the same person every week. He didn't want a woman who was a player, so he wanted to see what I did. I'm not a player, so every week I asked a man to walk me out to my car, but I drove home alone. Steve was watching this from the house.

This went on for a month, with me having no idea Steve was there for anything but the tango. How could I? He showed no particular sign of interest in me! But one of my resolutions for the new year was to use my many invitations to wonderful events to get to know new people. The current invitation was for the annual American Ireland Fund dinner, a big hoorah with a nice meal and way too many speeches. In Washington, I learned early on, there is nothing as interesting as the sound of one's own voice pontificating about something. Pair that with the Irish love of talk, and you've got a loooong evening ahead of you.

But I like any excuse to dress up and put on sparkly earrings, so even though there was no dancing, I usually went. But who should I invite this year? Steve hadn't made a move; I thought he was younger than I was, and I really had no idea he was interested in me. But I did think he might have an Irish background, and I knew he had a dinner jacket because he was wearing it when we met. So one week at tango I asked him, "Steve, are you by chance part Irish?"

"Yes, I am. How could you tell?"

"Just a guess actually, but anyway, I have two tickets to this Irish event in two weeks. Would you like to go with me?"

"Sure, great - this will be our first date!"

That stopped me in my tracks. Throughout 1997, I'd been dancing tango and swing with a man I liked a lot. Sometimes we went out five nights a week. We had great fun. But it was always just dancing, never a "date." He was getting over a painful divorce and made it clear he wasn't interested in anything romantic, so he set this rule – his rule - from the beginning. And, since I wanted to keep dancing, I had to live with it. Everyone in the tango community EXCEPT this man could see how much I liked him, but, you know, if you're not ready, you're just not ready. This was the reason for my New Year's resolution to do something different with my life. I'd spent a year "just dancing," and it wasn't enough for me. Many nights, after dropping him off, I drove home with tears streaming down my face. I was so lonely. So for Steve to say this would be our "first date" made my heart take a little leap.

The night of the dinner, Steve came to my house for the first time. He was carrying a small box, which, to my surprise held a wrist corsage of tiny white roses. I was touched but didn't know what to say. I hadn't seen a corsage since my senior prom in 1964. No adult I knew wore a corsage to a blacktie event. But he was so eager (and he looked so handsome in his tux) that I smiled and put it on my wrist. Since I have NO Irish in me, I was wearing a purple satin sheath and I could see he liked how it fit.

At the reception, Steve seemed to enjoy seeing all the celebrities he knew from politics and television. "Look - it's the Kennedys! Over there, it's Tim Russert! Is that Chris Matthews? Cool!"

Then we sat down to dinner with our hosts and their other guests. The conversation was going well and I thought, *This will be my chance to get to know Steve a little, since we've only ever talked about dance so far.*

I'm good at asking people questions about themselves,

getting them to open up and be comfortable. It's been an essential skill in all my jobs. So my ears perked up when someone at the table mentioned the year 1968. I'd been wondering how old Steve was, and I'm really bad at guessing, so I said, "I remember 1968 really well - it's the year I graduated from college," and looked at Steve inquiringly.

"I remember 1968 too," he said.

"Really? How old were you?"

"Seven."

Seven? I gasped. *Seven? Good Lord, he was just a child!*

I'm sure my face turned white and my eyes rolled back in my head. I was shocked down to my toes, and so disappointed. *Well, this will never work. Damn! I was starting to really like him ...*

But Steve reached for my hand and gave it a gentle squeeze. "Don't worry. I figured you're a little older than I am, and it doesn't bother me a bit."

"That's nice," I said, "but let's be clear here. I'm not a LITTLE older than you are. I'm FIFTEEN YEARS older. And that's a lot."

"Maybe so," he said, "but no one would believe it. You actually look younger than I do. So let's forget about it."

I nodded, but thought to myself, *Fifteen years is a really big age difference. I don't think this could ever work out long term. But, let's just have some fun now and see how it plays out.*

Well what did I know? That was the beginning of our now twenty-year relationship. He's the love of my life. We have been through a lot of good times, and some bad ones, and he's the one it was worth waiting for. Let's hear it for the universe!

CHAPTER TWENTY FIVE ~

OUR EGG ROLL MAKES HISTORY

Every year we tried to change the Easter Egg Roll in some way, and in 1998 we aimed for the biggest change in White House history: we decided to cybercast the whole event from the South Lawn. It would be the first cybercast from there in history. My partner in crime, so to speak, was Howard Lefkowitz, then a senior VP at EarthLink, the Internet provider. Our event producer, Gary Jacob, solicited their sponsorship for a technology tent - rows of Apple computers for kids to use to email the President. They were "in" for the computers, but Howard is a BIG thinker, and once we met, and clicked, he came to me with a proposal for this grand production.

"Hey, this will be great! We'll just lay some wire around the lawn... I've got friends who will bring in the production and broadcast trailers... we'll make history here! Computers are the future, let's show the world how savvy the Clintons are!"

It all sounded so... easy!

Howard, who soon became a good friend, is a really persuasive person. He's so full of enthusiasm and optimism about what he wants to do, and so obviously smart about what he's doing, you know you'd be a fool not to go along. Over the years I've known him, I learned to pay close attention to his seeming flights of fancy about the future of technology. Time after time, things he predicted that sounded incredible and impossible came true only a year or two down the road.

He's just under six feet tall, with curly dark hair, lively dark eyes, and a neatly shaped, short dark beard. He virtually VIBRATES with brilliance and a "can do" attitude that's irresistible. I liked him when Gary brought him to lunch with me at the Mess, for the first time.

I especially remember that meal because one of my other guests was an Internet exec from Disney who we were courting for another Egg Roll sponsorship. The Disney guy showed up in a gray suit with a vivid purple and white striped shirt and a lilac tie. We don't see that look much in Washington, and I wished I'd brought my sunglasses to the Mess.

While we chatted about the Internet he breezily asked me, "Do you know what's the most frequently searched word on the Internet?" (Remember – it was 1998, so, early days!)

"No, what?" I innocently asked. (Please skip this next part, kids!)

"Bestiality!" he said, loudly enough for colleagues and guests at other tables to hear.

I spit out my soup and coughed. Heads around the room turned our way. Eyebrows were raised. The room fell silent. I tried to see from the corners of my eyes if my boss was in the room. *Please, God, no ...*

I squirmed in my seat, but he was oblivious. "And you know what's the next most searched word?"

Desperately hoping for something, anything, more ... wholesome ... to come up, I whispered, "Gee, no, I can't imagine." I mean, the man was from DISNEY, for goodness sake.

"Bestiality misspelled!" he cheerfully blurted out, looking very pleased with himself for being so darn smart.

I choked, and slid further down into my seat, wishing I could end up under the table. Poor Gary, who brought this guy to us, sat speechless, with his mouth open, staring at us in horror. Howard appeared to be trying very hard not to laugh. Me too. What else could I do? I'm relatively sure this was the first time - hopefully ONLY time - that word was uttered in the White House Staff Mess.

Well, we didn't do the deal with Disney, which was just as well, I suppose, but Howard made a compelling pitch for both the Internet tent and the cybercast. If I'd had any real idea of how hard it was going to be to make it happen, I would've thought twice, but there you go - I like to aim high, and I knew Hillary wanted her Egg Rolls to be special and memorable. This sounded like just the ticket. New technology! First ever! We'll make history! Those words were like catnip to me.

There's nothing simple at the White House, so figuring out how we could make this happen was a challenge. We had to have approval from so many offices - counsel, administration, domestic policy, and the dreaded and dreadful Gary Walters, who of course controlled the grounds. We arranged a meeting to bring all the players on board and make our pitch for the project. Howard and his technology partners arrived from California wearing nice dark suits I suspected they didn't need very often. I found them in my reception room, looking intimidated, shuffling their feet and fidgeting with their dress-shirt collars.

The meeting was over in the Old Executive Office Building, which gave me a chance to walk these men through the House on the way over. Never underestimate the power of friendly intimidation. We weren't adversaries - on the contrary, I already thought of them as colleagues - but it can help to remind people of just how high the stakes are for any White House project, and how small is the room for error. I think they got the point.

We headed into a large, Victorian conference room, with a loooong dark table. Introductions all around and then we sat down, all the White House people on one side of the table and all the technology people on the other. We reached into our briefcases and took out pads of paper and pens or pencils. THEY reached into their pockets and took out PDAs. Everyone on our side took one look at these cool little devices, the height of technology (at the time) and sucked in our breath with envy. There was no way in the world the White House would issue these expensive little babies to us, and we were sooooo jealous. As Jimmy Carter once said, "I lusted in my heart."

Howard and I pitched the idea and got all the different offices on board. Then we began to plan. Since I had every other part of the Egg Roll to coordinate, most of this fell to Gary Jacob, as our event producer, and Howard, which was fine with me. I mean, it sounded so do-able!

And then we came to the part where we actually had to make it all happen. The trucks showed up on Friday, and I walked the Lawn with Howard, the production guys, and Dale Haney, Chief Horticulturist, who'd tell us what we could do and where we could do it. Saturday morning they began to lay cable. Remember, back to those dark days of yesteryear when everything had to be WIRED?

Well, everything had to be wired! And it was going to take a lot longer than we planned. They worked through Saturday, late into the night, and started again early Sunday. I was there to encourage, supervise and keep us all on track.

At one point we were working up close to the Rose Garden and Howard noticed the President come out of the Oval Office with Buddy, his beloved Lab, sit on the step and play fetch. He watched for a while, trying not to stare, then turned to me.

"My God, Melinda. I never thought about how lonely the job of President must be. He looks like the weight of the world is on his shoulders - and I guess it is. Thank God he has the dog!"

The day wore on, everyone was working really hard, but we were far from finished. The sun went down and we were working in the dark. Now I had a little fun with Howard's team.

"Hey, everybody, pay attention here for a minute! No matter what task you think you need to do in some new part of the Lawn, you have to remember not to go anywhere unless we send someone to escort you. 'Cause if you do, well, there are counter-snipers on the roof up there. (I pointed) and if you happen to see a little red light on your chest, that would be a sign you've got to stand very still, don't move, and call us to come get you - OK?"

They looked horrified, stared up at the roof, shook their heads and went back to work. At one point we called in a specialist from the phone company to adjust a connection. The box was in the ground, just outside the Oval Office, and we could see the President at his desk inside, working very late.

In order to activate the line, the technician had to call his office. I heard him say, "No, I can't wait until tomorrow morning! You've got to turn it on now, damn it! I'm standing outside the Oval Office - yes THAT Oval Office - and I need this wire live now, and you're going to make it happen now!"

Howard looked at me.

"Yes, that's how it is here pretty much all the time. You get used to it."

Around midnight, Easter Sunday, we finally had almost everything done. It was time to quit. One of the most important parts of the project was Howard's set up in the China Room: two computers, carefully hooked up to the broadcast truck, ready for the President and Hillary to sit down and view our cybercast in real time.

I was excited to finally get to this point, because it had been a real pain to make everything work. And I still had all the other parts of the Egg Roll to review and finalize. We were happy to walk away from it that night, exhausted but confident we'd be ready to go the next day, showing the Clintons their event this new way, making history ... So, can you imagine my shock and dismay to discover the next morning the Usher on overnight duty had shut off the power to that room after we left? And we didn't know, on Easter Monday morning, if we could re-set everything in time. Holy cow! If ever I wanted to shoot someone, this was the moment.

Gary said it was just their normal procedure to save energy, but I don't think so. I'd been perfectly clear about what we were doing. And, he'd been in the meeting! I can't prove it, but I sure think the Chief Usher tried to sabotage us again. It would have been hugely embarrassing to me if we couldn't demonstrate our project - it was on both the Clinton's daily schedules and I'd been talking about it for weeks. I would have looked like an idiot if we had to cancel their viewing of the cybercast at the last minute.

I'll never forget the look of stunned disbelief on Howard's face when he realized all their programming was lost. His team stared at me in horror. But, only for a minute. Howard is Mr. Can-do. No time to indulge outrage or point fingers. I watched them huddle together and snap questions and answers back and forth. After a few minutes, he turned to me, "Go on out to the Lawn. We think we can get it back up in time. Trust me - I won't let you down."

I couldn't help, because, of course, I didn't know a thing about the technology, and because after I arrived at oh-dark-thirty (as the military and USSS like to say) I had to be outside doing stand-up about the event with several networks and C-span, always a favorite part of the day. Then we had the breakfast reception for the sponsors, a gorgeous spread on tables in the East Room, with sugar Easter eggs three feet tall as centerpieces, little quiches, juices, coffee. The Clintons always stood in the Blue Room for a receiving line, so every sponsor could shake hands and get a photo with them. They especially liked it when people brought their children, dressed in Easter finery, for a picture they'd keep all their lives.

All this time people were entering the Lawn for egg rolling and other activities. My staff and volunteers, and Gary's staff ran everything there, so I could be on the State Floor. After the receiving line I walked the Clintons down to the China Room for our big moment. The President and Hillary sat down, and Howard, looking sharp in his very best suit, leaned in to show them how to use the mouse to select different feeds from all over the Lawn.

It worked! Halleluiah! I almost fainted with relief. There was our event, on the monitors, with kids, including Howard's daughter Laura (who understood the technology far better than I did) acting as correspondents, interviewing other kids, celebrity readers and "President Lincoln."

I watched with satisfaction and pride. The President and Hillary clicked between the feeds, watching it all.

"So, this means," the President asked, "… people all over the world can see the Easter Egg Roll right now, for the first time in history?"

"Yes, sir," Howard responded.

"Amazing," Hillary murmured, staring at her monitor. Then she looked up and smiled at both of us. "Good job!"

It was so wonderful it was worth all the heartburn. I was proud of Howard, and grateful to him and EarthLink. The technology tent was a big hit too - lots of kids who had never used a computer before sent email messages to the President. Lots of little wooden eggs were tucked away in Easter baskets, and about 30,000 happy guests spent the day at our event. And at the end, all of us in the Visitors Office, and Howard's team, and Gary's, collapsed onto the soft, green grass with exhausted giggles, and looked at each other to say, "Can you believe we did THAT?"

"This making-history stuff is HARD!"

"I know, let's start planning for next year now!" This last was hooted down with shouts of protest. There was no way we were going to do that now. We'd wait until, oh, I dunno, next week?

***

In May our Georgetown class returned for our second White House party - our thirtieth class reunion. How could this possibly happen? In the '60s, we'd told ourselves not to trust anyone over thirty and now we WUZ the enemy. Good God Almighty, we were fifty three! I didn't feel old. Thanks to a workout program I never learned to like, but still forced myself to do, I was in great shape. My friends all looked good to me. And if the proof is in the pudding, well, we all still had plenty of energy to party hard. After the first two days of celebrating at various events an exhausted Steve looked at me, shook his head, and said, "Where the heck do you all get your energy? You party twice as hard as anyone my age."

Yes, the crew planning our reunion events had something going every minute. There were golf games, charity neighborhood clean-ups, boat dinner cruises, parties on the lawn at Georgetown, a polo game that really brought back memories ... the minute one thing ended it was "Where's the next party?"

And off we'd go. I love the photos from these events, showing people I've known for a lifetime, as we all have grown and changed, smiling happily at each other and the camera.

On Saturday, the Clintons hosted a small group for brunch at Blair House. Hillary teased Steve about dancing, and he gallantly responded "I hope you'll save a dance for me?"

Me, Myra Greenspun, Tim Chorba, Gayden Thompson

She laughed. "Oh, no, you should save that for Melinda. The world is a better place if I don't dance or sing!"

Speaking just for myself, the older I get, the longer it takes to get tarted up for special events. When you're young, you can just throw on something, grab a bracelet and some heels, and be ready to go. It's a lot more work as we age. After brunch I had to rush home to give myself a facial and wash my hair again (damn Washington humidity!) I'd been dieting for months, and it paid off - I looked great in my short, white satin, embroidered dress and bolero jacket. Long, dangly pearl earrings and ivory dance shoes, and I was good to go to our second White House reunion dinner.

We planned for about 1,200 people, so we put up another hangar-sized tent, and then filled it with damask tablecloths, ivory and yellow roses, chandeliers hanging from the distant roof, and, most important, a large dance floor and stage.

We gathered in our best finery inside the blessedly cool White House for cocktails, and then moved out to the tent for dinner. Unpleasant Washington reality - the annual humidity festival, that normally doesn't start until July, was in full, wretched bloom. Inside the tent felt like a sauna. We were all sweating like crazy. My hair quickly went flat, and my make-up tried to melt. We ladies could at least take off our wraps, but the men in their wool tuxedo had a very unpleasant time of it. They mostly kept their jackets on until the dancing after dinner.

Once again I got to give a little speech to the Clintons, in front of all my classmates, to present our class gift, another surprise for them. All the speakers, including the President and Hillary were seated on gilt ballroom chairs on the stage. Other people got up and talked about the money raised for the University, and scholarships.

Then the President spoke, welcoming us to their home, and joking about our college days. Normally the President always speaks last at an event, so I'm sure he and Hillary wondered why I was on stage.

Then it was my turn. I spoke for only a few minutes, reminding everyone of our gratitude to the University, and our gratitude to the Clintons for another warm (literally!) welcome to the White House.

Finally, I invited them to step over to a table at the edge of the stage, where a drape covered a formless object. Hillary gave the cloth a tug and it fell away to reveal a set of cobalt blue glass bowls by Dale Chichuly, one of their favorite artists. Dale created the stunning glass flower ceiling in the *Bellagio Hotel in Las Vegas* as well as countless other fabulous installations and is internationally known. The Clintons admired his work for years. They both looked delighted and surprised - and surprising the President and First Lady is a real challenge. The photo of the three of us looking at this gift is one of my favorites from all eight years. It's on the back cover here.

After dinner and the speeches we were thrilled to hear the Righteous Brothers perform, and I really had to laugh. At the planning meetings, the younger women in the Social Office had worried that when the music started, no one would want to get up and dance, so what would we do to get the party going? Huh? They thought at our advanced age we would be embarrassed to dance? I kept trying to say I didn't think it would be a problem, but they weren't listening. I promised them at least Steve and I would get right up and dance (our second favorite thing), but I wasn't concerned. Of course, the minute the music started, a couple of hundred people rushed to the dance floor to shake their booties in happy frenzy. We KNOW how to party! I suppose we'll be doing it well into our dotage, and it won't be pretty to watch, but we won't care. We'll be too busy having fun.

As the evening wound down a social aide came by and I got the coveted tap on my shoulder and whisper in my ear: "The President would like you to join him up in the solarium after the party ends."

An invitation to the world's most exclusive after party - what fun! Steve and I headed for the elevator, gave our name to another social aid, and rode up. It's a very beautiful elevator - covered in fine rosewood paneling. An usher or a butler in white tie and tails pushes the buttons. The Residence has two floors and we went up to the top. It's set back from the balustrade you can see from the street, so people don't even know it's there. This second floor is mostly smaller bedrooms, but there's a large, cheerful solarium too, where Presidential kids like to entertain their friends, and Presidents and First Ladies host meetings and casual get-togethers. I'd seen the solarium before, but this was my first time as a guest.

When we arrived the room was full. About 30 people, all the closest Georgetown friends, roommates and spouses, filled comfortable chintz sofas and overstuffed chairs, listening to the President and Hillary discuss British politics. (No, I've no idea why they chose that topic.) I'm no expert on the Labour Party, so I was happy just to enjoy the moment, memorizing the details. It would have been tacky to break out my camera and start taking photos of this very private space.

After a few minutes Steve and I stepped out onto the patio area to look out to the south, past the giant tent, the Lawn and fountain, to the Washington Monument lit up in the distance. I thought about how many Presidents and their families had used this spot to relax away from the demands of their public lives, standing where we were standing now, looking at the same beautiful view. The breeze ruffled my hair, and I smelled the trees. The moon was close enough to touch. Below us the tent glowed like a lantern and workers scurried around, cleaning up from the event. We looked back at the White House behind us, gleaming in the dark, the President, Hillary, and my dear friends laughing and talking in the elegant room, filled with light and flowers. The most rarefied view in Washington, and we could hardly bear to turn away when it was time to leave. *What an honor it is to be here. I'll never forget these moments.*

Unspoken in our festivities was the reality that our next major reunion, in 2003, would be held in some far less exalted space. Where would it be, and who would come? I thought we'd end up with fifty people at the Marriott, but we actually about 400 came to a beautiful dinner in a grand old Washington hall. We just really love each other and any excuse to connect.

***

The holiday decorations this year were an opulent blend of silver and gold metallic finishes. Hillary's theme, *A Winter Wonderland*, was executed with ornaments from the country's most talented artists and craftspeople. Everyone knew Chelsea studied ballet, so there were several fantastical ballerinas, my favorite made of gold wire and wearing a jeweled tutu. There were gilded and silvered magnolia leaves and pinecones, just like the ones I made with my mother when I was a child. The strangest thing, of this or any Christmas, was a huge wreath, a full fifteen feet in diameter, dripping with gold and silver decorations, swags, and icicles, installed in the center of the East Room ceiling, in place of the chandelier. There it hovered for the entire month of December, eliciting gasps of wonder and disbelief. We quickly dubbed it *the Mother Ship*, as every time I looked at it I whispered to someone, "ET - phone home!"

The Pageant of Peace was incredible this year, with Tony Bennett and Jose Feliciano as our headliners. Our producers, Bob Johnson and Joe Fab of the Johnson Group, kept coming up with great talent for us, and ran a tight show - they had to, it was televised every year. I loved working with them. After years of prodding, I had finally persuaded the Pageant Board it was time for Washington, a majority African American city, to have an African American Santa Claus: Al Roker. And he was great in the part, returning in 1999 and 2000 to "HO, HO, HO" his way into children's hearts.

There are many celebrities who behave one way on screen and very differently in person. Al Roker is a truly nice man, with a sweet and very engaging spirit.

At the reception following the tree lighting, I asked Tony and Jose if they'd like to see the Oval Office, and then took them on a tour. Tony is an accomplished artist with paint as well as music, and we had a great time looking at all the art in the West Wing and Ground Floor. And, may I say, it doesn't matter how old he is, he's an incredibly sexy man!

The universe picked this moment to remind me of how silly life can be. At the beginning of December each year, I made several copies of my calendar of events, writing in what I planned to wear to each, and who (before Steve) would be my date. I kept one copy in a drawer in my desk. I posted another at home on the door of my second bedroom/office, which I turned into a dressing room, with all the outfits, shoes, jewelry, handbags, etc. I needed for the month, in easy-to-grab bags. Since I rarely had time to go home to change before showing up somewhere looking festive, I'd just reach for the day's stuff when I left for work in the morning.

On this day I'd thrown a new package of pantyhose into my bag of clothes for the evening, without looking at the size. When I took them out to put them on, I could see they were too small, but they were all I had. And oh my, they were waaaay too small. I had to tug and pull, and pull and tug to get them up, and honestly, if I'd had a little Crisco to slather on my hips I would have happily used it. You ladies who are slender, or you men, have no idea what a problem this was, but if you're curvy like me you can imagine my distress.

Well, I did get the pantyhose up where they belonged, but, they didn't want to STAY THERE. No, they wanted to rooooooll down my hips! So all evening, as I walked East and West around the White House with these distinguished guests, looking composed and authoritative in my favorite red silk suit? Panty hose were heading…SOUTH. Rolling slowly down, heading for my crotch.

Please believe me when I say I mean this in the nicest possible way, but, I was so glad Jose Feliciano is BLIND, because every time Tony Bennett turned away for a minute, I had to grab the waistband of those damn pantyhose and yank them back up where they belonged.

I think it's important to always tell this story when I can. I've spoken and written about all the glamorous and exciting elements of my job, and how the Universe swung open an incredible job for me – all of which is true - so I think it's equally important to talk about what can happen when the Universe shows it has a sense of humor!

CHAPTER TWENTY SIX ~ 1999 ~ A CENTURY CHANGES

As you've seen, there were a lot of fabulous events at the Clinton White House. Fabulous is the NORM at the White House. I was always thrilled to be a guest, or just to be working behind the scenes and get to watch. I organized many arrival ceremonies and assisted at many state dinners, but I'd never been a guest at one. These invitations are so highly sought, and space is so limited, I didn't expect to, either.

Then in January, the Clintons welcomed Argentine President, Carlos Menem. What's my connection? Tango! I'd fallen in love with tango two years before, and spent all my free time practicing, taking classes, and dancing. Argentine tango is very different from the flashy "show Tango" you may have seen on television. There's no head jerking, no leaning away from your partner. It's a slow, seductive, physical conversation between the man and woman, responding to exquisite music. It's not choreographed. It's spontaneous. It's also VERY difficult to learn - but if you get to do it with someone you love, what could be more fun?

Hillary knew – heck, EVERYONE knew - I loved tango, and she asked me to help arrange the entertainment, a mix of American and Argentine influences. I immediately asked the actor, Robert Duvall, (Bob to us), with his Argentine girlfriend, now wife, Luciana Pedrazza, and Pablo Veron, tango god and star of the movie, *The Tango Lesson*. Bob is a passionate tanguero (man who dances tango). For years he's traveled to Buenos Aires to learn and dance. When he's not on a film set somewhere, he lives on a farm in Virginia hunt country, with a barn made over into a dance space.

Steve and I were dancing there one frosty night, and I told Bob about the upcoming state visit. "I'd love to get Pablo Veron," I said, "but there's no money to pay him - nobody gets paid to perform at the White House. Do you think he'd do it anyway? And, isn't he performing in Paris now?"

"Tell me the dates again?"

I did, and to my great delight, Bob said, "Pablo will be here, in Virginia with us, right at that time. I'll call him - I'm sure he'll be honored to perform for the Clintons and his own President."

So, the dancers were arranged. Then I lined up a local ensemble, QuinTango, and, through another tango friend, Raul Jaurena, a maestro of the bandoneon (a small accordion that's the heart of tango music) and recent American citizen. The entertainment was going to be spectacular.

I was surprised at how exciting it was to be a guest, instead of an anonymous staffer at the back of the room. I walked proudly through the area where the press gathers to eyeball the guests and ask questions. I always thought it was funny to watch how different people handle this moment. Government people usually scuttle through like timid mice, with heads down, bland smiles and eyes averted, clearly hoping no one asks them a question. God forbid you say the wrong thing and end up on the front page of the Post! Corporate guests walk through in a kind of daze, and celebrity guests stroll along with big smiles, happy to have their photo taken and say something for the television press.

We received our escort cards (the small notes in envelopes that tell you what your table number is) and walked upstairs to the East Room, where guests gathered for cocktails. The two Presidents and First Ladies were up in the Residence, waiting for the signal to march down the stairs to greet the guests. We found Pablo, his girlfriend, and his dance partner, the elfin and exquisite Victoria Vieyra. I told them a little about the art and the history of the House, and introduced them to Salma Hayak, Hollywood fabulous in a silver slip dress and shiny straight hair.

The principals (shorthand for the two presidents and two first ladies) came and stood at the foot of the stairs, and we all waited for the receiving line. The President gave me a hug and introduced me to President Menem. Hillary smiled warmly. I kept thinking, *It's funny how odd this feels. I'm sure I should be over there, at the back of the room, checking on some last minute details - shouldn't I?*

We took our places at tables dressed in scarlet damask, with red, orange, yellow and hot pink roses. Hillary often used the Reagan china, with its wide red and gold border. Before the Reagans donated the service to the White House, there was no complete set of china for First Families to use - can you believe it? Thank you Ron and Nancy for your wonderful gift.

I was seated next to an economic advisor to the Argentine President, and our conversation was slow going. But, you only have to talk to the person on one side during one course. You get to turn to the other side when the next course is presented to you. Let's hear it for protocol! The dinner was delicious, another triumph for Hillary and her chef, Walter Scheib. Her inspiration and encouragement and Walter's skill had turned the White House kitchen into a world class restaurant, with the best and most interesting American cuisine served anywhere. No more stodgy French food, with its heavy sauces and sky high calories, for this Presidential couple.

When dessert arrived, everyone at the table stopped talking and said, "Ooohhh!" as the waiter presented a silver platter with an oval, dulce de leche bombe/dome (traditional Latin American caramel ice cream). At the back of the platter, a pair of chocolate tango dancers embraced under a chocolate palm tree. Another triumph for Roland Meissner, White House pastry chef for twenty five years.

After the toasts of mutual friendship, and the dinner, (and just one more chocolate in the shape of the Presidential seal) everyone moved into the East Room, where the carpets had been removed to create a dance floor. Performances after a state dinner last only about twenty minutes. You've got to squeeze a lot of passion and brilliance into a short time. Pablo and Victoria danced, QuinTango played, by themselves and with Maestro Jaurena. Bob and Lucianna danced. Then the four dancers performed together. I looked around the room and saw every guest, American and Argentinian, in rapt attention, gasping at some of Pablo's more acrobatic moves. The women were exquisite and graceful in their partner's arms. The men were handsome and intense. Even those unfamiliar with tango could see the "conversation" taking place between them, as their feet glided and kicked and spun them around. I sat on the edge of my gilt ballroom chair, mesmerized.

When it all ended, there was thunderous applause. A friend who had been to every state dinner, turned to me and said, "I believe we've just seen the most exciting and beautiful entertainment ever at any event here"

Yessss!

After the performance, the President was inspired to ask an Argentine lady to dance, and President Menem asked Hillary (who NEVER dances). They gamely moved across the floor to recorded tangos as we all watched. The President, while no dancer, is a musician, so he knows how to move to the beat. Good for him for trying. I was also happy to

see him, usually so depressed and burdened by his legal problems, relaxed and happy – at least for one evening.

When they finished and left the East Room, we all went out to the Foyer, where the Marine Band struck up happy dance music. Steve and I got out there right away to show off our steps. No tango, but plenty of swing and fox trot. I was out of breath when Pablo walked over and asked me to dance a swing with him.

He led me out on the floor and we danced a lively jive. This is one of the top dancers in the world, but he had only recently taken up American swing. We had a great time, and when it ended he smiled, kissed my hand and said, "You're a really good dancer."

Now, imagine if Fred Astaire told you you're a good dancer. I was over the moon.

***

On the Hill, the lunatic Republicans were unmoved by our win in the '98 midterms and all the polls showing the American people were opposed to their persecution of the President. They didn't care. They were going to impeach this man, no matter what the public wanted. One of the President's aides asked Newt Gingrich why they were proceeding in the face of this clear opposition. His answer?

"Because we can."

That about sums it up. Newt lost his own job over this - for failing to protect the GOP majority when all the zealots thought they should have racked up huge wins. Then the new speaker-designate, Robert Livingston, had to resign the post and his House seat when he realized news about his own sexual escapades was about to go public. Henry Hyde, who pushed the hardest on the House side, had to admit to an affair with a married woman that ruined her marriage. He brushed it off as a "youthful indiscretion." He was in his 40s. Dennis Hastert, later Speaker of the House, was found to have been guilty of paying a young man to keep quiet about sexual abuse. The hypocrisy would choke a horse, but that's politics for you.

On February 12, three weeks after the President's defense ended, the impeachment motions failed. The President told the American people he was profoundly sorry for what he had done, and the burden it had placed on them. He rededicated himself to "a time of reconciliation and renewal for America." He was determined to move on.

The same day the President sent a letter of apology and thanks to White House staff. He acknowledged how difficult the past year had been for all of us and thanked us for keeping focused on getting the job done. He promised to work even harder for the goals we all shared.

His sorrow and exhaustion were written in the heavy bags under his eyes and the weary slump to his shoulders.

We were all hurting and angry. Our service to him and to the country, service we had sacrificed so much for, and been so proud of, would forever be tarnished by his selfish and stupid actions. But now it was time to put it all behind us. If the President and Hillary could do it, of course we should too - and there was so much to do.

My disappointment in the President paled in comparison to my disdain for Ken Starr.

The President had been punished enough, by any normal

standards. The public humiliation, the pain he caused his family, the persecution of innocent colleagues and friends, the astronomical legal bills...?? The out of control "independent" counsel had destroyed too many lives in his relentless pursuit of non-existent "scandals." Seventy million dollars and six years - for what? He later admitted to Congress he had absolved the Clintons of any wrongdoing in *Whitewater* (you know, the so-called scandal he was supposed to be investigating?) months before the mid-term elections. He just didn't bother to share the news with anyone until later, so most Americans had (still have!) no idea. What a despicable man.

In the end, it was the President's fault for fooling around outside his marriage. But! Was he the first? Hardly. Was he the worst? Hardly. He just had the bad luck to be hunted to hell and back for it. And, what's the result? You can argue Al Gore would have won a theft-proof victory; 9/11 would have been prevented by a Gore administration; we would never have gone to war with a country that didn't and couldn't attack us; we wouldn't have squandered lives and treasure we can never recover ... and on and on. Certainly, there are thousands dead and in their graves because of this persecution. I wonder how Ken Starr sleeps at night.

***

Of course, the most wonderful events of 1999 - heck, of the decade! Of the century! - were the celebrations around the coming new millennium. Yeah, yeah, you can argue all you want that it didn't really arrive until the following New Year, but to us normal people, New Year's Eve 1999 was the last one we'd see of the 1900s, and that's all we needed to know.

The President had been talking about and working for the America of the twenty first century since the 1980s. Hillary planned a year of public events around the country, "honoring America's past and imagining America's future". My favorite program was *Saving America's Treasures*, a partnership between the National Park Service and the National Trust for Historic Preservation. The mission is "dedicated to identifying and rescuing the enduring symbols of American tradition that define us as a nation." The first project was saving the flag that inspired the *Star Spangled Banner*. The sponsor? Polo/Ralph Lauren. Isn't this a great fit?

There were celebrations and symposia around the country. Hillary wanted everyone to be involved in appreciating their connections to America's past and thinking about ways to improve America's future.

At the White House I had nothing to do with these, just got to enjoy what I saw and read. But New Year's Eve was the biggest of big deals, and I was thrilled to be invited.

Millennium New Year's Eve at the White House. Doesn't it sound incredible? Well, it was! During the day we watched midnight reach other parts of the world: Hong Kong, Australia, Russia, Rome, Paris (where the fireworks lit up the Eiffel Tower in glorious bursts), and London. We were next!

The Clintons hosted a dinner that night in the East Room for the glitterati - the most accomplished and famous musicians, writers, actors, actresses, singers, poets, thinkers and doers in America. What a gathering! The President sat between Sophia Loren (OK, not, strictly speaking, an American, but pretty swell anyway) and Elizabeth Taylor. One of the butlers told me later Ms. Taylor caught the President eyeing Ms. Loren's impressive breastwork, and said, "I see you're still an admirer of beautiful women."

The President's face turned red and he replied, through clenched teeth, "I don't notice that anymore!"

To which Ms. Taylor cheerfully replied, "Bullshit!"

After dinner, these guests put on their fur coats and boarded trolleys for the trip to the Lincoln Memorial. I bet a lot of those ladies in their evening gowns were freezing. Steve and I dressed at home in long johns and heavy clothes to go to dinner with friends at the Occidental, and then headed to the NPS Visitor Center, where we also boarded trolleys.

The Memorial was brilliantly lit in the frosty air, and the program was a procession of stars and local talent, singing, playing, acting, and reading poetry and inspirational thought from American history. We huddled in our coats and kept our hands tucked into our mittens. (Thank goodness the Park Service always kept me well supplied with chemical hand-warmers, the little packets you shake, and then put into your gloves, or pockets, or shoes.) One amazing star after another performed, and I couldn't tell you a favorite. I kept looking around, at the glittering audience up close, and far behind us the public, watching on Jumbotrons. It was hard to see in the dark, but it looked like hundreds of thousands of people.

The highpoint was fireworks around the Washington Monument, brilliantly lit for the year 2000. We were surprised at how small the fireworks display was, but it turned out this was the plan.

Since I'm an expert on lines of all kinds, I knew it would be difficult to get back to the White House quickly. The moment it all ended, I grabbed Steve's hand and we headed to the parked trolleys. We boarded one of the first, it quickly filled and began its slow trek through the crowds. We were thrilled to see there were lights on in the government buildings we passed. Remember Y2K? Plenty of smart people believed everything controlled by computers would fail at midnight, leaving us in the cold and dark. Thank God they were wrong.

As we sat waiting at an intersection, I glanced south and saw, above a row of buildings, fireworks. I nudged Steve and then motioned to our neighbors, "Look over there!"

For reasons that escape me, the brilliant Quincy Jones, producer of the entertainment, decided to blast off all the best of the fireworks display AFTER midnight. Most people had left the Mall and were already on underground Metro platforms. Instead of an audience of hundreds of thousands, barely thousands got to see them. We craned our necks and watched the best we could. What a shame.

We reached the White House and headed for my office, where I'd left our evening finery. Shed the coats, boots, scarves, hats and gloves for a long gown and heels (me), dinner jacket and dance shoes (Steve). We had to dress fast, because Mary Wilson, of the *Supremes*, and her two ladies were there to perform and needed to use my office as a dressing room. Fine with me. For a week after, there were random sequins and feathers floating around, reminding me of how much fun it had been. I told the cleaning lady not to work too hard at picking them all up.

A few months earlier, I'd had laser eye surgery, and my eyes were significantly under-corrected. It left me with seriously blurry vision (SERIOUSLY blurry vision), and it couldn't be corrected until six months passed. Meanwhile, I'd be in a room with guests and the President and vision so bad I'd have to whisper to another staffer, "Please nudge me when the President nods he's ready for this guest. I can just barely make out which one he is, because of his height, but I can't see the expression on his face right now."

This had been an incredibly aggravating problem for me, but one I had to live with until the docs said I was ready to be operated on again. I wasn't thinking about it when we headed out to the party, but I soon began to realize how it was going to impact this special evening.

"Oh, look!" said Steve. "It's Robert deNiro! Oh, sorry, I forgot you can't see him."

"Wow, over there, doesn't Trisha Yearwood look gre ... oh, sorry, you can't see her."

"Isn't that ... Martin Scorcese? Wonder Woman (Linda Carter)? Tom Jones, talking to John Mellencamp? Oh, sorry, you can't see him/her/them ..."

Can you imagine how upset I was? A once in a lifetime event, and I literally would have had to trip over these celebrities to see who was there. Damn!

I was happy to recognize one guest who wasn't such a well known celebrity. The master glass artist Dale Chichuly had created a pair of breathtaking glass Christmas trees for the North Foyer that dazzled us and the tourists all December. Clear, milky white, opalescent, and gold glass in long gourd shapes hung from center supports, lit from within. Magical!

I was standing by one of these trees when Mr. Chichuly, dressed in a bright red suit and his distinctive eye patch, walked by. No one else seemed to know who he was, but I stopped him and gushed. "Mr. Chichuly - Happy Millennium New Years. I'm on staff here, and I've been a fan of yours forever. I helped select the blue bowls my Georgetown class gave to the Clintons for our reunion in 1998. I'm thrilled to meet you."

He smiled, we stood for a moment admiring the glass tree together, and then he moved away into the crowd.

Steve found me and started again with, "Oh, there's Will Smith ... Mohammed Ali ... oops, you can't see them ..."

Well, if I couldn't identify most of the guests I could still see and enjoy the transformation of the House, and it was incredible.

The Jacqueline Kennedy Garden, on the East side, was tented in miles of iridescent purple satin, with a midnight blue ceiling covered with tiny lights, like stars. It was a jazz club, with bars and cabaret tables scattered along the edges. The grass had been left uncovered. We checked it out quickly, then moved back into the House, and on to the West Wing. The Rose Garden was also tented, transformed into a New York disco, all in white and silver. White cloths covered small tables, and we sat on small silver ballroom chairs with white velvet cushions, next to groupings of white velvet ottomans for lounging. White orchids topped each table. A DJ spun dance music, and there were bars in the corners.

On the West side of the Garden, the steps leading to the Oval Office were lit and guests were allowed to go up to the French door there and look in. The Resolute desk shone. Hanging on the wall was the White House's Christmas present from Stephen Spielberg and Kate Capshaw - a Nelson Rockefeller painting of the Statue of Liberty, showing the grand dame against the bluest sky. Beautiful!

We wandered from there to the State Floor, where famous artists took turns performing. There were crowds everywhere, and I squinted and stared to try to see all the celebrities. I'm sure people around me thought I was scowling, but I wasn't. Just trying to see a little.

Finally, we settled in the Rose Garden disco, on the ballroom chairs. Friends came by and lounged on the velvet ottomans. We laughed, took photos of each other, drank champagne and ate delicious food from trays passed by butlers. We watched the President dance with Chelsea, whirling her around the floor, everyone giddy with the excitement of the moment.

Millennium New Year's Eve! At the White House! I can't believe we're here!

I thought that we'd always have the photos of this magical

night to remind us of our moment in history. I carefully put them into one of more than twenty albums of photos, programs, agendas, notes I sent the President or Hillary, notes they sent back to me – all kinds of mementos I had kept and lovingly organized. Because I'm a very visual person, these albums were the prompts that helped me write this book. (And it's a good think I did that, as none of us could keep a journal – it would have been subpoenad by some aggrieved senator or counselor during the unending investigations. Ugh.)

Sadly, somewhere in our move from Washington to Baja, Mexico, in 2006, that album disappeared – the only album out of twenty we can't find. It's a tragedy!

But somewhere back in a closet I still have my black velvet dance shoes, with the champagne glasses and "2000" embroidered on them. Maybe someday I'll have a granddaughter to hand them down to.

***

Diagram of the State Floor reception rooms where events take place.

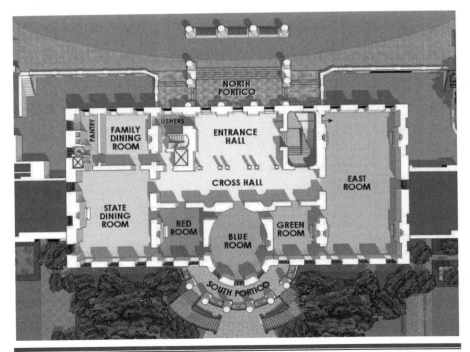

CHAPTER TWENTY SEVEN ~ THE LAST OF IT ALL

With the click of the calendar to the new millennium we ran smack into the reality that this would be our last year. Every annual thing we did would be our last - State of the Union, Egg Roll, July 4, President's Birthday on the Lawn, turkey pardoning, Christmas ...

Things move so fast at the White House, it sure didn't feel as if seven years had gone by. The pressure is so intense, so relentless, we joked that one year of White House life was the equivalent of seven years in the "real world." So, our seven years was really more like forty-nine normal years somewhere else. And yet, it was intoxicating, and addictive. To get to go to work every day in the most famous House in America, to walk through the gardens, look at the art and antiques, to share it with the most interesting people in the world, to meet world leaders seeking peace, to serve the public, to serve a President and First Lady I loved and admired, to work with the smartest people I'd ever met - this was the most exciting time in my life, and I was not going to let the final year pass without treasuring every moment.

I was **still** pushing the envelope to improve the tour process, now electronically. But once again we ran into obstructionist bureaucrats demanding ridiculous conditions no one could meet.

"There's no time for all that," I pleaded. "Hello? Does the date, January 20, 2001 mean anything to you? We have this one, last chance to reinvent government, and you won't help us?"

Well, no, they wouldn't.

Feel free to roll your eyes here, at the intransigence of bureaucrats, standing in the way of better government services. I know I did.

In the end, the best we could do was put everything in place so the new system would be available for the incoming administration (which I assumed would be my friends from the VP's office). Maybe they'd have better luck working with the bureaucrats. It was a big disappointment to me.

In our plans for the final Egg Roll, we came back to technology again. After the hassle of wiring the lawn in 1998, we passed on cybercasting in '99. But 2000 was our last chance to make history, so I was up for whatever it would take. Well, glory, halleluiah, the technology had advanced, and now we could do it wirelessly. Hooray!

Once again, Howard Lefkowitz was the man to make this happen for us. He brought in everything we needed to cybercast our event out to people around the country and around the world. Once again, the Clinton White House Easter Egg Roll goes global!

On Holy Saturday I welcomed Leonardo DiCaprio to the White House, walking him, his mother and uncle around for an hour or so. I know he's one of the best actors in the world, and one of the handsomest men, but he walked around with his baggy pants drooping off his ass, and I had to stop myself from stepping up behind him to yank them up. To me, he looked like a soft, spoiled boy. But a boy with very nice manners - his assistant sent me a bottle of wine. And he certainly did grow up into a gorgeous and politically involved man.

Since it was our final Egg Roll, I decided this year, for the first time, I'd read to the children myself. I found a sweet book, *Princess Prunella and the Purple Peanut* (it grew on her NOSE), and practiced my dramatic reading, while my staff, laughing uncontrollably, gasped out, "Diction! Diction! Make sure you pronounce that last word very carefully!"

A friend of Hillary's from New York, Jane Rosenthal, is a good friend of Robert DeNiro, and casually mentioned at lunch one day he might enjoy reading at the event.

"Really? You think Robert DeNiro would read at the Egg Roll?" I mean, Robert, "you talking to ME?" DeNiro? I had difficulty imagining this, but what did I know?

"Sure, he has twin sons who are toddlers - he's great with kids. If you like, I'll ask him."

"Wonderful! Just let me know."

Every year a different artist is invited to do the artwork for the program cover and the wooden eggs. We'd had some beautiful covers, but I liked this one the best of all. Mary Engelbreit, whose colorful and whimsical designs are collected by fans all over the world, agreed to be our artist. In fact, when she was asked, she responded, "I'll be delighted to do this. You know, I was asked during the Reagan and Bush years, but I told them as much as I was honored, I preferred to wait for a Democratic President to ask me."

Her distinctive style and bright colors were perfect for this project.

The morning of the event I watched Robert De Niro feed cookies to his adorable twin boys in their stroller in the Green Room. They sure were cute. Everyone took pictures of the magnificent, three-foot tall sugar Easter eggs on the buffet table in the East Room, then nibbled pastries and drank coffee. The sponsors and celebrity guests went through the receiving line in the Blue Room and then out to the Lawn. When they had all left, I turned to the President.

"Mr. President, I asked the Curators to check their history, and, as far as we can tell, you and Hillary are the only Presidential couple to personally host eight Egg Rolls. So, you've made history here as well . Isn't that interesting?"

The President looked shocked. "What do you mean? Didn't everyone do this?"

"No, sir. Other couples hosted a year or two, but then they got busy or disinterested and turned it over to the Vice President or a Cabinet Secretary. You two are the only ones."

"Well, for goodness sakes. It's such fun - I wouldn't miss this for anything."

He turned and walked over to Hillary, standing by a window talking to the Social Secretary.

"Hillary, Melinda tells me we're the first Presidential couple to ever host all eight Egg Rolls - isn't that something?"

"Really? That's great! Another record set in our last year, and such a fun one! The kids are so adorable."

I briefed them on the particulars of the day, and they went out from the Blue Room Portico, to the elevated stage on the driveway. The President made his welcoming remarks and then, for the first time ever, thanked me in public.

"... and we'd like to thank Melinda Bates, who's been organizing these events for us and for all of you. She's done a great job and we appreciate her so much." (Or words to that effect.)

I'd been absently listening while checking things off my very long mental list. When I heard the President say my name, I was startled and grateful. The number one rule of staff is to be anonymous, and I was always happy to be in the background. But it was very sweet to hear him thank me. Thank YOU, Mr. President, for giving me the opportunity to do the job all those years.

As he finished speaking, I checked my radio, pager and phone, and got ready to go out to the Lawn where I'd spend my day racing around from activity to activity to make sure everything went well. Before I could move, I saw a woman waving at me from behind the snow fence. I braced myself, assumed a complaint was coming my way, and walked over with a smile.

"Hello, how can I help you?"

"Aren't you the woman who organizes this event? I saw you on TV."

"Yes, I am," I smiled, "how can I help you?"

"I wanted to tell you, my child is disabled, and you invite her and the kids from her special classes to come here early, to roll eggs, listen to readers and decorate eggs. We do lots of activities together, but for everywhere else we go - **everywhere** - these kids are the last ones to get to do an activity. You put them first here, at the White House, and I wanted to tell you how much we appreciate it."

Dang! I expected a complaint, not this gracious thank you. My eyes teared up, and I choked out, "Thank you for telling me. It makes all the effort so worth it." And, it did.

I grabbed Steve, who was carrying all my communications equipment, and we headed out, eager to see the activities and watch the children. I did a video interview with Laura Lefkowitz for the cybercast. We watched "Abigail Adams" talk to a fascinated audience of kids and their parents sitting on the grass. There were eggs everywhere - in Easter baskets, on crafts tables for decorating, and in the Egg Roll lanes, where the word "roll" was (as always) loosely interpreted by the kids who found it easier (or more fun) to flip and toss them. I pretended not to see the parents trying to scam additional wooden eggs from the poor volunteers. God bless them.

I read my story to a group of kids and parents who had no idea who I was (no reason they should) and seemed to enjoy it anyway. I sure did.

Then Steve and I wandered over to the stage where Robert De Niro was reading. We stood at the back, but we couldn't hear him over the chatter of two women nearby having a loud conversation. After a few minutes I gently said, "shhhh!"

They didn't even pause.

Again, I put my finger to my lips and said, louder, "shhhh!"

This time they looked my way and said, "Get a grip, lady. We're outside, and it's noisy. Get over it."

Normally, my mission was to make every guest feel comfortable, happy and welcome. Not this time.

"Yes, I know exactly where we are, because I am THE WOMAN WHO ORGANIZED THIS EVENT, AND NOW I WANT TO HEAR ROBERT DE NIRO READ TO THE CHILDREN, SO PLEASE JUST SHUT UP OR I'LL HAVE YOU ESCORTED OFF THIS LAWN!"

That got their attention. They looked shocked and hustled away. Steve looked shocked and then laughed. He put his arm around me, I leaned into him and we listened to one of American's greatest actors gently read a children's story.

As we walked the Lawn, checking all the arrangements, I kept muttering, "Remember this. Remember this. It's our last time out here at Easter, so lock these memories away in your heart forever."

In the first years after we left the White House, there were many, many things I missed, but I didn't (and don't) miss organizing the Egg Roll. It's a huge and complicated event I wouldn't want to work on again. Not to mention, I never did like rising at "Oh-dark-thirty" to be professional and coherent before dawn. In 2001 I deliberately slept late, watched a little of the coverage of the first Bush Egg Roll (nothing special as far as I could see) and took bunches of flowers to the people who had worked on Egg Rolls for me.

***

July 4th was especially emotional. Once we got our 14,000 or so guests onto the Lawn, and the sound system keyed into the National Symphony Orchestra, Steve and I sat on the Blue Room Portico, looking out at the starry night. I clutched his hand tight, and tried to keep from weeping as the rockets' red glare flashed over the Washington monument. *Hold onto this!*

Howard's family was with us. I looked over and saw Harriet crying too, and whispering to Laura, "Remember this forever, sweetheart. This is so amazing ..."

***

By the summer of 2000, the smarter Clintonites were lining up swell new jobs. I had a conversation with a man from the Chief of Staff's office who gave me a friendly warning: "You need to look for your next job now, while the President is still in office, and your connection to him is a powerful draw to some high-level firm."

I thought about this, but not hard enough. My heart wasn't in it. My heart decided long before that I began with the President in January 1993, and I wanted to turn out the lights on the final day with the President, in January 2001. I knew if I did this I'd make history - the first Director of the Visitors Office to serve all eight years of an administration.

And, I was confident about my future for several reasons. First, like all of us in the Clinton White House, I admired Vice President Gore very much, and believed he'd win the 2000 election. When he did, we Clintonites would stay in place at our jobs for a while, and then slowly transition out to great new careers as the Gore people stepped into their positions. Oops! Well, we were right about him winning (don't bother to go there, you'll never convince me). We just didn't figure he'd have his election win stolen by the Supreme Court and handed to the loser. Who would have imagined that?!

So instead of looking for a new career, I focused on enjoying the final year.

***

The summer flew by, to the President's August birthday, his last in the White House. I gave him a set of children's playing cards from the early twentieth century, with pictures of the Presidents up to TR, and text about their accomplishments. The following year, when I visited him in Harlem, I saw it in his office, next to a lot of very expensive gifts from other people. I really love eBay!

Glenn Maes made the last of his amazing cakes for the President's birthday party on the Lawn and we all celebrated. Brilliant sunshine poured down on us, smiling and laughing as we joked about how old the President - and we- were getting. He looked wistful, wandering from group to group, chatting with staff. When he saw me, he gave me a hug and stood with his arm across my shoulders as we compared notes about our advanced age. I loved reminding him I'm almost three weeks younger. When he moved along I stood in the shade of the trees and looked back at the blinding white of the House, the puffy clouds in the blue sky, and the intense green of the grass and trees. I took a deep breath, closed my eyes and memorized the smell of it all. The most perfect Washington summer day.

Then came my own last birthday in the White House. I was glad many of my staff had stayed, and some came back to celebrate with me. I became very close to the people I worked with over the years. They were like family, and now we were looking at each other with sad eyes, knowing the "family" was soon going to splinter and go off in a thousand different directions.

CHAPTER TWENTY EIGHT ~ MOVIN' ON OUT

Our final big project in 2000 was the creation of manuals covering every aspect of Visitors Office responsibilities. Not the most exciting project we'd done, but the President committed himself, and all of us, to the most comprehensive and effective transition in history. His heart was in the right place. Of course, we all thought we'd be transitioning to our friends in the Gore administration, so there was no lack of enthusiasm for the task

We wrote, edited, rewrote, and edited some more. Every couple of weeks I delivered our latest effort to White House Counsel, so they could review and tell us what to change. Then we'd start all over again. It went on for months.

In hindsight (remember? the ONLY kind of insight in politics?), this was a complete waste of time. If we'd known we'd be replaced by the Bush administration we could just not have bothered. They hated Bill Clinton, everything he and we represented and everything we did for him. So, no matter how successful and effective a program or process was, if it was associated with Clintonites, it was poison to them. The manuals we labored over so carefully? Useless trash. And this was true from the most important public policy to the relative unimportance of the Visitors Office. We later heard their mantra was "ABC" - anything but Clinton. Doesn't seem to have worked out very well for them, did it?

***

In November, the President invited me to fly on Air Force One for the last time. I left the White House carrying a garment bag with my evening clothes, on the staff bus to Andrews Air Force Base. We were only going to New York, for a charity fund-raiser, so the other staffers and I didn't bother with the regular staff cabin. We just settled into chairs around the conference table, glancing idly at the television screens and taking turns changing into our evening clothes. I was the only one on board not a frequent AF1 flyer. To the President and Hillary's aides it was clearly no more exciting than hailing a cab.

But for me, knowing it was my last flight, the moments were exciting and bitter sweet. It felt as if we barely got into the air before we touched down at JFK. Then things really got interesting. We boarded a pair of shiny Marine helicopters and took off for the Wall Street landing zone, passing the Statue of Liberty on our way in, with a swell look at the New York skyline.

At the landing zone we ran out of the 'copters, piled into the long line of cars in the motorcade and took off uptown, at, I'd guess, 60 mph. Now that was fun! We raced through the city, and I could see the cross streets all barricaded for our passing, the police holding back pedestrians, the people standing and waving. New Yorkers have seen everything, but they liked Bill Clinton, and Hillary Clinton had just become the junior Senator from New York. People stood and cheered.

New York events are always so much more interesting than Washington ones. In Washington, everything is about political power, position, and policy. For women, it's dangerous to dress too nicely. You won't be taken seriously. Even women who might like to look glamorous, or could afford to dress elegantly, seldom do. People would frown and wonder what you're trying so hard to prove.

But in New York, the power is all about money and style - a language I love. Women dress in exquisite, sometimes exquisitely eccentric style. They're not afraid of serious jewelry. They don't think it's frivolous to be beautiful. On the contrary, if you don't make an effort, you are inconsequential. I love New York!

The Clintons' friend, Denise Rich, had organized a fund raiser in support of cancer research. As always, staff stood off to the side and watched. Just a few feet away I spotted her big celebrity guest, Michael Jackson. He was so weird looking it took all my effort not to stare. His face was dead white, and he had long, flowing, glamorous, '40's movie star hair. Every time I glanced his way, I shivered at the creepiness of it.

The President's speech was fascinating, as usual, and I remember turning to his aide, shaking my head, and saying, "Eight years of brilliance and eloquence. How much are we going to miss this?" I had no idea.

On our flight back to JFK the helicopter pilots took us up high enough to see the canyons of New York's avenues opening up before us, and the skyscrapers, all brilliantly lit and sparkling like stars against the dark of the night and the streets. Breathtaking! Then, when we headed out, we flew around the top of the Statue of Liberty. I never thought I'd get to see her from up there. Thank you, Mr. President.

***

For our final Pageant of Peace tree lighting, our producers, Bob Johnson and Joe Fab arranged a fabulous coup - *the Three Tenors*. They came to me early in September with the news that Placido Domingo, a good friend of the Clintons, had offered this incredible act. There was just one little hitch: they were only available ONE night in early December. We had to schedule the event that night or they were out. Maybe you think this shouldn't have been a problem. Tsk. You haven't been paying attention. Even after almost eight years, the Clintons were just as difficult to schedule as ever. It's nothing personal, it's how they are.

So, with my fingers crossed, I sent the scheduling requests to the President's office and Hillary's scheduler, Patti Solis Doyle (who later ran her 2008 campaign). I waited. Waited some more. Weeks passed, and I re-sent the memos, but heard nothing. Now our producers, and Sony Music, were getting nervous. Hell, I was getting nervous. *The Three Tenors!* Hello?

In November I saw Patti at lunch in the Mess, and she whined, "I don't know why you keep calling me about that event."

"Um, because you're the scheduler for the First Lady, and traditionally she accompanies the President to the tree lighting? It would be a shocker if she didn't, in her last year. Can't you please talk to Presidential scheduling and lock them in for this date?"

It's OK, you can roll your eyes here. I know I did.

"I don't know, I don't know. We'll have to see ..."

Bob and Joe, who had no idea how difficult this was, couldn't understand the delay and kept pressing me for a commitment. Finally, just a few weeks out, I sent Patti yet another memo: "The Clintons have an opportunity to host the most prestigious talent in the history of the Pageant of Peace, but the offer expires at close of business **tomorrow**. If we don't commit to the date for *the Three Tenors*, it will be too late to line up any other big stars, and we'll be stuck with *Crusty the Clown* as our headliner. I don't think any of us want that. Please respond."

Well, the threat of a Simpsons character got their attention. By the following morning I had a "Yes" and could tell our producers to go ahead. We were all thrilled. *The Three Tenors!* We'd put on a final tree lighting people would talk about for a decade.

But, best laid plans, well, you know.

Two weeks before the event, Luciano Pavarotti bailed. He hadn't thought about how cold it would be (although we'd been clear about it); he hadn't realized he'd be singing outside, with no cover, and might be rained or snowed on (although we'd been clear about that too). We heard Mr. Domingo had pleaded with him, but without success. Holy cow! NOW what would we do?

Bob and Joe gave the folks at Sony an earful about commitments, and Presidential expectations. I was enraged. After all the pushing, and making a nuisance of myself, I'd look like a fool. Can you hear the "smack!" as my palm hit my forehead?

The Sony people, perhaps marginally embarrassed, offered up Charlotte Church. I'd never heard of her, but this adorable young girl was huge in Britain, singing everything from operatic arias to pop with a voice like an angel. She came, and charmed us all. Her voice was exquisite.

Our last Christmas was as over-the-top as all the others had been. Instead of a new theme, Hillary decided to use decorations from the seven previous years. They're beautiful, whimsical, clever and original, true works of art. I guess now they all live in storage at the Clinton Library, tucked away in boxes. What a shame. First Ladies don't reuse decorations made for their predecessors.

The exquisite collection of American crafts Hillary had assembled in 1993 came back from touring museums for final display on White House tables and mantels. Works in glass, metal, ceramic, wood and paper by the country's most gifted craftspeople were my favorites of all the artistic projects she commissioned.

***

All this time we'd been carrying on our work responsibilities while watching in stunned disbelief as the 2000 election results were disputed in the press, in the courts, and in voting districts across Florida. Had American suddenly become a banana republic with crooked elections decided not by actual voters, but by party operatives and shady judges? It sure looked that way. We pored over the papers, watched the news non-stop. He had won, hadn't he? Al Gore had actually WON, hadn't he?

Well, yes, but it didn't matter. The Supreme Court ruled a complete recall would irreparably damage candidate Bush (you think?) and called it off. Did the VP and his team make mistakes? Sure. Did they underestimate the slimy trickery of the Republicans? You bet. But, you know what, after eight years of what they had done to Bill and Hillary Clinton, how could Democrats make these mistakes? Are we just slow learners? In denial? Relentlessly naive? All of the above?

We alternated between rage, hope and heartbreak - and that was minute to minute. I couldn't imagine what our friends in the VP's office were going through. I couldn't bring myself to talk to any of them. It was too painful, and, what could I say? What could they say?

The day of the final ruling by the Supremes, the day the VP graciously conceded, was the day the Gores had invited dozens of people to a holiday reception at their home. I called their aide and asked, "Surely you're canceling tonight? I mean, they don't want a house full of people tonight of all nights?"

"Please come. They want the party to go on; they'll be here, and you should come to say goodbye to them."

Steve, my son Noah and I headed out for the strangest, saddest "party" I'd ever been to. The house was beautifully decorated for the holidays. There was a tent, bars, food, everything very festive. But we all walked around in shock, clutching each friend to say, "Can you believe it? How could this happen in America?"

The Gores came out, and both spoke briefly. They were composed and calm - which was more than most of us were. Such great people, so devoted to public service. Despite what the press told everyone, some of us didn't buy their loony preference for "the guy you'd most like to have a beer with." I wasn't planning to DATE the President, so "brilliant" and "engaged" were important qualities to me. He would have been a fine President, and so much better than what we got. I don't know how the Justices can sleep at night. I don't know how the Republican operatives can sleep at night, after handing us one of the worst Presidents of the last hundred years.

After the reception we trudged back to the White House. The VP was going to make his concession speech from his office in the OEOB, and I wanted to be there. We watched on television in my office, tears streaming down our faces. Then we went out to the steps of the building, a crowd of several hundred, to cheer them as they left. (There I am on the right, in the hat. You can't see my tears.)

This pretty much sucked all the joy out of our last Christmas. Now we knew all our work on the transition would benefit, not our beloved Vice President, but an upstart "legacy" from Texas, who we already knew was unqualified for the job. I had to grit my teeth and remind myself, "He didn't beat MY guy. He could never beat MY guy. And my guy asked us to do a good job of this, so I'm doing it for HIM, not for W."

I was a huge fan of *the West Wing*, as so many in the White House were. Over time I got to know the writers, actors and producers, taking them on tours, and to lunch in the Mess. Every week or so I got a call from someone asking, "Melinda, we want to show a meeting about (name your topic here) and we need to know who would be in that meeting? Where would it take place? Is this plot line plausible?"

Of course, I loved this. In my heart, I wanted to be a writer for the show when our time at the White House ended.

On December 20th, Steve and I had been to yet another holiday party, got home late, dropped our finery, pulled on our 'jammies, hopped into bed and turned on the television. My TiVO was programmed with a "season pass" for *the West Wing*, and I couldn't wait to see the latest episode. We snuggled up and watched the opening scene. There was a problem of some kind, and CJ, the President's Press Secretary, shouted to someone, "Get me the Director of the Visitors Office!"

Well, that got our attention. I sat up in bed, excited.

"Wow! Oh boy! This is so great! They actually wrote me into an episode!"

But then, then ... their "Director" walked in, and he was a MAN. A seventy year old man, with a British accent and a snooty attitude.

I couldn't believe it. After all my help they done me wrong.

We watched the end of the episode, and I was still upset. Too upset to sleep, so I went into my home office, sat down, and wrote a little poem (remember, it was Christmas):

Ode to *the West Wing*

'Twas five days before Christmas and all through the House
Not a creature was stirring - 'cause we were all out.
The TiVO was set, all the "favorites" chosen
So *West Wing* and *ER* would not be forgotten.
Around about midnight, when we had come home,
And settled in bed, and turned off the phone,
Steve in his 'jammies and I in my gown
We turned on the TV and guess what we found -
West Wing was recorded - just as we'd hoped
(otherwise I would have ranted and moped.)
So we lifted a glass, and had us a nosh
To see what the writers had planned for ol' Josh.
His face was quite grim as his problem was told,
And we sighed as we watched his sad story unfold.
The choirs, the trees, the bell ringers too
Reminded us both how the House is a zoo
In December when holidays brighten our lives -
But one more soprano will give me the hives!
Then what to my wondering eyes should appear
But a story you guys had requested I hear.
I sat up in bed, I settled the blanket
When CJ said, "Bring me the VO director!"
I thought about calling my friends just to gloat
'Cause all of us Clintonites just love to dote
On this program so clever and carefully made -
The writers must all be so handsomely paid ...
Imagine my shock, my angst and my grief
To discover the VO director's a creep!
He's snobby, cantankerous, rude and affected.
And worst of all cases, his gender was bended!
A man? He's a man! Oh, the shame of it all!
How could you resort to a theme so banal!
I've been trashed, I've been thrashed, I've been run thru the mill

(For a Clintonite, life in the White House 's a thrill.)
But I never expected a stab in the back
From you Hollywood folks who are born with a knack
Of twisting and turning the truth on its end
So even a mother would not comprehend
That her daughter is really quite good at her job,
And never - no NEVER - behaves as a snob.
So we muttered and wailed and were too mad to sleep
(I just must say again - that old guy is a creep!)
We turned off the TV and turned out the light.
Just be glad you were too far away for a fight!
May the mudslides and earthquakes and fires all get you!
Or worse - may the Bushies all try to adopt you.
Let's just see how your President Bartlett gets on
With the right-wing Hezbollah when we are all gone.
Enough of this rant, it has quite spoiled my day
To consider your treachery, goodness! Oy vey!
May your holiday stockings all be filled with coal.
(It's likely you'll need it for an energy hole.)
May your dreams all be filled with McLaughlin and Matthews -
A pox on these spinmeisters, now let THEM bash you.
A Republican stew, yes that's just what you'd like!
Merry Christmas to all, and to all a GOOD NIGHT!

OK, I'm not the world's best poet, but it did capture my mood! The next day I faxed it to *the West Wing* writers' office and got a quick call back.

"Melinda, we're so sorry! The story line and script all called for a woman like you in the part. We wanted to show our appreciation for all your help. But at the last minute Aaron (Sorkin) came in and changed things. We had this guy, who was supposed to be the White House curator, and we had to move him into your job. We're sorry!" Well, boo.

On December 23, as I had for all our White House years, we attended the Messiah Sing Along, in the President's box at the

Kennedy Center. The lump in my throat made it hard to sing (just as well, as I'm not any good). I clutched Steve's hand and blinked away tears. My son, Shiloh, came too, I think as much to cheer me up as for the history of it. What a privilege it had been to see concerts, shows and operas from the center box with the elegant lounge behind. We drank our last champagne from the little bottles with the Presidential seal around the neck, and took photos of each other there for the last time.

***

Hilary redecorates the Blue Room back in 1993....

CHAPTER TWENTY NINE ~
AND NOW, THE TIME HAS COME ...

We're careening towards our end date, January 20 2001, and hold onto your hats, boys, it's going to be a bumpy ride.

Time's up - for everything. No time for any more improvements to our work. No time to tweak the transition manuals anymore and, really, I don't want to. I've done my best at this last service to my President, and I'm done. I don't give a rat's ass about the incoming Bush people. If they use it, they will succeed. If they don't, they'll fail - fine with me.

No time to pack, and that's a huge problem for the President and me. I have an office full of eight years of mementos and some really nice, personal furniture. Steve has been helping me pack for weeks, little by little, wrapping things up, taking them home, where they sit in my living room. I have no time, or emotional energy to unpack them there. Let it all go up to the attic, so I don't have to deal with it any more. And still, there's more stuff. How can this be? I mean, it's only ONE room, after all.

Just think how much worse the problem is for the President.

From his Cabinet Secretaries on down through every level of White House staff, he's demanded lists of projects to try to push through at the last minute or set in place with an executive order. Unlike the rest of us, he never says a critical word about his successor, and it's clear he doesn't want to hear it, either. But he must be frantic at the thought of the hatchet George W will to take to his life's work, slicing and dicing his way through the most successful and popular programs, achievements of a lifetime. Little does he know!

And now he insists, against all advice and pleading, he wants to pack up his things himself. This is plain crazy. The President does not pack. It's not presidential. There are plenty of other people glad to step up, and likely to do a fine job of it. I guess he's worried about some small memento, some important piece of history ending up at the wrong place - the Clinton Library, the gorgeous apartment above it, the farm house in Chappaqua, or the elegant brick mansion on Embassy Row. It's not as if things could not be found - and moved - later, but no, he's going to do it himself. The problem with this (the worst of many problems with this) is - of course - he is not actually packing, just *promising* to pack. He keeps putting it off. Because he's too busy? Because he wants to postpone the inevitable? Who knows? Whatever the reason, it's driving everyone crazy.

Now his persistent problem with time we've all gotten used to over the years and adjusted for, is really making problems. When you are President, the world will (more or less happily) wait while you finish an unexpectedly interesting conversation with a film star or Nobel prize winner. When you are President, the plane - Air Force One! - does not take off until you are ready.

But January 20, 2001 is a deadline set in stone. Or, the constitution, which is really the same thing. If he doesn't either let someone else do the job, or get to it himself (which, face it, is not going to happen), the staff will be left to frantically toss things into indiscriminate boxes at the last minute, and then God knows where the stuff will end up - maybe in a government box in a bureaucrat's warehouse, like Indiana Jones' Arc of the Covenant.

Now that date is rushing to overtake us all, as we race to finish up, tie up, and move out. I am beyond tired myself, running on fumes, doing my best to stay focused and get the final job done. Not a moment to think about how it feels to be going through this unusual experience. There will be plenty of time for that later. And sleep. There will be time for sleep and rest later as well. Exhaustion is simply a garment we all wear, hanging loosely over our aching bones.

Every day is filled with farewells, as my staff leave, one by one, for their new jobs, new lives. It's like watching my children leave, except I know I'll never see some of them again. Before they go, the President calls us over for a photo with him in the Oval. Very thoughtful.

I make my rounds in the East and West Wings, saying good bye to those who, like me, stayed to the end. There aren't a lot of us. The smart people are already ensconced in swell, new jobs, watching this from the outside.

Now I get a call for a different photo: all the people who have been with the Clintons in the White House for all eight years. I think, *how many could that be?* Will we fit in the Oval? Well, no problem. There are only about ten of us - **ten** - who made it for the whole ride (as the President says). And, I can't believe it, but there are faces in this small group I've never seen before. Where have they been for eight years?

I take friends to lunch in the Mess every day. Soon we'll be lunching at *Au Bon Pain*, I think, so why not grab all the experiences we can?

One week to go, and the Social Office puts on a final great event for everyone - a big party, in a tent on the lawn, for all present and former staff they can reach to invite. Steve and I have been packing, (yes, still!) We clean up and go out for yet another heart-wrenching afternoon of laughter and tears. I'm saying farewell to people I've grown to love and admire, and it's tough. The Clintons both speak. He is nostalgic, wistful, proud of all we've accomplished, and grateful for our hard work. I can actually feel my heart breaking.

Hillary is full of excitement at the new life ahead of her in the Senate. You go girl! We're all over the moon at this new history she's making. Some people ask me why I'm not going to the Hill with her, but it wouldn't make sense. I never worked directly for Hillaryland, and my area of expertise is visitor services, events and administration. There's no fit for me, and truly, I'm hoping for a better job (read: a higher salary) out in the real world. I watch her happy and passionate staff - they're already thinking about the future, not the past. Our past.

Just as we think the event is ending, the curtains open, and Stevie Nicks walks out singing *Don't Stop Thinking About Tomorrow*. Then the rest of *Fleetwood Mac* joins her, and we all go wild at this last rendition of the Clinton's favorite theme song. Remember, he's been called the first "Rock 'n' Roll President," an appellation he wears with pride.

Now, in our final week, the Clintons open up Camp David for all of us to visit. We ride on buses to the Catoctin Mountains in Maryland, climbing through scrubby forest, along fast-moving streams. We pass through intense security and get off in the center of the compound of small, rustic cabins, peeking into the rooms where Presidents, their families, and visiting heads of state stay. It's a real camp, not fancy, at least to look at, with hiking trails, tennis courts, a pool and other recreational facilities. But my favorite space is *Evergreen Chapel*, a gift from George and Barbara Bush, built like an Alpine chalet, with a high, peaked ceiling and exposed wood rafters. It's peaceful, calm, and beautiful.

I wander the trails, thinking about the meetings the President held here with Israeli and Palestinian leaders. He worked so hard for peace, so constantly, right up to the last minute, and still couldn't get Arafat to agree to terms to give his people hope and a better future. Now, all these years later, how many have suffered and died, because of that man's intransigence?

I spent eight years working with people who understood power is meant to be used to benefit the people from whom it comes - not for personal riches or position. The Clintons viewed their time at the White House as an opportunity and sacred trust. Remember this? "What are you doing today, to make people's lives better?"

I wonder if the people who follow us will understand this, and care about it? I don't think so.

Steve brings me a moving truck, and we load all my furniture, art and boxes. Thank God, when I brought it all in I made a list of these personal things and put it on file in the White House decorator's office. I have to produce it for a skeptical Secret Service officer, who doesn't know me, at the door to the East Wing. Later, when I hear the nonsense about Clinton staff supposedly taking public property as they leave, I'm really glad I handled it that way. (I hope you know that "scandal" was a total lie. Everything they took belonged to them, not the government.)

The Archives people come and take away all the documents we carefully packed into numbered boxes and labeled for them. The piece I'm saddest to see go is the red book - the Bush I tours record. All these years I've held onto it as a reminder of how far we've come. Now it will probably live in a dusty box, and no one will understand why we kept it. I take a final peek, close this last box, and watch them load it on the dolly.

Next to go will be the computers, so I write a final message to all my friends, colleagues and family, thanking them for their support and many kindnesses that meant so much to me over the years. I remind them we made history every day (every day!) and they will always be a part of it. I hope they are as proud as I am of all we accomplished.

I look at the monitor and realize I won't be seeing the seal of the President every morning in my new life. No Presidential schedule coming my way, so I know what he's doing, and what's happening in the House. He and Hillary are going off to new lives I won't be part of. It feels strange and unsettling. I guess if I had an exciting new job to go to, to look forward to, this might not be so painful. But I haven't. I don't know what I'm going to do next and can hardly bear to think about it. But, I'm not worried. Every time some pesky reality reminds me I won't have a paycheck in two weeks, I close my eyes and remember Scarlet O'Hara. "I'll think about it tomorrow. I'll think about it tomorrow."

Eight years ago the carpenters told me the secret of how to leave my permanent mark on the Visitors Office. I move a chair over to the double doors Darryl and I installed in January 1993. I climb up, pull out a Sharpie, and write, on the top edge, where no one can see, "Melinda Bates, Director, Visitors Office, 1993 -2001." I hope it lasts forever.

There's snow on the ground. Not a lot, but enough to frost the trees and shrubs in the Rose Garden and turn everything more beautiful in shades of gray and white. I take my last photos there. Out on the North side, on Pennsylvania Avenue, the Inaugural reviewing stands are up, but I'm not interested. I look away.

Then, on January 19th, I say my last farewell to the President, in the Oval Office. We weep a little, we hug, we exchange gifts. I'm barely holding on to my emotions as we finally part and I walk away for the final time. And, how many of these does he have to do? He must be numb. I know I am.

I don't get to even say goodbye to Hillary, who's already off working as the new, junior Senator from New York. I'm very happy for her, and proud too. She's a remarkable woman, and it was a privilege to be her friend and work for her. I know she'll work her heart out for the people of her state and for the country. ("What are we doing today, to make people's lives better?")

So, that's it. I sit in my empty office, staring at the blank walls, waiting for the Bush people, who finally arrive hours later. They don't seem interested in my help, so I provide a basic briefing and turn over the manuals, and the boxes of supplies I hid from the Archives people so they'd have a way to at least get started. I'm paying back (and hopefully paying forward) the help the Bush I ladies gave me eight years ago. I offer to come in to help the transition next week, and they're politely non-committal. Fine with me. It would be creepy to be the only Clintonite in an office of excited Bush II people. They offer cool thanks and are gone.

Now, it's just me and some final bits of business. I'm numb as I walk through the dark and silent House to the OEOB to close out my White House life. I see new Secret Service officers everywhere, who don't know us, and they frown at me. When the staff leaves, the USSS reassigns the officers they've worked with. There's a new sheriff in town, and new people at every level. It makes sense, but it makes me sad. In the last minute rush I didn't say goodbye to all those men and women I so liked and respected. I hope they know how much I enjoyed working with them. I hope they read this now, and remember the amazing things we did together.

There's a crowd of mostly younger staff in the checkout office, giddy with the moment. Their noise is grating to my ears, although they mean no disrespect. I turn in my pass, my pager and phone. I am officially a "civilian". Now I need an escort to get back to my office. It's so painful. The White House has been my home for eight incredible years, but now I'm an outsider.

In the office I linger briefly, but there's no excuse to stay. All of this is someone else's responsibility now. So, just as I've imagined for eight long years, I turn off the lights and gently close the door. I walk down the hallway to the East Door, with my bag and some small boxes. Out on the driveway, one of the laborers, a very nice man I've seen countless times over the years, stops me to say, "You know how it is here. We all work for whoever is the President, and his family, one hundred percent. I'll be honored to serve the new President, as I was honored to serve President Clinton. But I have to tell you, I LOVE President Clinton. In all the years I've been here, he and Mrs. Clinton are the first ones to make a difference in my life. Because of them, everyone in my family got a job. Because of them, my kids are the first generation in my family to go to college. They'll have a better life. We saw how hard they worked, and we love them for it. I needed to tell you that."

I give a little smile, nod my thanks, pick up the boxes again and keep walking.

Officer Russ Appleyard, a very classy guy, sees me heading to my car and stops me. He takes the boxes from my arms without a word and walks me down East Executive Avenue. We stand at the car and I'm incapable of speech. I stare at him sadly. I'm sure, like most men, he hates women's tears, but they're brimming in my eyes, and I think his too.

"Thank you, Russ. Thank you for everything. I hope you know how much I've loved working with you and all your colleagues. You guys are the best, and I'm proud to have known you. Give my regards to anyone I didn't see this week, will you?"

I have to get in the car before I lose it and fall onto his shirt in hysterics. To my surprise, I do this, smile, wave at him, and drive away for the last time. I watch the White House recede in my mirror and think, *Will I ever come back here? What an adventure it all was* ...

Plenty of time for tears now. All the time in the world.

In the weeks that follow, I find myself in a personal transition similar to dealing with the death of a loved one. I try to shake it off, but can't. I'm wracked with thoughts of things I should have done, never got around to doing, didn't think about doing until now. I call my friend Howard and burst into tears.

"I should have done more, should have worked harder, should have been a better leader to my staff and others ... I'm sure I wasted too many opportunities, and now it's too late. I can't forgive myself ..."

He's shocked. "Are you nuts? I saw how hard you worked, the endless hours you put in, the way you pushed yourself and the office to do better, always do better. You did a GREAT job and you should be nothing but proud of yourself and all you accomplished. This is ridiculous!"

"You really think so?" I snivel.

"Damn right I do. You made history there every day. You need to get over this right now."

But it goes on for weeks. I get frustrated, then annoyed with myself, until I take the time to think it through.

You may have a job you like - or love - and for some reason it's time to move on. BUT, when you leave you know you can return there to see the place you care about and re-connect with the people you miss. That's how it was when I left the National Gallery of Art in 1989.

When people leave the White House at the end of a President's term, the emotions are all much more intense, but the practical things are all different.

The place you've come to love, the heart of American political life and history, where you could come and go as you pleased? That place is now completely closed to you. You're on the outside of the fence, and there's no getting in again.

The people you loved and respected at work aren't there anymore. They're dispersed to a thousand different places, and you don't know when - if ever - you'll see them again. There will be no visits back, no re-connecting.

And then, if it were some ordinary place, maybe you could put it all out of your mind and just get on with your life. But this is the **White House**. It's on the news every night, in front of your face. And it's clear there are people there, people you don't much like, working in this place you love, and most likely doing things there you don't approve of at all.

It's painful! And there's no avoiding it.

Getting past it takes ... as long as it takes.

Maybe for some people it isn't difficult to cope with this loss, but even after the worst of it passes for me, I still keep dreaming about it. Several times a week. For a solid year. I wake up tired and irritated. Why can't I just let this all go? Finally I accept that dreams are a way our soul processes things for us, and it takes ... as long as it takes.

For me, it took a year. In January 2002, the dreams finally stopped. By then I was moving ahead with my life, refusing to look back, concentrating on the future.

But no matter where I go, the White House years will always be an enormous part of who I am. I'm marked by it forever. I grew there, and changed into the person I am now. I did what Bill and Hillary told me I'd have to do: reached down deep inside myself and learned how to be smarter, wiser, more patient, more compassionate, more creative and more forgiving than I ever imagined I could be. I'm proud to be a Clintonista for life.

Oh, and, it was a hell of a ride. A hell of a ride.

To Melinda — with thanks for everything Bill Clinton
Happy Birthday

Epilogue, 3rd Edition, Winter 2019

After the White House I had a great job with Barbara Boggs Associates, one of Washington's premier event firms. I organized international conferences and fund raising events for associations and press groups in Washington, events the President attended. Everyone told me what a great fit it was, and I knew, rationally, it was. But, I just couldn't settle into the ordinary-ness of it, after the excitement of the White House years. I missed the satisfaction and excitement of all we did. I wanted to do good, not just do well.

In July, 2005, I visited Baja California Norte, Mexico, the part of Mexico that's just south of San Deigo California. I found myself on the patio of a little villa on the ocean, in a place with white buildings and the blue sea that looked just like Greece – but was a lot closer to home. I turned to Steve and said, "This is it. I'm buying this house, quitting my job, selling the Virginia house (of thirty years) and moving here. I've always wanted to live on the ocean, and I see my chance to do that here."

He was as shocked and unwilling as any rational person would be, but, in the end, this is what we did. Now we live in the villa above the ocean, watching whales, dolphins and humming birds, when I'm not traveling the world giving speeches.

After my book was originally published, in 2008, I did a lot of TV and radio commentary about it. Turned out people loved hearing my stories as much as reading them. So, I became a professional speaker and leading authority whose expertise is White House social history. Now I travel on land and on luxury cruise ships giving presentations about many different aspects of life and work in the world's most famous House. If you belong to an association or organization that sometimes needs a funny, candid speaker with lots of surprising and inspiring stories, please think of me! People routinely tell me I'm "the best speaker we ever heard!"

I can be reached at: Melinda@WhiteHouseBook.com,
My website is: https://www.WhiteHouseBook.com

You can watch me tell some stories there and on Youtube. I'd love to entertain your colleagues and guests!

ACKNOWLEDGMENTS

Many people helped me in my White House career, and I offer profound thanks to:

President Bill Clinton, who gave me my opportunity, and a lifetime of friendship.

First Lady/Senator/Secretary Hillary Rodham Clinton, for her countless kindnesses, loyalty and support, and for inspiring me to always reach within myself for more. #AlwaysWithHer

Robyn Dickey, Ann McCoy and Margaret Whillock, the three fabulous Arkansas ladies who worked by my side as Deputy Directors of the Visitors Office, steel magnolias all.

Marc Hoberman who made sure the Visitors Office ran like a professional office, when some of the others did not, and who always challenged me to keep growing.

Holly Holt Thoden, who stayed with me all eight years and who I loved like a daughter.

The many staff members over the years who came to us starry-eyed and never lost the wonder, including Elizabeth Cheek Jones, whose light touch managed our volunteers (no easy task), Christine Maloy, Carla Duryea and Claudia Derricotte who helped us get off to a great start. Jared Powell and Gayleen Dalsimer who came to us young and inexperienced, but worked heart and soul for me and the President. Their only flaw was that as Californians, theytalkedtoofast! Aprill Springfield arrived a shy girl and grew into an accomplished and remarkable young woman. Shawn Johnson brought unmistakable Arkansas charm and smarts to all our work and went on to be an ADA in Little Rock. Thanks to Miguel Bustos, Josh Maddox, Tracy Pakulniewicz, Melinda Frankfurter, and Patty whose last name I'm embarrassed to have lost. It was a privilege to know and work with all of you.

Our talented and dedicated volunteers kept the office running and were a vital part of every success. To Joni Stephens, Mary Ann Thornburg, Jacquie Dinwiddie, Barbara Chapin and so many others,

I owe great thanks. We could never have done what we did without you! I hope you all know you are also a part of history forever

I had many bosses over the years, and the two I most appreciated were Mark Lindsay and John Dankowski, whose examples demonstrated the difference between managing and leading, and the importance of the latter. To Nancy Hernreich and the late Evelyn Lieberman, for being such classy dames and powerful women, and Capricia Marshall for her example of boundless energy and devotion in service to the Clintons, ladies, I am in awe of you.

In my writing life I'm grateful to Marsh Cassady, leader of the Baja Writers' Workshop, and our talented members, especially Alice Donenfeld, for teaching by example and encouragement and being dear friends in my new life in Mexico. I'm also grateful to the California writing teacher I won't name, who listened to me read and talk when I was just getting started, and suggested I get a ghost writer. Damn. Nothing like a challenge to rise to! (No thanks.) And to the countless authors whose remarkable books inspired me to keep going when I despaired of ever writing anything people would want to read. I'm not in your league, but I've tried to tell a good story.

In my personal life I'm grateful to my then-husband, Darryl Bates, a Republican to the bone, who nevertheless always supported and encouraged me and was proud of me, as were my sons, Shiloh and Noah. And for the last two years of my White House adventure, and twenty years of our lives, Stephen Ense, who brought joy, passion and fun to everything we did. He's the one who pushed me and pushed me to finally write this book. He's my publisher and partner. I love you Steve!

Credits: All photos in this book are either from my personal collection (taken by me) or given to me as official White House photos I'm in or of events I organized. White House photos belong to the public.

Cover designs -

Front cover digital art by Stephen Ense
Back cover official White House photo
Cover layout: Melinda Bates, Noah Bates and Alice Donenfeld-Vernoux
Final Print Layout: Image Design and Graphics, Josh Knapp, San Diego, CA

Consultant: Noah G. Bates

More photos ahead and can be seen in color at:
www.WhiteHouseBook.com

I love you, Mom.

Georgetown reunions, 1998 (above) and 1993 (below)

Will Smith and JFK

Roger Moore (The Saint, James Bond)

With Her Majesty, Queen Sylvia of Sweden, right before my faux pas of saying "bottom" to a Queen. Oops!

Robin Williams and Socks

Steve and I practice tango before the Argentine State Dinner

Judy Collins plays and sings "A Chelsea Morning" up in the Residence

With Sharon Stone on that memorable day with Larry Hagman

I was so proud to have my name on these tour tickets, next to POTUS and FLOTUS!

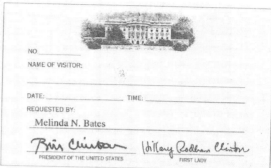

NON TRANSFERABLE	
(PLEASE DO NOT DETACH)	
THIS TICKET IS PROVIDED BY THE WHITE HOUSE WITHOUT CHARGE AND MAY NOT BE USED FOR PERSONAL PROFIT.	

NO _____

NAME OF VISITOR: _____

DATE: _____ TIME: _____

REQUESTED BY:
Melinda N. Bates

VISITORS ENTRANCE
EAST EXECUTIVE AVENUE

NO _____

NAME OF VISITOR: _____

DATE: _____ TIME: _____

REQUESTED BY:
Melinda N. Bates

Bill Clinton
PRESIDENT OF THE UNITED STATES

Hillary Rodham Clinton
FIRST LADY

1993 I welcome Robyn to a Washington winter. We were too excited about our new jobs to feel the cold.

Printed in Poland
by Amazon Fulfillment
Poland Sp. z o.o., Wrocław